Let's Talk About Egg Donation

Real Stories from Real People

Marna Gatlin
and
Carole LieberWilkins, M.F.T

Edited by Lauren Cross

ARCHWAY
PUBLISHING

Archway Publishing books may be ordered through booksellers or by contacting:

Archway Publishing
1663 Liberty Drive
Bloomington, IN 47403
www.archwaypublishing.com
1 (888) 242-5904

ISBN: 978-1-4808-7759-7 (sc)
ISBN: 978-1-4808-7760-3 (hc)
ISBN: 978-1-4808-7758-0 (e)

Library of Congress Control Number: 2019907579

Print information available on the last page.

Archway Publishing rev. date: 10/21/2019

For Manny, Nick, Jennifer, John, Carole, and all of the donor-conceived children who are changing the world one baby at a time. Without each and every one of you, this book would not exist. All of you have my eternal thanks, love, and gratitude.
—MDG

§

For Marna Gatlin and Lauren Cross, whose steady patience made the idea of this book a reality.

For Don, who saw me through the darkest days of infertility.

For Renee and Mary, whose sacrifices, generosity, and grace made me a mom. Their humility and graciousness through the years is beyond description and without equal.

For Jay, who picked up the pieces and loved us just when we needed him.

And for Alex and Daniel, who gave me my life and my passion and whose wisdom has helped so many throughout the years.

—CLW

On Children
Kahlil Gibran

Your children are not your children.
They are the sons and daughters of Life's longing for itself.
They come through you but not from you,
And though they are with you yet they belong not to you.
You may give them your love but not your thoughts,
For they have their own thoughts.
You may house their bodies but not their souls,
For their souls dwell in the house of tomorrow,
which you cannot visit, not even in your dreams.
You may strive to be like them,
but seek not to make them like you.
For Life goes not backward nor tarries with yesterday.
You are the bows from which your children
as living arrows are sent forth.
The archer sees the mark upon the path of the infinite,
and He bends you with His might
that His arrows may go swift and far.
Let your bending in the archer's hand be for gladness;
For even as He loves the arrow that flies,
so He loves also the bow that is stable.

Contents

FOREWORD

Listen to the mustn'ts, child. Listen to the don'ts. Listen to the shouldn'ts, the impossibles, the won'ts. Listen to the never haves, then listen close to me … Anything can happen, child. Anything can be.

—Shel Silverstein

During the thirty years that I have been practicing reproductive endocrinology and infertility, I've seen dramatic advances in medical technology that allow individuals and couples to have children. Many of those whom I have helped would not have been able to have families if they had been born a generation earlier. It's important to recognize that in vitro fertilization (IVF) is a relatively new fertility therapy—the oldest "test tube baby" is less than forty years of age, and the first pregnancy achieved through egg donation did not occur until 1984. Since the turn of the current century, various components of family-building through IVF—including egg donation, embryo donation, and gestational surrogacy—have become increasingly effective, safe, available, and commonplace. These methods often are highlighted by the media, which has increased their recognition and their acceptance by society at large. Nevertheless, the decision to utilize IVF as a tool to create one's family can be a difficult one to make. This is especially true for those in need of egg donation. For heterosexual couples and single women, their future child will not have the same DNA that the baby's mother has. This loss of genetic connection has profound implications and is often very difficult to accept. I've seen many women and men struggle through many months or years of contemplation and apparent indecision, while fully understanding that their only valid options are egg or embryo donation, adoption, or not having future children. Same-sex male couples and single men may be concerned about how their child will be affected by not having a mother, although the child will likely have ongoing contact with the gestational surrogate, with the egg donor, and/or with caring women who have a close personal relationship with the father or fathers. For all parties in need of egg donation, the financial costs are high, there are no absolute guarantees of success, and multiple important decisions must be made during the planning stages, during the treatment period, and following delivery of the baby. These decisions can, at times, seem overwhelming. Intended parents who will use assisted reproductive technology have to become educated in reproductive biology, genetics, psychology, and law to make the right choices on how to create their families. Ideally, the fertility clinic, reproductive mental health professional, egg donor and/or surrogacy agency, and reproductive attorney will provide clear guidance during this coordinated effort. Future parents must place their trust in many providers to complete a successful baby journey. Intended parents should be appropriately assertive to ensure that their providers understand their unique needs. This will allow them to develop the necessary level of trust.

Many of my patients have shared with me their anger, frustration, shame, and disbelief after they have been told that they have low numbers of eggs and that they should consider egg donation. They often feel isolated and that they have failed. They may not know of anyone else who has become a parent through egg donation. They want to share their feelings and learn insights from others who have faced similar obstacles. Same-sex couples, transgender individuals, and single men and women have the same need for peer guidance and support in order to learn how to achieve their goal of becoming parents through assisted reproductive technology. The process is especially daunting for international patients who are traveling to North America for care.

Those who are considering becoming parents through egg donation, those who have children from egg donation, and these individuals' family members and close friends will find *Let's Talk about Egg Donation* an essential resource. Carole LieberWilkins and Marna Gatlin, the authors, are two women who have created their families through egg donation and who have devoted their lives and their professional careers to helping others do the same. The insights that Marna, Carole, and members of the online community Parents via Egg Donation share in this book are invaluable and not readily obtained through other resources.

I first met Marna Gatlin in 1999, when she became my patient at ORM Fertility. I was immediately impressed by Marna's intelligence, warmth, thoughtfulness, and candor. I thought that this was clearly someone who had done her homework and knew what was possible to achieve the family that she and her husband had long desired. Knowledge of medical factors and egg donor options is certainly empowering. Too often, those in need of egg donation feel like they have been on the losing side in their effort to become parents. Knowledge instills acceptance and hope.

Marna's experiences compelled her to found the large international nonprofit organization Parents via Egg Donation (PVED), which has been an important resource for many years for those who are just starting out on their journey to parenthood, those who are already pregnant, and those who are now parents. Marna is the executive director of this organization. Many of the comments and stories in *Let's Talk about Egg Donation* are from participants in the PVED internet forums. Having compromised fertility is highly stressful and can become all-consuming; the PVED organization offers a resource for hundreds of current and future parents to connect and exchange insights, new ideas, and encouragement.

I have had the opportunity to participate in several conferences in which Carole LieberWilkins has been a speaker, and I am always impressed by her thoughtful comments. I gain a deeper understanding of the psychosocial issues associated with creating families through egg donation every time I talk to Carole. She is well known for her work regarding the sharing of information with children, having helped hundreds of former patients feel more comfortable about talking with their kids about how they came into this world. Carole sits on the board of directors of PVED as its director of mental health. She is a licensed marriage and family therapist in private practice in Los Angeles, providing counseling to individuals and couples. A specialist in the field of reproductive medicine, adoption, and family-building options since 1986, she became a founding member of Resolve of Greater Los Angeles in 1987 and served on the board of directors of Resolve in various positions for the next fourteen years.

The careful quality-control measures and high technical expertise of top fertility clinics have allowed those in need of egg donation to achieve pregnancies through IVF at rates that were hardly imaginable twenty years ago. The intense focus on technology by fertility clinics has not always extended into the realm of psychological preparedness for the future parent. This book is an outstanding resource for those who are struggling with the concept of becoming a parent through egg donation and the resulting issues associated with raising a child who was conceived through egg donation. During my medical career, I've seen hundreds of happy, healthy, loving families that have been made possible through egg donation. It's not always an easy journey for the intended parent(s), but it is one that can have profound, life-changing rewards. The expert authors of *Let's Talk about Egg Donation* have astutely addressed the important issues faced by couples and individuals who are contemplating this journey. They clearly demonstrate that both the kids and the parents are "all right." They are normal families with the same joys and sorrows that all families experience.

John S. Hesla, MD
Medical Director, Parents Via Egg Donation
Medical Director, ORM Fertility

INTRODUCTION

There's only one story in the world—your story.

—Ray Bradbury

Everyone has a story. Our stories are the narratives of our lives. Intimacy develops when people share stories. Connection between people comes from sharing the stories of where we have been and where we are now. How we touch each other through our life's narrative is the thread that binds us as human beings. The stories shared in this book are from scores of families created through egg or embryo donation. Although edited for clarity, the stories have not been altered in any way. In most cases, we've used people's real names; pseudonyms are indicated with an asterisk.

Carole became a parent via egg donation after a shocking diagnosis of extremely early menopause. Marna's story was one of nine pregnancy losses before her son Nick finally came into her life. Kitty* chose egg donation after a pregnancy loss revealed a rare chromosomal disorder. Tommy and Rich joined the club for the obvious reason that they were two men who wanted to be dads, and they needed the parts a female would contribute.

Stacey and Steve had their first and only child through egg donation, but Jenn,* April,* and Diana became moms through egg donation after first having children with their own eggs. Carole and Don were blessed to become parents first by adoption and then were able to give birth to their second child with the help of an egg donor.

The stories shared here are from younger parents as well as parents who are older than they thought they would be when they became parents. These parents are single and partnered, gay, straight, and transgender. They live in the United States, the United Kingdom, Switzerland, and Spain. Their donors were their sisters or their cousins or strangers who gave frozen eggs to an egg bank, or the parents were matched to donors through an egg broker program, sometimes called an agency. Donors may have donated in an arrangement they believed to be anonymous, or the parents may have sat in a room with donors, exchanging information, hopes, and dreams for the future.

The stories herein tell how we came to egg donation, but no matter how we got there, there are common pieces that bind us. We all brag about our kids and exclaim how much we love them. We all struggled. Most of us grieved the loss of genetic relatedness. We all worried or wondered who our children would be, since we had lost the expectation that they would be like us or look like us. We all wondered how and when and with whom we would share our family creation story. We all hoped our kids would end up feeling good about how we created our families. We chose donors and then may have fretted over whether we were making the right decision. Our stories have so much in common, regardless of the varying paths we took.

Here is a collection of stories of real families created through egg and sometimes embryo donation. We hope the stories we share here will educate and inform you, inspire and comfort you. We hope they will help you to absolutely know that you are not alone, that we have felt what you feel, and that you are part of a community of families with a common difference. We hope the stories reassure you that you have the exact right family and that your future will have challenges and joys, disappointments, and successes, just like all families.

We welcome you to share your story with us at
www.letstalkabouteggdonation.com.

MEET THE AUTHORS

Marna Gatlin

Founder and Executive Director, Parents via Egg Donation

Having kids and being a mom was something I always thought I'd do. When I was growing up, if you had asked me how many kids I wanted, I would have told you I wanted four kids—two boys and two girls—and I wanted each of them born in a different season: winter, spring, summer, and fall. I even had all of their names picked out; that's how sure I was that someday I would become a mom.

But that's not the way it worked out—at least not for me. I struggled with infertility for many years, until the winter of 2000, when I had my son through egg donation. I, like many of you, struggled with the loss of my own genetic link as I wrapped my head around the idea of egg donation.

When I first learned about egg donation, I was curious, excited, and above all, hopeful that this process might be the conduit for me to achieve my lifelong dream of becoming a mom. As I began my quest to learn about egg donation, I was extraordinarily frustrated by the lack of information available about this particular kind of assisted reproductive technology. I wanted education and support. I also wanted to be empowered. However, back in the late 1990s, there wasn't much in the way of education, support, or empowerment. In fact, during my pregnancy I was pretty much on my own, except for my husband, my family, and a small email support group that I clung to. This support group was truly my lifeline.

After my son was born, I felt isolated and alone during what should have been the happiest time of my life. I didn't want anyone considering egg donation or parenting after egg donation to go through what I did alone, so I decided to create an organization that would embrace every parent who had chosen egg donation to grow their family. I wanted to welcome traditional parents, single mothers and fathers, and gay, lesbian, and transgender individuals into a warm community. Like me, many of these individuals didn't feel they had the support to become educated, be empowered, or have a voice. Often they felt lonely, isolated, or like they didn't belong. And so Parents via Egg Donation (PVED) was born.

My broader vision was to create a global resource for unbiased, timely, and accurate information about egg donation, eliminating the need to scour the internet for answers. Today, PVED is home to thousands of members who share emotional support, as well as legal concerns, anecdotes, mental health questions, protocols regarding egg donors, clinics, agencies, and medications, and other information about egg or embryo donation, on a daily basis.

Carole LieberWilkins
Marriage and Family Therapist

The process of egg donation has come a long way in the last thirty years. I did not choose a donor. The donor was chosen for me.

In 1987, there was no such thing as a "solicited" donor. There were no matching programs, and egg donors were not compensated. Eggs given from one woman to another were from IVF patients, from women undergoing IVF because of endometriosis, blocked tubes, or male infertility. Their ovaries worked fine, but they were infertile for a multitude of other reasons. There was also no cryo-technology, so eggs not used in one cycle were not fertilized to create embryos for a subsequent cycle. Because of this, some women opted to give the eggs they could not use to women whose ovarian function was compromised. These were women who had diminished ovarian reserve or premature ovarian failure or who carried heritable diseases they did not wish to pass on to their offspring.

Similar to the "shared" cycles that currently take place in some clinics in the United States, information about the donating woman was limited to whatever information the physician would have on any IVF patient. Unlike a more contemporary donation process, there was no psychological evaluation. No psychosocial information was obtained. Patients going through IVF were not screened as donors are today. No questions were asked about family history or about what her major was in college. Doctors would have no reason to ask an IVF patient if she had even gone to college. They would not know if cancer, depression, or Alzheimer's ran in her family. They would have only information relevant to her own fertility struggle.

After being diagnosed with significant premature ovarian failure at the age of thirty, I first became a mom via adoption to my son Alex. We were present at the moment of birth, and his dad cut the umbilical cord. Then, wanting to add to our family, I became the ninth person in the world to receive a "donated" egg in the way described previously. Because there was no matching process whatsoever, and because the doctor could not know whether a patient would have enough eggs to give away, patients wanting to receive someone else's gametes were put on hormonal treatments to simulate a normal cycle, so that at any given moment she could be ready to receive a donor's egg.

On a Friday afternoon in June 1987, I received a call from the clinic saying that a donor was available and that I needed to be there in two hours to undergo surgery. But first we had to call a family member to babysit a one-month-old Alex!

When I arrived at the clinic office, I asked a lot of questions about the woman whose eggs I would receive. The staff told me the chosen donor's height, weight, and eye color. The reproductive endocrinology fellow who was attempting to answer my questions was not a native English speaker. She told me the donor's eyes were yellow. I guessed that she meant a kind of light brown or amber color and that perhaps the fellow just did not have the word to describe this. There was no photograph or profile of the donor because she was a patient and not a donor as we think of donors today. The patient had undergone an egg retrieval for her own IVF and had more eggs than she could use, so the clinic had called me because I was on the thirteenth day of a simulated cycle, induced through medication. We were "matched" through an accident of timing and nothing else.

In attempting to answer my questions about the donor, the staff told me the woman was Scandinavian. I asked what she did for a living because I wanted to know something about her and thought that knowing what kind of work the donor did would say much about her. Someone who is a math teacher has a different personality from an opera singer, who is different from a social worker. I was told the donor was in marketing. The doctors and the nurses kept asking me, "Why are you asking these questions? This is going to be *your* child." There was a complete lack of acknowledgment that the genetic history and characteristics of the woman whose eggs were about to be put inside of me mattered at all to me or would matter to the child that I would ultimately have.

But those details did matter, because every shred of information was helpful years later when I started talking with the son who resulted from that procedure. I had written it all down on a scrap of paper, including the reasons the donor was having IVF.

Eventually, many years later, the donor and I were introduced to each other and have had a relationship ever since. It turned out she was not Scandinavian at all. The height I had been given was right, but the eye color was wrong.

In some parts of the world outside of the United States and in a few clinics in the United States, this is how egg donation is still conducted. Twenty-nine years later, recipients still may not receive a photograph and still may be told that the information they want is unimportant and will not be crucial to the healthy identity development of donor offspring. Fortunately, much *has* changed, and most clinics in the United States now provide photos and some basic information about education level, family history, and hobbies. However, three decades have taught us so much about donor-conceived families, and it is our hope that those programs still functioning in a fashion now considered backward will soon recognize their added responsibility to help create healthy families.

Chapter 1

DIAGNOSIS

It's hard to wait around for something you know might never happen; but it's harder to give up when you know it's everything you want.

—Unknown

Most people assume that getting pregnant is the easiest thing in the world. Everybody can do it. You choose a partner, have sex, and don't use birth control, and within a year you will have a baby. That baby will grow into the perfect combination of you and your chosen partner.

There are exceptions, of course. Some people know ahead of time that they will have difficulty conceiving. Same-sex couples or single people know they will need the help of donors and physicians to become moms or dads. However, our individual responses to learning we cannot have a child genetically related to us will be unique to our own life experiences and personalities.

A person who receives an infertility diagnosis is often filled with shame. Everyone around us seems to be having babies, so why can't we? It's hard to be a patient. It is hard to have a medical condition of any sort. It is harder still to be a patient for something we don't think of as medical. We think of becoming pregnant as a part of life, something that comes with adulthood or partnering or growing up and becoming ready to parent. Having to be patients in a way that intrudes on every aspect of our lives adds insult to injury. Reproduction without sex interferes with our marriages, our friendships, our family relationships, our jobs, our finances, our sexual lives, our identities, and our self-esteem.

Most people learn that egg donation is their best option to become pregnant after many prior attempts at pregnancy. Sometimes years of attempts with their own eggs have preceded this news. Some women already have a sense that their ovarian function is insufficient because of their age or prior information. For most, this is a crisis point. For many, it is devastating. Ultimately, for the men and women who choose egg donation, this path is the way forward.

Here are a few of the stories shared with us about the moment when people realized they would not be having children who were genetically related to them.

Terrie and Dave

> I barely got the key in the door, shutting it behind me [before] I leaned my back against a wall, slid down it, and fell apart. I completely lost it. My heart was pounding in my ears. I knew I was in shock and felt so alone. I remember thinking that no one knew what I was feeling. I broke down and finally let it out.

When Terrie and Dave married at thirty-eight, they knew they wanted and needed to start their family pretty quickly. So they tried— and tried some more. Although Terrie worried that her clock was ticking too loudly, she also struggled with the idea of seeking medical treatment for something she felt she should be able to do on her own. So rather than going to a doctor, she tried going "all natural."

> I started eating all organic ... We went to see a nutritionist. We did body cleanses and detox regimens. Nothing. Months went by, and I finally gave in to seeking medical help. By

this time, I was quickly approaching forty and didn't want to waste any more time.

Now, of course, Terrie thinks of that time with an ironic view of herself, wondering why it was so difficult to ask for help from traditional medicine. Why is it that we feel like a failure if we go to a doctor but not if we just change our diets? Maybe the latter helps us to feel like we are in charge, like there are steps *we* can take to become fertile. It is painful to feel so helpless, so we try other avenues first.

> *I started with my gynecologist, who first ran tests on my husband and me. Dave was diagnosed with unobstructed azoospermia and was referred to a urologist. After ... many more tests, the urologist suggested donor sperm.*

When Terrie remembers this time, she is surprised at how blithely they made that decision. It did not seem traumatic to either one of them, and they proceeded because it was the "next logical step." In hindsight, it is ironic for her to see how that was not the case when Terrie's own genes were on the line.

> *The plan was to try three cycles of inseminations with donor sperm, but we only did one. The other two, I never got to an insemination. By that time my FSH [follicle-stimulating hormone] was well over the desired limit of 10. At its highest, it was 19. When I went for the third try, my doctor called me into his office. Of course, that was the one time Dave didn't go with me. I was alone. So alone.*
>
> *It was December 20, and I was filled with fantasies of giving Dave the Christmas present of a Big Fat Positive for the first time. I was wearing my favorite comfy jeans and a cozy powder-blue sweater. The weather was crappy, which of course was not surprising for late December in Pittsburgh. Gray, overcast skies and snow flurries followed*

me to the appointment, but I was still hopeful as I went in for our third try.

The doctor called me into his office to give me the talk about moving on to donor eggs. He said I would have to do egg donation if I wanted to be pregnant. I went deaf and numb. After the first few words, I couldn't hear him. I needed to go home. I looked to my right and saw only the empty chair my husband should have been in. I knew he would feel dreadful that he was not there that day, and no one could have predicted it would be the Day of Trauma. The shelves behind the doctor's seat were filled with books that certainly should have told him how to help me conceive. The titles blurred. I desperately tried to hold it together.

I had a forty-five-minute bus ride to get home, and I knew that when I got there, Dave would not yet be home. I willed myself, one minute at a time, not to completely disintegrate right there on the bus with all those people. Ten minutes, then eleven. Twenty. Halfway there. My brain was oatmeal. I focused on not missing my stop—the stop I knew like my I knew my own name. Half an hour passed. I couldn't call anyone because I could not think. Forty minutes. At last.

I barely got the key in the door and shut it behind me when I leaned my back against a wall, slid down it, and fell apart. I completely lost it. My heart was pounding in my ears. I knew I was in shock and was so alone. I remember thinking that no one knew what I was feeling, and I could finally let it out.

When Dave finally got home and found me in that state, he thought someone had died. He could never—and I completely understand this—have imagined that a meeting with my doctor had created my devastation. He was right. Someone had died, and it would be quite a while before I would understand how that would so significantly affect our lives.

The tug-of-war that many women like Terrie feel is natural. On one hand, we can hear our biological clocks not just ticking but shouting from the rooftops: "Have a baby, already!" But on the other hand, we dance the 'I-should' dance and do nothing because we feel that having a baby *should* be something that occurs naturally.

Terrie thought she was doing all the right things—seeing a nutritionist, eating all organic, doing detox regimens and body cleanses—and that these things just might do the trick. But they didn't. Nothing happened, and all the while, time was ticking by.

The isolation and loneliness we often feel throughout this process can be overwhelming, especially when we finally have the talk with our doctors. No one can prepare us for being told that we will need the help of an egg donor to have a baby—and for most, this does feel like a death.

The hardest thing about reproductive loss is saying goodbye to someone we never said hello to. Our sadness and depression over the loss of our genetic offspring are a form of grief. But unlike the grief we feel when a real person dies, infertility grief means saying goodbye to someone who was never really here. When there is an actual death, we have ritual around it. We have funerals and wakes, or we sit *shiva* and make social calls. We may go to our places of worship, and often we light candles. People bring casseroles to our homes and say, "I'm so sorry for your loss." But when we are told that genetic children aren't possible and that we will need someone else's DNA in order to conceive, we have to confront that our child may not look like us, be like us, laugh like our grandparents, or have our partner's intelligence. It is a big deal—but no one brings you a casserole or says they are sorry for your loss. There is no name to give to a person who died, even though you feel exactly as if a real person has passed. That's because the person—your genetic child—has been so real to you for so long, even if you didn't realize it.

Carole and Don

Carole was only thirty when she learned that she had the ovaries of a menopausal woman. No one knew why her ovaries had stopped working. The news was a complete shock. What does it feel like when the choice to have a child, when you want to have one, is taken away? She learned that she had a medical condition and that she would never be pregnant or have a child that looked like her, all at the same time.

Having married at twenty-five in the late 1970s, Carole and Don were not trying to conceive when they received information that would change their lives forever. Don was seven years older than Carole, and although he was in his thirties, he wasn't ready to have a child.

Carole had never had regular periods. Sometimes she would have one every month for many months and then wouldn't get another one for ten weeks. Then she'd bleed again three weeks later. In her early twenties, she had gone to a few different doctors to find out why she was so irregular. Their response was to tell her that if she wanted to conceive, it would be difficult because she did not ovulate regularly; when she was ready, the doctors would prescribe clomiphene (aka Clomid), but since she did not want to be pregnant at that time, they recommended estrogen to regulate. Since children were not in the immediate plan, she didn't want to take hormones. She never took the estrogen, and she and Don continued to use birth control. Random ovulation meant they could never be sure when they might be fertile.

Five years into their marriage, Carole changed gynecologists simply for geographic reasons. They had moved and needed a doctor a bit closer to where they were living. Upon taking a history for the first time, the doctor was concerned and baffled by the description of a thirty-year-old whose periods had always been so erratic. She requested that Carole come to the office every week for four weeks so that she could run some blood tests.

At the conclusion of the four weeks, Carole and Don were referred to a reproductive endocrinologist (RE) affiliated with the local major university. They had no idea what an RE was, but they figured that since Carole's hormones were off, it made sense to see an endocrinologist.

It was a typically sweltering July day in 1984. They had planned lunch after the doctor appointment, completely naïve to the news they would receive. They held hands on this unexpected midweek date with each other.

> *The doctor said, "You are in menopause. There is no cure for menopause. Once you don't have any more eggs, they are gone. If you want to have children, you will 'have' to adopt. I'm sorry."*

> *My vision was blurred as we walked outside the building. I remember the heat, the stillness of the leaves on the sidewalk trees, and my breathing felt labored. Don asked me about lunch, and I thought he was speaking a language I didn't know. Words didn't process, and I could not understand why he was asking me about food when I felt so nauseated.*

The menopause the doctor was describing was actually a diagnosis of premature ovarian failure. The parties did not know it at the time, but 1984 saw the first birth of a child created through the donation of an egg. Since that process was virtually unheard of, no options were available for a woman with an FSH of 167 and no estrogen whatsoever.

Carole wondered what it meant to be in menopause at age thirty, aside from the infertility. Menopause was something that had happened to her grandmother and mother, and it didn't look at all appealing. Suffering through hot flashes and tremendous mood swings, Carole worried she would soon dry up and look wrinkled and aged. What would happen to a thirty-year-old who was aging prematurely? Aside from starting to understand that motherhood would be elusive for a long time to come, she wondered about her marriage and her health.

She told Don he should leave her. She said she was going to shrivel up, be unattractive, be barren, and be dark and sad for a long time. He deserved better. He said all the right things—he had married her not for her baby-making ability, but for the *her*-ness of her. She didn't believe him. His words sank into the bottomless vessel of her insecurity.

Everyone in their lives knew they had received this diagnosis, but no one really understood the magnitude of the emotional turmoil it created. Feeling alone, terrified, and depressed, Carole began the long, meandering, uneven process of grieving and planning for an uncertain future.

Marna says:

> An infertility diagnosis at any age is painful; there's no easy way around it. For many infertility diagnoses, there is a work-around—new medication, various procedures, intrauterine insemination (IUI), or IVF. However, when women like Carole receive a diagnosis of premature menopause at such a young age, their world can look extraordinarily bleak.
>
> It's hard to know what such a diagnosis will mean. Many of us conjure up images of really old, arthritic women who shuffle with the help of a cane. We worry, as Carole did, about aging prematurely.
>
> Carole didn't have the opportunity to put off childbearing because of life choices such as education, career, personal relationships, or the adventure of travel. She just thought that she and Don would have children like everyone else on their timetable, when the time was right.
>
> At that time, there was no internet, and there were no organized support groups or therapists who specialized in infertility. Carole was pretty much on her own. Like the majority of us when we receive such a diagnosis, she felt alone, depressed, and terrified. That is when the grieving begins, and that process can be very long and hard for many women.

Marna and Manny

Marna concisely described her vision regarding the way she wanted to begin her family, but she was sideswiped by nine miscarriages over a span of seventeen years. What was incredibly frustrating to Marna and her husband was the lack of answers. No one could give her any reasonable explanation for why this was happening over and over to her. There was nothing definitive to point a finger at. There was a lot of head-scratching and "maybes" thrown around by the many different doctors Marna saw over this period of time.

From the time I was old enough to articulate thoughts about children, family, and growing up, I always knew I wanted to be a mom.

When I married and began my quest—or rather, my mission—to have children, I conceived easily without much effort at all. My challenge was staying pregnant. By the time I was thirty-six, I had experienced nine separate losses between weeks six and twenty-seven of pregnancy. They say that the first miscarriage is the toughest and a little piece of you dies when that happens. I want to say that they were all tough, and a little piece of me died with each of them—I wouldn't wish the experience of miscarriage on anyone.

Time marched on, and over the next seventeen years, I would go to various gynecologists, who would talk to me about losing weight, eating differently, taking different medications, and trying IVF, meditation, and more procedures than I could shake a stick at—it was crazy.

This stuff also causes an unfathomable amount of stress on relationships. I don't mean just intimate relationships; I mean relationships with everyone around you—personal, professional, and familial—as well as the one with your partner. I was one of those statistics—my relationship took a huge hit and didn't make it, and though I can't blame infertility for all of it, I will say with confidence that it was a contributing factor.

More time passed, and I met a man who knew all about my reproductive challenges and loved me in spite of them. We had many discussions about children, about adopting them, fostering them, and even living childless—and we knew that becoming parents was extraordinarily important to us. So we decided that we were going to now call in the big guns and research specialists whose focus was solely on infertility.

I can clearly remember sitting in my reproductive endocrinologist's office and feeling resentful that I was spending part of my thirty-sixth birthday at a doctor's appointment. As I sat across the table from him in his office, holding my husband's hand, I watched intently as he pored through my chart, which seemed to me so very thick with "stuff." After what seemed like a very long time, he looked across the table at me and said, "I feel confident that we can help you get pregnant, but it may be a challenge keeping you that way, and donor eggs are going to be what you need to become a mother."

He then went on to explain that he felt like I had an egg issue, and later, when all of the testing came back, my hormone levels were indicative of someone who was well on her way to menopause—something called diminished ovarian reserve. I remember exhaling and feeling actually relieved and grateful that this wasn't all in my head—I wasn't just imagining all of this. However, I was devastated that I would be giving up my genes and would need the eggs of another woman to become a mother. I didn't know what any of that meant.

The office was very kind to us as they helped us make another appointment to begin actual treatment. They gave me a little pamphlet about egg donation and then sent us on our way.

It is extraordinarily frustrating for patients who want nothing more than to become parents to hear from their doctors, "We just don't know" or "This is all unexplained" or "You are a big mystery," and that is exactly what happened with me.

Infertility of any kind can affect the strongest of relationships in such a negative way that the stress can create cracks in many marriages. Unfortunately, Marna's first marriage ended in divorce. The other stressor that many women carry around is that they don't talk about the issue when entering into a new relationship, knowing that they have something wrong but not sure what that something is. They often feel as if they are presenting themselves to a potentially new partner as "damaged goods."

For some women like Marna, there is a moment of relief upon finally having an answer about what really has been wrong—it wasn't all in her head but really was in her eggs! But it was devastating to learn that her lifelong dream of those four genetic children was not going to happen; instead, becoming a mother would mean borrowing genes from someone else.

Kitty and Mike *

Who would be the person to replace my DNA?

In Kitty's own words, she describes what happened when she learned, in stages, that her eggs were unlikely to ever create a healthy child. A chromosomal anomaly diagnosed at age thirty-five explained everything and changed the course of her life.

It all happened so fast, and yet it's a bit long and complicated.

For as long as I can remember, I'd dreamed of being a mom and was fascinated by pregnancy and childbirth. I was the four-year-old who pretended to breastfeed her dolls; the seven-year-old who played with (and casually looked after) the neighbors' toddler; the teenager who showed her stepdad how to change her baby sister's diaper. In a nutshell: my reproductive story reaches back a very long way ...

I spontaneously conceived after only a month of trying. I was almost thirty-five, so was relieved that I'd conceived without any issues. A few weeks later, I couldn't shake the thought that something was wrong with my tiny baby. I called the nurse, but at six weeks' pregnant, it was too early to do an ultrasound. When I had my first prenatal visit a couple of weeks later, I learned that [the] baby had died on the day I thought something was wrong. I was horrified that I knew but also [was] comforted by my intuition. (It has served me well in this donor egg pregnancy.)

The next few months were a whirlwind of grief. When I began to emerge, I was determined to conceive again— quickly—and this time carry my baby to term. After a couple of suspected chemical pregnancies, I began to have an uneasy sense that this was going to be a difficult journey for me, despite coming from an extremely fertile family on both sides.

Five months after my miscarriage, I had an appointment with a specialist in endometriosis—I'd been diagnosed with the disease at twenty-three. My plan was to maximize my chances of getting pregnant again while minimizing my chances of miscarrying (something endometriosis puts you at higher risk for). To my shock, the doctor—on a hunch—said I might be "less fertile than a woman my age." I didn't faint, but I remember the room growing darker and my voice smaller until it was reduced to a whisper.

The doctor ordered blood tests for Kitty, and the results were devastating. One of her hormone levels came back in a barely detectable range. Kitty's reaction was powerful and intense:

I don't know how to describe my reaction exactly. I remember wanting to claw off my skin. This can't be happening. I stared helplessly at the results on my computer screen. Point one seven: I was practically menopausal at thirty-five. A four-year-old has more AMH than I do.

I hoarsely called over my husband. I remember sitting weakly on the edge of our bed, trying desperately to remain calm. I tried every mindfulness technique I could think of, but it was useless. I remember saying to my husband, "I think I'm about to lose it."

And I did.

I started screaming and screaming and screaming. Once I started, I couldn't stop. I guess at the point of exhaustion, my screams turned into raspy sobs of "I don't know what to do. I don't know what to do. I don't know what to do." A stuck record playing the rhythm of a moving train. I remember wanting desperately to rewind time. The tiny baby I'd mourned for six months seemed more precious to me than ever.

I eventually ran out of steam. I lay on the floor, and my husband and I talked for a while. "I have literally clawed my way out of the darkness, only to learn it's all been for nothing. I'm at the bottom of a well, and now I'll never get out. I don't know what to do." … I remember telling him he should leave me. That he deserved better than this broken woman.

Grief wears many faces. Some women cry, scream, and have intense physical reactions. Others retreat within themselves, bottling up their feelings and still experiencing the same type of overwhelming grief.

In Kitty's particular case, the doctor diagnosed her with diminished ovarian reserve (DOR). When a woman is diagnosed with DOR, it means she has fewer eggs than a typical woman her age. This physician told Kitty that her best chances of conceiving again would be via IVF and referred her to a reproductive endocrinologist.

In another layer of complexity to Kitty's infertility issues, the RE discovered that her DOR was likely caused by a chromosomal disorder. This meant that Kitty and Mike also had to meet with a genetic counselor, who educated them about Kitty's chromosomal issue. It was discovered that in addition to Kitty not having many eggs left, the ones she did have couldn't be used because they wouldn't create embryos that were compatible with life.

Kitty shared with us her biggest fear:

My biggest fear—having to use an egg donor to achieve the pregnancy I'd been imagining since I was a little kid—loomed large. But the reality was that paying tens of thousands of dollars for IVF with my own eggs didn't seem like a good idea. I wrestled with the idea of not trying with my own eggs first. My head said it was a waste of time and money. My heart asked if I could live with "What if I'd tried?" Would the question hang over me for the rest of my life?

I sat with the decision while allowing myself to explore egg donation. Would it really be so bad not to pass on my genes? I quickly learned that for as many sensationalist stories as there are portrayed in the media, there are twice as many stories of regular families who used an egg donor with neither regrets nor exploitation.

I started looking at profiles of fertile young women. How would I choose? Who would be the person to replace my DNA? If I were going to use an egg donor, she had to be like the best of me ...

Marna says:

Like so many women in the stories we share, Kitty wanted nothing more than to be a mother. For a young woman in her thirties, learning that her body didn't work the way it should was shocking.

We see that grief comes in so many different forms and has no timeline. The feelings of disbelief, denial, anger, fear, and finally acceptance make their way through us as we strive to reconcile within ourselves the reality that we will not have a child with our own genes.

Stacey and Steve

It was much tougher for my husband, who romanticized the union of my egg and his sperm.

Stacey was a stage IV endometriosis patient who had undergone multiple surgeries for maladies such as blocked fallopian tubes, fibroids, and cysts, as well as the endometriosis from which she had suffered for years.

A reproductive endocrinologist informed Stacey and her partner, Steve, that they needed to use donor eggs to create their family. However, they opted to do one round of IVF with Stacey's eggs because that cycle would be covered 50 percent by insurance.

After producing only two eggs during their first IVF cycle and having a negative outcome, they moved on to egg donation. At the time of their failed cycle, Stacey was thirty-nine. The following year, Stacey transitioned to egg donation, and she gave birth to her son at age forty-one.

The diagnosis part of this journey is different for everybody. By the time some patients receive their diagnosis and the news that they will need to use an egg donor to create their family, that news is a relief. The thing that is wrong with their body actually has a name. The inability to have a child is not just in their head—it's very real.

For Stacey, the transition to egg donation wasn't difficult because she'd had some time to process the idea of using the genes of another woman to help her become a mother.

> It wasn't that difficult for me. I'd had some time to digest the idea. It was much tougher for my husband, who romanticized the union of my egg and his sperm. He told me he [had] always imagined our children getting the best of both of us. I told him even with both of our genes, the kids could be psycho. I gave him some time to process it all, and he came around much more quickly than I expected. Then we were off to the races.

> There were times I was sad that I wouldn't be able to pass on my dad's genes. I loved him dearly. However, I came to realize [that] the most important qualities of my dad's that I would pass on to my child were not about looks, but more about love, loyalty, friendships, and relationships.

Once Steve was on board, they began the process of looking for a donor. When prospective parents are looking for donors of a particular race or ethnicity, the process often can take much longer and be more arduous. Because Stacey is African American, they knew it might take a while. And so their search began.

It can't be said often enough that although there are definitely universal truths about infertility, genetic loss, and donor-conceived families, each person's response to the news or the process is unique. We respond to crises with whatever defenses we already have. People who tend to be matter-of-face and soldier through life's challenges will do so in this process as well. People who tend toward depression will experience news about their ovarian function with sadness and darkness. For Stacey, the transition to ovum donation was easier than it was for Steve. He had more specific fantasies about the biracial/bi-personality child they would create and had to let go of his dream of creating a genetic child with the woman he loved.

We have learned over the years that unfortunately, the dads are often forgotten about in the process because in most cases they still have the ability to hang on to their genes. Because intended fathers express their feelings differently, they may not show they are struggling, but they also may feel sad at the loss of their partner's genes. The reality is that many partners do mourn the loss of their wife's genes and feel uncomfortable at the prospect of looking for genes from another woman.

Kris

> I was so focused on finding my baby that I didn't look back ...

Kris was a forty-year-old single woman when she finally took action to become a mom. Like many women her age, she had always known she wanted to be a mother and had always thought the next date would be the man with whom that would finally happen. But it didn't happen that way.

Kris started with inseminations with donor sperm from a cryobank. Although she worked full-time, she had a middle-class income and had to be very careful with finances. Multiple insemination tries were unsuccessful. Finally, her doctor ran additional tests and told her she had less than a 5 percent chance of conceiving with her own eggs, even with in vitro fertilization. She did not have the money for IVF with donor eggs and donor sperm, so she looked into embryo donation. Either way, she would be a single woman with a child not genetically related to her.

Embryo donation was a path to parenthood that felt very comfortable in every way. According to Kris, it was not a particularly difficult decision at the time. She said, "I was so focused on finding my baby that I didn't look back after learning of this option."

For many women who become single mothers by choice, it is not the lack of genetic connection that they grieve as much as not giving their child two parents. As Kris put it, "Afterwards I did feel guilt, like *What was I thinking?* I always wanted my child to have two parents. That part of things took a while for me to become comfortable with. To be honest I still mourn that."

For many, receiving a diagnosis that will mean substituting their own genetic material with someone else's is terribly sad and disappointing. For others, it opens up options they never could have imagined, leading them to the children they never thought they would have.

> *I still needed to figure out who would be willing to donate to me the embryos they would not be "using." Being single, I thought it would be very challenging. So I turned to my community at Parents via Egg Donation and started the search. What an incredible journey that would become!*

It's hard to feel alone. Finding a community of people who understand what you're going through can be very helpful.

Jenn

> *You could have knocked me over with a feather. Here I am, ready to get on the infertility train, only to find out I wasn't going to be let on to the train at all.*

Jenn had no problems getting pregnant with her daughter at thirty-five. In fact, she and her husband got pregnant on the first try. She told us:

> *My husband and I joked about how incredibly fertile we must be. At thirty-eight, we decided to start trying for a second child and assumed it would happen quickly. After about six months, I started getting nervous. My primary care doctor and midwife both said not to worry. They told me as you get older, sometimes it takes longer. They both said since I already had a child, I should be fine.*

So as instructed, they tried a little longer but still did not get pregnant. Jenn decided to take action—sort of.

> *On my own I made and cancelled two appointments with an RE (mind you, none of my doctors recommended I see someone). I kept saying, "Let's try one more month." Finally, I couldn't shake the feeling that something was wrong. I made a third appointment and kept it, seven weeks before I turned forty. I thought maybe I'd take some Clomid, do a few rounds of IUI; I just needed something to kick-start things. It is so hard to admit there may be obstacles to achieving something that was so easy the first time. "Maybe next time" is the familiar cry of hope.*

> *My reproductive endocrinologist recommended I do the Clomid challenge. When he called with the final results, he said: "It's bad news. I'm sorry, but your chances of having a baby using your eggs are less than 5 percent. Your best option is using a donor egg."*

> *You could have knocked me over with a feather. Here I am, ready to get on the infertility train, only to find out I wasn't going to be let on to the train at all. None of those options*

would be available to me. I went from start to finish in one phone call. I was not given any more information. My RE didn't even book a follow-up meeting with me!

After two weeks of crying and hurting and not sleeping, I started researching donor eggs. I wish I had some guidance in those early days. I have never felt so alone. I tried to reach out to a couple of friends who'd done traditional IVF, but they weren't much help. Nobody knew anything about donor eggs. Luckily, I found PVED, and that is where I found a community who could understand and give support and information.

After a few weeks of learning about DE [donor egg IVF/ egg donation], I realized it was totally different from what I thought. Suddenly it became an option.

It was indeed a very difficult decision. No one talks about DE. It's like this huge secret thing that women are doing more and more, but there is hardly any information out there. I had to explain the basics of donor eggs to my own primary care doctor!

The hardest part is figuring everything out. I had so many questions, and since no one talks about it, it is hard to get answers. I tried to work with a therapist, but she didn't quite get it either. Finding a new therapist who specialized in infertility and who had worked with women who had done DE before was very helpful. Also, joining PVED was a huge source of information and support for me.

In the end, we decided that we wanted to invest our emotion, time, energy, and money into whatever would get us closer to having a child. Trying to use my own eggs would have been a waste of time and would only work with a miracle. Using donor eggs would give us the best chance, so we started down the DE path. I don't regret moving forward so quickly with donor eggs. I think we saved ourselves a lot of heartache.

Carole says:

Once again, we hear a woman's shock and horror upon receiving a diagnosis. Jenn remembers the exact words her physician used with her when describing her probability of conceiving with her own genes. She remembers being so confused, with no one to turn to. When physicians don't address the psychological impact of the information they have communicated, patients feel alone and devastated. Luckily, Jenn was resourceful and found information and a community that could understand what she was experiencing. Fortunately, we now live in a time when more people feel comfortable talking about egg donation.

Shock and trauma take their toll. Expectations are powerful, and when our expectations are not met, there is a period of adjustment when we have to figure out what the future might look like. We wonder where to go from here—who will understand, hear me, and help me? Readjusting to choices that are new takes time.

Bella*

Getting to a place where I could accept having a child that would not look like me or be like me was very painful.

Bella* is a thirty-eight-year-old premature ovarian failure (POF) patient who underwent three unsuccessful surgeries to attempt to preserve her fertility.

I was diagnosed with POF at thirty-eight. I had just completed the first of three surgeries to preserve my fertility. I had two laparoscopic procedures to alleviate the symptoms of endometriosis and a myomectomy. I was absolutely devastated to learn that after three attempts to try with my own eggs, I would "have" to have [a] donor egg. While my insurance covered everything for three IVF and IUI attempts, they wouldn't pay for [a] donor egg. Almost two years later, we finally began a DE cycle.

Moving on to have a child through ovum donation was a very difficult decision for Bella for several reasons.

I come from a very fertile family with very antiquated religious and social beliefs. I am also African American in a community that is slow to embrace alternatives to reproduction, particularly DE. In addition, donor egg IVF is very expensive, even with shared cycles. Lastly, I would be lying if I said that the genetic loss doesn't hurt. Getting to a place where I could accept having a child that would not look like me or be like me was very painful.

Carole says:

It *is* very difficult to accept that the child you have been imagining is never going to come into your life. It is especially challenging to keep trying to fix medical issues with the expectation that the surgery, medication, or procedure will finally make you fertile. Fertility treatment such as that which Bella was involved in for a few years takes you on a roller coaster of the worst kind. Hope and disappointment rotate through your life with regularity, eventually robbing you of any hope at all.

Bella's challenge was compounded by her social and cultural environment. As hard as it might be for her to embrace mothering a child who was not genetically related to her, she feared that it would be even harder for her family and friends. We would encourage women in Bella's circumstances to not be too quick to assume that they and their child will be outcasts. Though people can certainly reject an idea, very few people actually reject children. Once a woman is certain that she can be proud of overcoming obstacles to find a way to build her family, the people around her will most likely follow suit.

Final Thoughts

When the last procedure, ultrasound, or blood test has been done, and the results are in, the news that having a genetic child isn't probable is almost always devastating.

Now what?
I don't understand.
How come?
Why me?

These are all common and reasonable reactions that many women have when they receive their diagnosis.

It's important to know that it's normal to be sad or even angry about losing our genetic link to our future child. The grieving process can be lengthy. We encourage you to give yourself time to grieve this loss and seek help from a therapist to help sort through the many complicated feelings you might be experiencing.

What are my options?

As you leave your physician's office, you may already be wondering what to do next. You might need time to digest the news. Take that time. You probably didn't receive your diagnosis overnight, and it's okay not to make a decision right away.

Your physician probably mentioned egg donation and/or surrogacy as a way to create your family. This is one option. Embryo donation (where the intended parent receives embryos from people who already have completed their family) is another.

As you begin to research your options, you also might think about adoption, foster care, or even living childfree. Explore all the many paths to parenthood to figure out which option fits you the best.

If you decide that egg donation or embryo donation is your path, you might feel overwhelmed, and it might seem like an eternity before you meet your baby.

We want to reassure you that regardless of your choice, you will find the path that is right for you.

Ready?
1 …
2 …
3 …
Deep breath!

What are my next steps?

There are so many things to think about in this process, and at times the process itself can be incredibly overwhelming.

Once the decision to have a child with the help of an egg donor has been made, you may wish to select a new infertility physician and clinic. The physician who gave you your original diagnosis might be the physician you want to receive treatment from, or you might decide that you would like to explore different clinics and their egg donor programs.

Your next step is selecting an egg donor from a clinic's egg donor pool, an egg donor agency/matching program, or an egg bank. Or there may be a friend or relative in your life who would be a very good candidate for helping you build your family.

The hardest step to take in all of this is the emotional step—up to this point you've been just dangling your feet in the water, but once you've selected an egg donor and committed to cycling, you are "jumping in the deep end." The deep end is extraordinarily emotional, and although this route is a wonderful option for many, coming to terms with letting go and grieving the genetic link is a very big deal.

The fantasy child we tried to create can take up a lot of room in our heads, our hearts, and our homes. There isn't enough room in our home for the child we originally wanted and the child or children we will eventually have. So we need to say goodbye to the child we can't have to make room for the children we can. We will address this in more depth in chapter 6, "Letting Go, Moving On."

> 🦜 *Our take-home message to you is this: Your feelings of loss are real. Take the time you need to mourn.*

This is the time when you may wish to seek a counselor or therapist who specializes in the field of infertility or third-party reproduction to talk about your feelings. A therapist can also guide you on how to share your decision to create your family this way with other members of your family and circle of friends.

We encourage you to check out the resources on the PVED website and join the PVED forum, where you can connect with other people who have walked this path, and to utilize the other support networks referenced in the Resources section at the end of this book. We also encourage you to express your feelings therapeutically—journaling, creating art, going for walks in nature—and to take the time to pamper yourself. Be kind to yourself. Up until this point, it's been a rough ride.

> 🦜 *Marna says, "Fasten your seat belt because the adventure you are about to embark on is going to be the ride of a lifetime!"*

Chapter 2

SELECTING YOUR EGG DONOR

Love is a decision—not an emotion!

—Lao Tzu, *Tao Te Ching*

By now you've most likely had the big conversation with your physician about the need to use donor eggs to expand your family, so let's take a moment to regroup. You might need a little time to process this mind-boggling news, what it means, and the steps it will take to complete an egg donor cycle from start to finish. This is likely one of the biggest decisions you are going to make in your life, so feeling overwhelmed, anxious, apprehensive, uncertain, or even afraid is completely normal.

It is normal to be sad about losing our genetic link to our future child. For some women, a lengthy grieving process can ensue. We encourage you to give yourself time to grieve this loss and to consider seeing a therapist specializing in third-party reproduction to help you sort through the complicated feelings and unique grief you may feel.

Remember that no matter which egg donor you select, your child will be one you and your partner (if you have one) create and give life to. The child will be exclusive and special to your own family, and he or she wouldn't be coming into this world if not for the love that you have to give. Most importantly, regardless of eye color, hair color, height, or other physical characteristics, you are going to love, honor, and cherish this child—because this child is going to be *your* child.

How Do I Choose?

It's very helpful to find support at this point in the process. Parents via Egg Donation (PVED) is a nonprofit organization with an active online forum (www.pved.org). Thousands of parents and intended parents from all over the world communicate daily on PVED regarding all aspects of egg donation, embryo donation, and surrogacy. (Other support networks are listed in the Resources section at the back of this book.)

Next, get your head in the game. Donor selection is not like purchasing a big-ticket item, such as a car or a house. This is about creating life and having a baby—you can't trade your child in! This means that you will be giving a lot of thought to the physical, emotional, social, and spiritual qualities you believe are important when choosing your donor. Some intended parents find it helpful to make a list of the qualities important to them.

Susie* shares her experience regarding her donor selection process:

> *My first donor was a known donor/good friend. That was an easy selection because she volunteered. There are pretty much no physical characteristics shared between us, but ideologically we are basically identical. We did the counseling; we were all on the same page; the doctor cleared her, so we moved forward. However, that cycle was catastrophic in so many ways that I almost quit. When I was ready to try again, nine or so months later, we went anonymous. I was not capable of dealing with the heartbreak of another known cycle, even though she was more than willing to try again.*
>
> *I stayed local and used a clinic with a relatively small in-house donor pool (though out of curiosity, I just went back to look now, and it's grown by leaps and bounds). By the*

time I got to the point of [an] anonymous donor, I had no requirements other than healthy, proven, and donation(s) resulting in a "take-home" baby. I didn't care about similarity in looks, about education, about hobbies, etc. I narrowed it down to two donors. My husband didn't even want to see pictures. I brought home the health information and their essays, we went over them, and we made our choice before bedtime. All told, it took less than twenty-four hours to settle on a donor.

I ended up with a donor who didn't really resemble me in the slightest. My ethnicity is Indigenous. Hers is Irish, German, and Swedish. My eyes are green; hers are blue. I'm 5' 7"; she's 5'5". She weighs a good twenty-five pounds less than I do, when I'm actually at my ideal weight. Even our skin tones are different, with me being pale and [her] having an olive complexion. Pretty much our only similarity is brown hair, but mine is darker, thick, and wavy, while hers is light, fine, and stick-straight. In the end, it came down to the "take-home baby" aspect. They both had stellar family health histories. They were both proven in that they had successfully donated before. However, Donor A, while having a child of her own, had not yet produced a take-home baby for intended parents. There was a woman who was six weeks pregnant, but in the end, that wasn't enough for me. I needed to know a baby had made it all the way home. So we went with Donor B, whose donations had resulted in two take-home babies.

Egg donors can be found in the in-house egg donor program your clinic might have. Although those pools are generally small, they are a place to start. There are also egg donation agencies, sometimes called matching programs or brokers, as well as egg banks, which specialize in the recruitment of donors and therefore have a much larger and varied selection of donors to choose from. An in-house program might be the right choice for you if you want to choose someone whose fertility is proven. An agency might be more helpful to you if you are a person of color or you wish to be matched with someone who shares your religion.

Frances*

> I was using my clinic's in-house agency, so I got log-in information and started looking. How I narrowed it down? First, I wanted to make sure that we would be successful and get viable eggs.
>
> 1. Proven donor
> 2. Preferably young (early twenties)
>
> Then I went for attributes that resembled me and my family:
>
> 3. Caucasian
> 4. Blue eyes (I have blue, [and] my husband has green, so [our] children should have light eyes if naturally conceived)
> 5. Over 5'6" (I'm 6'1" and knew that finding a donor that tall would be impossible, but I definitely wanted on the tall side—I ended up going with 5'8")
> 6. Preferred college-educated but selected someone attending college
> 7. She looked friendly
>
> I got the paperwork, and I liked what she wrote about why she was doing this. It just felt right. In hindsight I may have looked for someone open to contact after [my child turned] eighteen, but then I wouldn't have my little guy, so maybe I wouldn't have cared!

Remember, there are different kinds of egg donor agencies. Some are very large and well established, whereas others are small and new to the industry. Regardless of where you choose your donor (in-house pool, agency, or egg bank), it's important that you learn as much as possible so that you can make an informed choice. Above all, egg donor agencies are service providers, meaning you are in the driver's seat—they work for you. They may have the egg donor you need to grow your family, but in the end, you are writing the check, and they need your business to stay in business. If there is information you want or need that has not been provided, be sure to ask. It is easier to ask for as much information as you can at the beginning of this process than it is to go back and try to get it later.

Sometimes the first egg donor we select isn't the egg donor we end up cycling with, as Lorraine* experienced. She shares with us that it's okay to change your mind regarding egg donor selection and criteria.

Lorraine*

> *We had to pick two donors. [With] Donor A, the cycle failed. I went with an in-house pool and shared cycle at my clinic. I loved that donor. She was a first-time donor but had a child of her own. She was like a much younger and cuter version of me. Her childhood pictures could have been mine. We had nothing in common, on paper at least, but she looked like me! That cycle was a disaster, and I was heartbroken. It was one of those cases where a twenty-four-year-old has crappy eggs—I guess we did have something in common after all.*

> *When it came time to pick a second donor, I had switched clinics [to a clinic] with no in-house pool, and I needed to find an agency. I looked at a few different ones and decided to pick the agency first. I went with an agency that seemed to vet their donors well, and most of them had a college degree. It was a semi-smaller pool of donors, and I almost liked the limited selection. Drawing on our first experience, I realized that I didn't care so much about the physical appearance of my donor. I only required light eyes.*

I have greenish-blue and my husband has crystal-blue eyes. I didn't want our kid to come out with brown eyes for the simple fact of someone asking, how did s/he get brown eyes? I swear, eye color is the only thing people remember from that one week of basic genetics in high school biology! Ended up that the donor we picked looks nothing like me, but we have several things in common. And she ended up being a rock star in the egg department!

I'm just eleven weeks [pregnant], and I don't think much about the donor. I do wonder what this child is going to look like, but I guess if I had my OE [own egg] baby, I would probably wonder the same.

Judith*

I studied all of the donors within our clinic's in-house donor pool. I felt that since my genes were the ones not being represented in our child(ren), I should make most of the decision. I initially picked a donor out of the in-house pool, but she failed the psych evaluation. A brand-new donor was suggested to me (clinic donor pool), and I absolutely fell in love with her. Much of her profile was similar to my own, and she was the "one." Now we have a wonderful four-year-old boy and the memory of his twin sister (lost at fourteen days old).

As you read through the stories of others in this chapter, you will find that donor selection is a highly individual process. In Sharon's case, she and her husband "wanted a proven donor who was intelligent and looked like she could be related to" Sharon.

Sharon

> *I didn't have a strong desire for a child who would look like me, but my husband thought it would be less likely that people would wonder later why our child(ren) bore no resemblance to me if there were similarities between the donor's appearance and mine.*
>
> *I also hoped to find a donor with a similar ethnic background. My father is Irish, and my mother is a mixture of Scottish, English, and German, so this was more possible for me than it might be for someone who is not of European descent.*

Other people discover what's important to them by looking at multiple donor profiles. Only then are they able to figure out what to prioritize. This was the case for Cheryl*.

Cheryl*

> *We (or really I) first looked at our clinic's database, but it was small, and nobody on it even came close to resembling me, and I also wasn't comfortable with the fact [that] our clinic didn't have adult pictures. I then started looking on agency databases and [at] some other great clinics that have good databases.*
>
> *The process of looking helped me clarify what my priorities were: proven donor; great health history and family longevity; adult pictures available and possibly open to contact if the kids want it; some physical similarity to me; intelligent (measured by what they said about how they wanted to live their lives, what their taste in books and movies and hobbies was, etc., rather than in college degrees); artistic/musical; good-looking; good temperament*

(optimistic, caring, etc.). Basically, I felt like a sci-fi fairy godmother, choosing what gifts I wanted to give my children, and the process of searching made it more and more clear to me what gifts I wanted to give them the most.

At first I was looking at brunette white, Asian, Jewish, and Hispanic—basically any shade of brown hair and any skin tone between Irish and Mexican/Indian—but then I saw a video interview with a young woman who was donor-conceived and [who] said the only thing that made her at all uncomfortable was the fact [that] she looked nothing like her mom. I'm white and fair-complected. Also, I learned that it's much harder for nonwhite and Jewish women to find donors who are a good physical match, and I felt it would be unfair of me to take an Asian, Jewish, etc. donor "off the market" and use up one of her six allotted cycles when I wasn't Asian or Jewish, etc., myself.

We ended up going with a donor who has my exact coloring, presumably because she happens to be a close ethnic match (Northern European on one side and Spanish on the other, same as me).

Moms like Stacey felt strongly about selecting a donor who had donated previously.

Stacey

Being a rocket scientist wasn't a requirement. We looked for someone who seemed warm, nice, and interesting. Looks-wise, we definitely look like we could be related, which was also important to me. Additionally, it was important to us that our donor had donated previously, so she'd know what she was getting herself into.

Some parents have an easy time selecting their egg donor, but for others, such as Jaclyn* and Lindsey*, it is a challenging and lengthy process. And that's okay. There is no official timetable regarding how long it should or shouldn't take you to make your donor selection—it's really your own process.

Jaclyn*

> *It was a long process. I started looking even before [my husband] was 100 percent on board because I knew it would take time. I looked at agency donor lists first and found a few donors that I thought would be wonderful. I actually fell in love with one donor, whose essay I could have written myself. But she was [on the] East Coast, and I didn't want to have to travel because I had a full-time job and a toddler at home. It was hard to let that donor go! In the end, because we could barely afford to cycle at all, I decided to use a clinic donor. I actually looked at clinic donor profiles before I chose a clinic, just to see what our options would be.*

> *I felt comfortable with one clinic's donor list in particular and met with their top RE and really clicked with her and also the donor coordinator. For me, that connection was very important because it was such a personal thing to be going through. At first, it was important to me to find a donor with at least some of my ethnic heritage, but on the West Coast that was proving to be very difficult. My options were very limited. So I had to let that go eventually as well. I found a donor I thought would be great, but by the time I called the next morning, she had been taken!*

> *At that point I became very focused. I set my parameters for "young and proven," with at least some of my physical characteristics. I found four and rank-ordered them. I gave*

the list to my husband, and independent of my input, his #1 was the same as my #1. That seemed like as good a way to choose as any. I spoke to the nurse coordinator who had worked with the donor in her previous cycle, and she said that [the] donor was very responsible and took donating seriously and that she had a beautiful smile (I knew that part already from photos). I should say I did have child and adult photos of her. [My husband] thought she resembled me, but I didn't. Anyway … that's how we chose. At the time, donor choice was very important for me, but I didn't really get how important that would be to my kids until they were maybe two years old. That's when I began to regret using an anonymous donor. I likely could not have convinced [my husband] to use a known donor, but that is a regret that I have because I have come to believe it's a child right to know who their donor is. In the end, I love my boys to death and would not change a thing.

Lindsey*

Donor selection for me was very tough. I went site to site, looking and looking for someone who would jump out as "right" to me. I eventually realized that I was looking for a carbon copy of myself. I eventually went through a clinic in the Czech Republic that had anonymous donors only— no pictures. I sent my and my husband's picture, and the doctor matched us to donors. My requirements were in terms of height, age, eye color, and hair color. I know little more than that about the donor. It worked for me/us. It took the decision out of my hands—I didn't have to search for something that wasn't out there anymore. Now I wish I had a little more info that I could share with my daughter about her genetic origins, but I have few regrets.

Prioritizing What Is Important in Donor Selection

Characteristics to consider in donor selection include physical traits, education, personality, and family history, as well as genetic traits. However, matching physical characteristics is mostly a way to hopefully make the means of conception less public. Choosing a donor who looks like you does not mean you will have a child who looks like you. It is important to explore the reason you are looking for a physical match. Are you denying that this child will not be your genetic offspring? Sometimes the donor search reveals a lack of readiness to move forward. Is it a way to help you not have to think about the donor? We want you to be able to think about your donor with gratitude and heartfelt appreciation, embracing what she imbued in your child. Having a physical match will not make you forget that your children came to you after infertility.

Nevertheless, if everyone in your family is tall and has red hair or blue eyes and freckles, it makes sense that finding those qualities in a donor might be very important to you. Aside from height and hair color, intended moms are often looking for someone who is from their specific part of the world. For them, that's a big part of their identity. And while they might be ready to let go of their genetic connection to their future children, many are not ready to let go of their heritage.

Marna says:

> It's no secret that beautiful egg donors are selected quickly, often have waiting lists, and are almost always used repeatedly. Does that guarantee you a baby who will look like a child model? In actuality, no. Genes are a crapshoot. Your child is going to be an unrecognizable version of yourself, the donor, and the sperm contributor or your partner (if you have one), so don't feel like you have to select somebody who is your mirror twin or a clone of what you think your future offspring is supposed to look like. The baby whom you're meant to have is the baby whom you're meant to have!

So if looks aren't the way to go, how do you choose?

Although many families start out looking for a donor who looks like members of the recipient family, physical resemblance may be one of the least important things to look for in a donor. Sometimes when family members don't look like each other, they get asked more frequently where a child might have gotten a particular feature, placing the parents in the position of answering more questions than they might be comfortable with. However, many families *don't* look alike. As we have discussed in previous chapters, this dissimilarity can trigger feelings of loss in the parent who has lost the genetic connection, and those feelings are what one is trying to avoid in looking for a clone. However, when the work of grief is done, we can fully accept that our child or children will be uniquely themselves and never will be a physical reflection of us.

Many mental health professionals recommend a very different way of choosing a donor than has been described. A "good fit" means way more than looking alike. A great way to select a donor is to choose someone whom it seems you would love to spend a few hours at a coffee shop getting to know. It is nice to choose someone whom you'd be proud to call your daughter, since in most cases, a donor could easily be the daughter to a recipient, who might be twice the age of the donor. Donors who are matched through matching programs usually complete a questionnaire profile that gives so much information that the donor's personality comes through. Even if she remains semi-anonymous, it's not hard to get a feel for who she is, and you may find yourself wanting to know more, or to know her. This is why patients often choose donors very different from the ones they originally set out to select; it may be that the one who looks like you isn't somebody who calls out to your heart, and someone who doesn't look like you feels like someone with whom you'd like to be friends.

Kinds of Relationships with Your Egg Donor

Let's talk a little bit about donor egg terminology. The kinds of relationships we have (or don't have) with our egg donors are organized into four categories: anonymous, semi-anonymous, known, and directed egg donation.

"Anonymous" Egg Donation

A completely "anonymous" arrangement is one in which the donor and recipients are unknown to each other, and no adult photo of the donor is presented. The identities of the egg donors and intended parents are unknown to each other at the time of the arrangement. However, intended parents will be informed about, and have access to, details about the egg donor such as her age, ethnicity, medical history, family history, religious denomination, sexual orientation, and educational background. This kind of an egg donor would often be found at clinics' in-house donor pools or at egg banks that do not provide photographs. There are not many agencies, egg banks, or clinics in the United States that, at the time of writing, practice truly anonymous egg donation.

This category can be confusing to many intended parents because although no identifying information is exchanged, sometimes clinics and agencies share childhood and adult photos. **When we place a face (photograph) with other potentially identifying information, that egg donation category becomes semi-anonymous**. These kinds of donors typically do not register with an agency such as the Donor Sibling Registry for continuing contact at a later date.

Ruth*

> *Our facility had anonymous only-donors. We received donor profiles (maybe four at a time) based on our characteristics, nationality, etc. If we didn't like any, we called the office to ask for more. Once we decided, we called the office to let them know. The donor was notified, and then we were off to the races. We had twin girls.*

Juana*

We used an anonymous donor. Our clinic had a database of about twenty women to choose from. My husband and I came up with a plan to go through their profiles separately and then bring our top three choices to each other. We both ended up picking the same one, hands down. Neither of us picked a second and third choice because we were so excited about the first choice! We liked her because she shared physical characteristics of me, but also her personality was very similar. (Our clinic has extensive profiles with several essay questions that give us a good idea [of] what kind of person she is). She seemed very real and not like she was just writing what prospective IPs [intended parents] wanted to hear. When we told our nurse which donor we picked, we also found that she had donated several times prior, and all had resulted in successful pregnancies, so that helped as well!

Jessie*

We used an anonymous donor. For months I scrolled through all of the donor websites looking for me! Of course, I couldn't find me, but when I saw her, I knew right away that was the one! That was as close to me as I was going to get.

Charlotte*

We used two different donors. The first time we volunteered for a study (the clinic was new to egg vitrification). Our donor was completely anonymous and chosen by the medical staff. We didn't even see a picture of her until the morning of our (successful) transfer. The second time, it was also anonymous. But we were able to choose her from the donor pool at the clinic.

I should also say that we tried to use my sister as a donor, but we had two unsuccessful cycles with her.

Sharon

We selected an anonymous donor from our clinic's in-house pool. We did not know anyone who would be an appropriate candidate to donate to us, and the process of finding a donor who would be willing to meet, at the time of the cycle or in the future, seemed too cumbersome to us. We received a lot of information about our donor from our clinic, and we were satisfied with that.

A Note about the Internet, Illusions of Privacy, and the Myth of Anonymity

However you choose your egg donor is the right way for your family—but one of the most important things to consider is future contact. Regardless of what we think or what we are comfortable with, kids are curious about themselves and the world. They will ask questions. We know that donor-conceived individuals care about that invisible side of themselves. Some people care more than others, but many have a healthy degree of curiosity. So it's in your and your children's best interest to have as much information available at your fingertips; think of it as your toolbox for your child's future. You may never need it because your child may never show an interest in future or continued contact with his or her egg donor. However, in the event your child *does* show an interest, the information is right there for you to share when the time is right. Regardless of what category your egg donor falls into, with current and future technological advances, we are connected in ways we never imagined.

We live in an age where we are able to communicate with the push of a button or a few simple keystrokes. The internet and social media have upended the traditional meaning of privacy. When we go online or send an email or text message, that information is stored somewhere, probably indefinitely. The advances in technology have given us the ability to search unlimited information. Even screenshots can potentially be viewed or recorded by a third party. The reality is there is no such thing as true anonymous egg donation; in this day and age, it simply does not exist.

Home DNA tests have completely changed the world of donor conception. No matter what a clinic or agency calls it, there is no longer any such thing as anonymity. Every single day, all over the world, people are learning of their donor-conceived status and/or are finding donor-related siblings and the donors themselves through DNA testing and matching. Be prepared for the psychological needs of your children, and do not delude yourselves that a donor will not be found if you or your children need or want to find her.

Consider asking your egg donor to register with a third-party entity such as the Donor Sibling Registry, or DSR (DonorSiblingRegistry. com), which is another way of creating future or continuing contact. The DSR is a nonprofit organization that acts as a third party to create a safe space for you and your egg donor to exchange or hold information. The matching program or agency through whom you matched with your donor may also have a system to help you with contact in the future.

Semi-Anonymous Egg Donation

Most egg donors registered with agencies, clinics, and egg banks fall into this category. Semi-anonymous egg donation means the identities of the egg donors and intended parents are unknown to each other at the time of the arrangement, but intended parents have access to information about the egg donor such as her age, ethnicity, medical history, family history, religious denomination, sexual orientation, and educational background. Photographs are always shared, and sometimes a first name or alias is also provided. A facilitator may arrange for a conference call or email address exchange between both parties and the facilitator, but no physical meeting takes place.

These donors may be on the fence about continued contact at a later date but are often open-minded and agreeable about registering with a registry of some kind. Donors in this category can and sometimes do become known egg donors.

It is important to note that both "anonymous" and semi-anonymous donation mean that the identities of donors and recipients are unknown to each other at the time the arrangement is made, even if they speak on the phone or Skype with each other. We know that in this age of the internet and with the voices of donor offspring becoming more outspoken, these originally anonymous and semi-anonymous arrangements may not stay that way forever. The terms refer to the status of the arrangements prior to the start of the cycles.

Marna

When we selected our donor, we used the in-house donor pool within our clinic. I had no idea what I was doing. There was nothing online to look at; all of the profiles were on paper. The clinic would mail three profiles at a time. We would look at three profiles, and if we didn't like them, we would drive them back into the city and hand them back. This went on for a month. Finally, our physician helped us select our donor. He selected a very lovely young lady he thought would fit within our family. It was a great match. It was completely anonymous. We had information provided with an in-depth profile, but no photographs, no names—nothing. We also had to sign an agreement that we wouldn't try to find her using a private detective, the internet, etc.

Much later, we reached back out to our clinic and inquired about our donor because our son had questions, and we asked if they would approach her to see if she would become a known donor and have continuing contact. This process took a long time—but they finally did [reach her], and she was on board with meeting us. The relationship we have with her now is extremely positive, and she has become an extended member of our family.

Kitty

I don't have an identical twin, so when I accepted that finding my clone was never going to happen, I had to make decisions based on who I thought could represent the best of me. I wanted someone proven and who would be open to future contact. After that, I wanted someone tall (over 5'8" because I am almost 6'1"), smart (but not necessarily academic), kind, creative—basically, someone who I could relate to and who had similar interests. My donor and I look a lot alike, as it turns out. She's an inch shorter than I hoped, but like me, she has an angular face, pale olive skin, and a lot of fine, wavy hair. Unlike me, she has large, beautiful eyes, which my daughter inherited. I've spent hours gazing into them, and I'm always reminded of my journey, and I'm always delighted to see my donor reflected in my daughter. How could I be anything but grateful to the special woman who gave me the gift of my exquisite girl, my best little sidekick?

Noreen*

I used an agency and spent my days scrolling through profiles like a dating website (I'm sure my new coworker that sat behind me was wondering why I was trolling female profiles while married—LOL). The donor was anonymous, but I have her pictures and profile (health, school, family, personal traits, and interests info). I ultimately went with a woman who had the most genuine smile. I truly think as soon as I saw her, I knew she was the one. Of course,

*we fully vetted her with our doctor and psychologist, and
everyone agreed with my gut feeling about her.*

Known Egg Donation

With known egg donation, intended parents are given the same
kind of information about the egg donor as in a semi-anonymous egg
donation, but also first name, last name, email address, cell number, and
other personal identifying information are mutually exchanged between
both parties, *and* there is always some sort of face-to-face contact. This
may occur over Skype or in a physical meeting. The intentions of egg
donors and intended parents in this category are to have continued
contact at a later date in the event a child is born. These egg donors
are almost always registered with an entity such as the Donor Sibling
Registry.

Marie*

*I narrowed it down from a pool of about ten that I had
selected from various agencies, then picked based on looks,
intelligence/drive, previous successful donations, and family
history ... and I wanted it to be open so my kids could find
her later if they wanted to or had questions. We talked on
the phone, and I discovered our personalities were very
similar. My doctor kept telling me how impressed she was
with her while she was going through the process, so that
was encouraging. Then I met her at her retrieval, and we
looked like we could be sisters. It was a great choice.*

Directed Egg Donation

Directed egg donation describes an egg donor who is a relative or
friend of the intended parent(s). This egg donor is not typically registered
with a clinic, agency, or egg bank. These kinds of egg donors almost
always have continuing contact with the family they donated to.

Jessica

My health insurance at the time was from Massachusetts, which has some fertility coverage. After going through two separate one-week trials of medication, I did not produce any eggs, so my treatments were both canceled. I was very vocal on my Facebook about the trials and challenges I was going through in an upbeat way. My insurance did not cover egg donors and would not cover the medication an egg donor would need. A friend messaged me and said she would give me her eggs. I honestly didn't care what she looked like, her personality, etc. I was just grateful that someone would be so generous. So we went through the counseling session and signed legal documents with a lawyer. I had just enough medication from both canceled treatment plans to give her, so I didn't need to buy medication. I was in no way in a position to be picky, but she was the best person to offer this gift to me. She is very much like me, and my daughter does not look that much different. No one can tell if I didn't tell them. Also, my cousin offered first, and once the doctor looked at her blood tests and physical, she was determined to probably have the same condition as me—"premature ovarian failure." My egg donor and I remained good friends until my child's first birthday party, in which we had a falling-out which was indirectly related to my child. I hope we make amends soon.

Lisa*

My husband was talking to her (our egg donor) at work about our struggle, and she volunteered. Wonderful experience. We went to appointments together, and I was at her egg retrieval and watched it on the screen. We have a good relationship, [and] we go over to [her] house, but

she feels uncomfortable coming over to things like birthdays
celebrations because my own family does not know.

Susie

The short version is that we worked with her because she
volunteered. Using a known donor never occurred to us.
She said, "I'm not using my eggs; I never want to use my
eggs. I would like you to have them if you want them."
It didn't work. It was awesome to cycle with her. We got
closer. I felt super involved. I was a part of everything.
What was awful was the loss. We did the psych evaluations
and everything like we were supposed to. We were prepared
for what would happen if it worked. We weren't prepared
for what would happen if it didn't. Not only did I have to
deal with my grief (and it was huge); I had to deal with
hers as well. I watched her beat herself up. I watched her
blame herself for causing me more pain when she was trying
to take some of it away. It was terrible. I think it would
have been less awful had it just been negative. But she was
there for the positive pee stick, the beta, the early heartbeats.
She was as excited as I was. Then I lost one. And four and
a half weeks later, I lost the other. We kind of went into a
tailspin together.

Who Can Be an Egg Donor?

An egg donor is a young woman who has undergone extensive testing at a fertility clinic by a reproductive endocrinologist (RE, or fertility doctor). She is in excellent health and has many eggs to donate. She has a clean health history and is free of any genetic diseases, disorders, or sexually transmitted infections. Last but not least, she is psychologically healthy and sound and desires to help others create their families.

Any woman selected to be an egg donor typically:

➤ Is between 21 and 29
➤ Has regular monthly menstrual periods
➤ Has undergone extensive testing to ensure that she is in excellent health
➤ Has a healthy BMI
➤ Is a nonsmoker
➤ Is not a drug user
➤ Has no reproductive disorders/abnormalities and has two ovaries and many eggs
➤ Is responsible (has the ability to follow complex directions and administer injectable medications to herself, has dependable transportation, and is willing to make the commitment to attend many doctor appointments)
➤ Has an excellent family history, free of serious inheritable diseases
➤ Is not using any sort of long-term birth control such as Depo-Provera, an implant, or an IUD
➤ Is free of infections
➤ Is psychologically sound and willing to undergo a psychological evaluation
➤ Is excited about the process of helping to build a family

The psychological assessment of egg donor candidates is a crucial part of this process. An assessment consists of an extensive clinical interview as well as the administration of a standardized psychological test. The interview gives the clinic staff a thorough psychosocial history; we learn about the members of her family and their functioning levels and general psychological health. To the best of our ability, we learn about any issues such as substance abuse, learning issues, attention deficit disorder, developmental issues, and mental illness. This is by no means an exhaustive list.

We also determine the woman's motivation to be a donor. It is not enough to just show up on time and take medication properly. A good evaluation will also inform and educate a candidate about the long-term risks and benefits of providing gametes to help create families. When a woman gives informed consent, we want to make sure it is truly informed consent. Part of the evaluation's purpose is to help a woman understand that although a donor offspring is not her child to parent, and we don't want her to feel a sense of "ownership" over the child, we do want her to feel a sense of responsibility for the future need for contact felt by the child she helped to create. We help her to understand that DNA tests have changed the landscape of egg donation and that she should expect to be contacted by either the donor offspring or the recipient family at some point in the future. We talk to her about the importance of sharing her participation with any future children she parents, as well any future or current life partner. A significant focus of a good psychological evaluation should be to help a candidate understand that egg donation creates new forms of kinship. Her children will have half siblings, and she will always be related to the recipient families, whether or not they ever know each other.

Ideally, psychological assessments should be done in person in the office of a mental health professional who has proven expertise in reproductive medicine and third-party family-building. The Mental Health Professional Group of the American Society of Reproductive Medicine is a good place to start to locate such professionals. Qualified professionals can be at https://www.asrm.org/.

Blood Types: Are They Important?

Some families find it important to select an egg donor who has the same blood type as one of the intended parents. There are some advantages to this—in the event you need to donate blood to your child, you can. But often intended parents are mystified by the issue of blood type.

Historically, doctors in the early days of donor-egg IVF would match intended mothers with donors based on nothing more than blood type. But times have changed. It used to be that egg donation was overwhelmingly kept secret from the child, and no biographical information was provided about the donor to the recipient family. When blood type was matched in order to keep the donation a secret, DNA testing was not readily available through such testing companies as Ancestry and 23andMe. Many people of all ages are learning that they were donor-conceived after doing a simple over-the-counter drugstore DNA test, like from Ancestry or 23andMe. Matching blood type will not protect such a secret in today's world. Even with the best planning, a child will find out that that his or her parents are not genetically connected.

Donor Personality

As you begin looking through egg donor profiles, you might notice personalities emerging as you learn more about the donors you review. It may seem silly to see basic questions such as "What's your favorite color? What's your favorite food? Book? Sport?" However, these kinds of questions can give you a glimpse into a donor's personality. You might read about what an egg donor was like as a kid, and this may be helpful to you when you think back to how you were as a kid. Are there similarities? Or big differences? Were you a bubbly, happy, free-spirited, outgoing kid? Or were you a quiet, serious, thoughtful, shy kid?

Some intended parents feel it's important to select an egg donor who has a personality similar to their own, as well as similar interests and values. Others may intentionally select a woman who is quite different from themselves—in fact, screening out for qualities the intended mom does not like in herself.

First-Time Donors versus Repeat or Proven Donors

First-time egg donors are women who have never gone through the egg donation process. This doesn't mean they have not already conceived (gotten pregnant). Many first-time donors are deemed to have "proven fertility" because they have successfully gotten pregnant.

Proven donors are women who have successfully gone through the egg donation process one or more times. This means that they have completed an egg donor cycle and undergone an egg donor retrieval, and the intended mother or gestational surrogate has successfully conceived.

Selecting a proven donor over a first-time donor doesn't always guarantee a successful egg donation cycle for pregnancy, but it does have some advantages. A proven donor knows what's expected; she previously took all her medications correctly and responded to them well. The clinic can predict from previous cycles how she might respond to the medication. The proven egg donor knows the drill regarding all those many doctor appointments and has undergone a successful retrieval. The majority of proven donors are asked back if the egg donation cycle results in a pregnancy—hence, the term "proven." There are a lot of unknowns when jumping into creating a family with someone else's genes, and some intended parents find having a proven donor very reassuring.

Where Do We Go from Here?

Many intended parents start off not wanting to know anything about their egg donor beyond what they see in the photograph or on her profile. Some will even tell you that looking at a photograph takes up too much "head space," and they feel they might be distracted in regard to parenting if they think about their egg donor. Fears and insecurities tend to bubble to the surface, and it's easier to push something away than talk about it or try to resolve it. But then what happens during this whole experience is the most incredible phenomenon. These little eggs are fertilized and become embryos, and these little embryos are transferred into an awaiting uterus of an intended mother or surrogate, and if everything works like it's supposed to, nine months later an amazing baby is born. Once this little being arrives into the world and we begin to parent, more often than not, our minds change about our donor and the information or lack of information we originally received.

Your location may play a part in the type of information you are provided about a donor, as well as your ability to have a phone or in-person meeting. Many parts of the world, such as Australia and the

United Kingdom, prohibit anonymity; in the mid-western United States, it might be more challenging to receive more than basic information. But many agencies are now supportive of extensive profiles and willing to facilitate a match meeting.

We receive telephone calls and emails on a daily basis from parents asking if it's okay to change their minds about future contact and if we can help them find information about their egg donor that they did not receive before. This change of heart is almost always because of their child. Maybe their child is at an age where she or he has begun to ask questions. Or maybe the parents have reached a point where they now would like to meet the egg donor to gain closure on their infertility journey, give thanks, and introduce their child to the special person who helped create them.

We want you to know it's okay to change your mind. People change their minds every day about myriad things. Deciding to learn more about your egg donor and her background is very normal and perfectly healthy.

What's important is that you can't have *too much* information about your egg donor. Whatever you were offered ethically and legally, take it and file it away. Who knows? Maybe your child will show no interest in knowing about their egg donor, ancestry, or heritage. But maybe your child will be very invested in their ancestry and learning about the other half of their genes. Regardless of how interested your child is, safeguarding your donor's information and photos means you will have answers to at least some of your child's questions.

If you need more help with your donor selection, feel free to reach out to the community at www.pved.org. Help is literally a click away. If you find that you need help with your feelings surrounding egg donation, we recommend that you reach out to a mental health professional who specializes in third-party reproduction.

Marna says:

Don't get too hung up emotionally regarding your egg donor selection because at the end of the day, the baby you have is the baby you were meant to have.

Chapter 3

FROM HERE TO MATERNITY

That first pregnancy is a long sea journey to a country where you don't know the language, where land is in sight for such a long time that after a while it's just the horizon—and then one day birds wheel over that dark shape and it's suddenly close, and all you can do is hope like hell that you've had the right shots.

—Emily Perkins, *Novel about My Wife*

The endless shots. The countless pills. The oh-so-many blood draws, ultrasounds, and doctor appointments. Infertility patients are pros at navigating the waters of infertility and have become experts at treading water while we wait. It's fair to say we play the hurry-up-and-wait game all too well. We've also become experts at researching and obsessing about every little detail in relation to our donor egg cycle, and still we wait some more.

We wait to see if our chosen donor is available. We wait to start cycling. We wait to see if she's responding to meds. We wait to see how many eggs we got. We wait for the fertilization report, the day 3 report, the day 5 report, and—for those of us who genetically test our embryos—the genetic report.

And finally, the day we have been waiting for so long: transfer day. And then we wait some more to find out if months of waiting for one thing or another has worked. Some of us wait for the official beta blood test. Others of us "cheat" and pee on a home pregnancy test. Some of us get a positive result, and some of us don't.

But if we made it to the BFP (big fat positive), we're in the game—but everything we've done so far has just been to get to the conceiving part. And for many of us, that moment is not what we expected.

Carole

From the beginning, it was not what I expected.

The doctor called as promised the afternoon I had my blood drawn, twelve days after my procedure, my heart beating in my throat. My breasts hurt, so I thought maybe I could be, not knowing at that time that progesterone can cause breast tenderness.

"Your blood test result is consistent with early pregnancy," *she said. Still, not the words I so wanted to hear.*

"Excuse me?" I asked.

"Your blood test result is consistent with early pregnancy," *she repeated.*

"What does that mean?" I asked. I was not being facetious; I really wasn't sure.

"Well," she said, "your blood test shows a very early pregnancy."

Okay. I think maybe she is telling me I'm pregnant, I thought. My husband was standing by and could not even begin to read the signals from the little I said and from my facial expression. I told him what she had said and that it probably meant that it had worked.

But still she did not say, "You're pregnant!"

And how could it be that my blood test showed early pregnancy? Even in that moment, it was completely surreal and seemed impossible. I was menopausal. I was thirty-three and had been completely in ovarian failure— in menopause—for years. So pregnancy was impossible. Women in complete ovarian failure did not become pregnant, especially not in 1987. And truly, what did it feel like to be pregnant? How could they be sure from one blood test? And so began months of denial.

We question ourselves daily. "Am I crazy?" "Am I doing the right thing?" "I'm over forty—what are others going to think?" "If this works, when my child is twenty, I'm going to be sixty-six years old." The ongoing conversations that sometimes take place in our heads can really make us question our sanity.

Marna

I took nineteen separate home pregnancy tests and did not believe the results from any of them. Infertility has this ability to cause such self-doubt and denial. For many, even when a blood test and ultrasound, or even feeling the movement of pregnancy, confirms beyond a shadow of a doubt we are pregnant, we don't believe it. And even after delivery, when we are finally holding that baby in our arms, we still can't believe it.

Chrissy

I was pretty apprehensive in the beginning and just kept hoping and praying I was finally pregnant. Then when the bleeding started, I was terrified I had lost them (but at least that happened at a Resolve conference, and I was surrounded by my peeps). The ultrasounds were so comforting, and the further along, the calmer I got and more excited. I never felt like they were aliens/strangers. Definitely love at first sight. They were always mine, and I talked to them and played songs for them daily—the same ones which they still love!

It's hard to say if the donor piece affected my feelings. It was a long process to become parents, so it probably makes me more appreciative, but I would have loved them no matter what with every ounce of my being.

The dreaded two-week wait can seem like an eternity. Every single ache or pain can be misinterpreted as something negative. Lack of symptoms can be misinterpreted as something negative. Spotting or bleeding can be misinterpreted as something negative. There is so much riding on that blood test that will tell us if our cycle has worked that our mind and body [often] work overtime at causing self-doubt.

And then the results are in ...

Maybe you watched two lines darken on a home pregnancy test, or maybe your clinic called with a beta number that confirmed it: You're pregnant! At long last, you really are pregnant! Can you believe it? This may feel like the finish line of the longest marathon you've ever run, but the reality is it's just the beginning of something so incredibly amazing that it's almost incomprehensible.

It's everything you have wished for and spent so many years working toward. Before you began this arduous journey to become a parent, you had a different identity. Maybe you used to be defined by your career, your relationships, your friends or family, or your hobbies and interests. And then infertility came along and redefined you, or a large part of you.

You wanted to have a baby, and it wasn't happening. Your life became centered around your treatment cycles, and the roller coaster of mood swings—fueled by disappointment, envy, frustration, and anger—often felt endless and brutal. Some days it felt like everyone around you was having a baby—family, friends, and colleagues all sporting that baby bump and having something that you so desperately wanted and kept failing at. If you are like many women who have gone through years of loss and infertility, isolation became your middle name. Suddenly, you really didn't know who you were aside from being *infertile*.

But now you're pregnant. Your situation has changed dramatically overnight. Yesterday you weren't pregnant, and today you are. But you're still infertile, and you may still be grieving the loss of your genes.

You have just joined one of the most anticipated, happy, scary, joyful, shocking, disbelieving, and fantastic groups on the planet: the Moms-to-Be Club. Welcome!

Pregnancy

Sometimes we feel very anxious about our pregnancies, especially if we have already experienced pregnancy loss.

We have invested so much time, effort, blood, sweat, tears, and money trying to get pregnant that we often worry about losing a pregnancy or about the health of our baby. After everything we've been through to get to this point, we find ourselves on high alert.

Infertility is a life crisis. It affects our friendships, our marriages, and our identity. The process often deflates our self-esteem and diminishes our hope for the future. It is no wonder that a positive pregnancy test does not universally evoke unmitigated enthusiasm. Unless you are the rare exception who always knew you would have reproductive challenges, the attempts to become a parent have taken their toll. Sometimes in those early weeks and months, we still expect disappointment. We expect to have hopes dashed.

When we get a positive pregnancy test, we are often confused because despite ourselves, we are overwhelmed with hope for the future. We are both excited and frightened. We are extremely reticent and not sure how to react. We often don't even share the news right away for fear it is not really true or that the truth will change tomorrow. Or we might tell everyone because we have waited so long to be able to make such an announcement.

Newly expectant parents via egg or embryo donation may have all the fears any parent has. *Will my baby be healthy? Will the pregnancy go well? Will I have complications?* But some parents also may have a healthy dose of fear as they try to imagine who their child will be, given that some parts may be a mystery. Many intended moms say they instantly fell in love with their growing baby; others tell us it took a few days in the hospital to fall in love. This is all normal, and all new parents have a wide array of experiences.

The stories told here tell the whole story of hope and fear, terror and ecstasy, excitement and a sense of wonder. Sometimes we may even have that moment of "Oh no, now what? We really are going to have a baby!"

One thing is certain—we are entitled to have all the feelings that all parents feel when they are newly expecting a child. There is no right way, and ultimately, we are parents like all others—with that extra layer of meaning because of how we got there.

Carole

> *Months before, I had received the now extinct GIFT (gamete intra-fallopian transfer) procedure with a donor's egg, just four weeks after our first son was born to his birth mother.*
>
> *At four months pregnant, I had a five-month-old infant in the seat of the shopping cart or in my Gerry carrier on my back. And as my pregnancy moved further along, I got more and more questions and comments. The worst and most disturbing were those that suggested that not only had*

this growing family come easily to me, but that we'd had fun doing it.

"Oooh. Somebody's been busy," people would say with a smile and a wink, suggesting a lot of sex.

"Wow, your husband is really potent."

"How did you have the energy, right after giving birth?" they would ask.

Truly, people would frequently say all these things to me in the middle of the supermarket, just as I was trying to buy milk and diapers and get out of there.

I now know that many people can just shrug this off and move on with their day. But for me, the thought that someone would not know how hard adoption had been and how much I had gone through to become pregnant was intolerable. I wanted them to know that not everyone gets pregnant through sex. That it was really hard. That I had no genetic connection to either of the children I was carrying (one in my arms and one in my body). That they should not assume that everyone who so desperately wants to be a parent can just get drunk on a Saturday night four weeks after giving birth and get pregnant again.

So I developed a repertoire of responses, depending on where we were or how tired I was.

"Well, first we were an adoptive family, and then, for this one," I would say, pointing to my belly, "I had a surgery where they put someone else's egg and my husband's sperm in my fallopian tube, and ..." Really, right in the dairy section. Most times people would just nod and run away, especially when I said "sperm."

Or I would say, "It's not so easy for everyone! I worked very hard for both these children."

Or "Oh, no. We did not have that much fun to create this family."

And a million other responses. And I did that until my children were about six years old.

Bonnie*

One of my biggest regrets is that I didn't enjoy my pregnancy. I was so worried that something was going to go wrong after my history of infertility. We had a bleeding scare early on, and then I was worried about premature labor, as I was pregnant with twins. I wish I had enjoyed the pregnancy moments a bit more. I have always felt that my babies were the babies that were meant for me, even when they were moments old. It didn't take me any longer to bond with them or feel like they were mine. While I never would have believed it prior to their arrival (three years ago next week), the donor egg piece really has not been as significant as I imagined it would be. People simply do not know and do not ask. I was very concerned about my daughters having my blue eyes. Turns out that they don't, and I still love them more than I had ever imagined.

Kitty*

My problem is not getting pregnant—it's staying pregnant. The morning after the transfer, I awoke to a humming in my womb. I knew the DE IVF had worked. I was pregnant, and this time, I was optimistic there would be a living baby at the end of it.

I felt a little detached for a while. I clung to the first beta result (2,000) and the second (4,063), and then I set my sights on the first ultrasound. There it was, a beautiful flicker of a heartbeat. I was mesmerized by its simple beauty. Life.

That's how I managed my pregnancy: I broke the time up into manageable chunks to assuage my anxiety. I counted off the weeks (Thursdays) and the half-weeks (Sunday nights). It wasn't until I felt my daughter's kicks that I was able to relax. I was lucky that I began feeling movement around fifteen weeks.

Susie

I was terrified during my pregnancy. I'd had so many losses before, and I was bleeding. I started bleeding before my first beta. I figured, just like times before, it was a chemical pregnancy. My first beta was pretty low, but much to everyone's surprise, they [the hormone levels] continued to rise correctly. I continued to bleed due to a relatively large SCH [sub-chorionic hematoma]. I bled heavily, with clots, for a solid thirteen weeks. I was on bed rest during that time; I think my OB put me on bed rest for my own peace of mind more than anything else. I was marginally relieved when it finally stopped, but I was still scared.

General Questions and Concerns

How honest do I have to be with my OB? Do I have to tell my child's pediatrician how the child was conceived? We are very private; we don't want the whole world to know how we conceived our child. Will my medical record show that my child was conceived via egg donation?

How you create your family is private but should not be secret. Medical and mental health professionals need accurate information in order to properly treat you and your child. No one else *needs* to know how you created your family, but along the way, you will figure out with whom and when and why you will share the information. If you need language or suggestions on how to start such conversations with your child, your health providers, and others, see chapter 9, "Let's Talk about Egg Donation," where we give you scripts to kick off those conversations.

What do I say to those in my religious community about all of this?

We are often asked what to say to people in a family's religious community. Many intended parents seek counsel with their clergy for support. The level of support you receive may vary depending on where you worship.

Marna

> *At the present date, I am a non-practicing Roman Catholic. When my husband and I were actively creating our family, I didn't bother to do any sort of research on whether or not having a baby through egg donation would be supported or accepted. As the date got closer to the time of transfer, I began to feel a little anxious about the special part of egg donation, and I really wanted to talk to a priest. I spoke to my parish priest, which was an incredibly uncomfortable and humiliating experience. He told me to go adopt. He told me that if I created a child via donation, I would be committing adultery. I'd had these expectations that I would receive a hug from the church and a blessing to go forth, be fruitful, and multiply.*

I wanted a second opinion, so I sought out another priest from another area of the church called the Jesuits. The Jesuits question everything and tend to be a little bit more controversial within the Church. So I met with the priest, who, after hearing my plight, said to me simply that no matter where my husband and I were, there was our marriage bed—regardless of whether that was at home, on vacation, or in a surgical suite having an embryo transfer. That was all I needed. I then went into my transfer feeling better; I had my transfer, and nine months later, I had my son.

Thinking all my troubles were behind me, I introduced my son to our parish priest and requested that he be baptized. After much discussion with our parish priest about baptism and the Church's stance on IVF, egg donation, and surrogacy, both my husband and I decided that this was one of those decisions we wanted our son to make for himself when he was older. So we chose not to have him baptized and have allowed him to choose his own spiritual path. This did not go over very well with our family. That was my experience with the Roman Catholic Church.

Cherie*

I'm honest and upfront with everyone, no matter what their beliefs are. If they don't like it or don't agree with science, and therefore the existence of my children, then we both should know that upfront, so we don't waste our time building a relationship.

How you choose to create your family is between you, your partner (if you have one), and whatever higher power you believe in (if you believe in one).

Will my pregnancy be any different now that I am pregnant with donor eggs versus pregnant with my own eggs?

Every pregnancy is different, regardless of how you conceived. If you have been pregnant with your own eggs before, you may think that a difference in your donor egg pregnancy is a result of using donor eggs, but most likely it is not. If you have never been pregnant before, you may feel like you're somehow missing out on an ability to compare this pregnancy with a previous pregnancy, but rest assured that plenty of moms who have genetic children *and* donor egg children say there is physically no difference in the pregnancies.

Joan*

Having never been more than six weeks pregnant with my own eggs, it's hard to say whether my DE pregnancy was different. (One awesome and important difference is that it resulted in two living babies at the end!)

Mentally, my pregnancy was one of the happiest times of my life. I can't imagine that I would have been happier or more excited if I had become pregnant with my own eggs.

But physically? I was constantly feeling terrible: extreme fatigue (like I had mononucleosis for eight months), all-day nausea, severe heartburn, to name a few things, and I developed complications (gestational diabetes, preeclampsia, and post-delivery hemorrhage). It's hard to know how many of these physical problems were related to our use of DE versus simply having a twin pregnancy at age forty.

Frances

My difference between OE and DE pregnancies was because of getting there and not the eggs. With my first [pregnancy], I wasn't taking multiple shots of progesterone and Lovenox every day. I also wasn't truly waiting for the other shoe to drop. But besides that, my DE pregnancy was better in that I didn't develop preeclampsia and went full-term before a very uneventful repeat C-section (versus two days of induction resulting in emergency C-section).

Cherie

It's hard to say, but I would imagine that the anxiety of "Will this stick? Will this embryo/fetus/baby be healthy enough to make it to birth day? Will my body be able to meet the needs of this 'artificially' placed embryo/baby?" would be significantly higher than in a natural pregnancy with a [presumably] healthy mother. Fewer doubts and fears would be present in the mind and heart of a mom-to-be if conception happened without any or much intervention.

What do I say if someone asks me if I used an egg donor?

This is one of the most common questions asked on a daily basis on the private forums of PVED. There is no right or wrong answer. Many women tell the truth because they feel that being transparent is best. Other women don't tell anyone because they feel like their pregnancy is nobody else's business.

As we will discuss in chapter 9, it's a good idea to have a repertoire of responses. How you respond is up to you. Here are some ideas:

> *Why do you ask?*
> *Yes, I did. My eggs were shot, and we were more attached to the notion of having children than to passing on my genes.*
> *That's a personal question.*

Or until your child is old enough to understand how you built your family, you could simply say nothing.

That said, even though it's a common concern, the question "Did you use an egg donor?" really isn't one that most people are asked.

Amy

> *No one has ever asked me this question! Ever! And when I do disclose, for whatever reason, [people] are usually fascinated. One person said, "Good for you!"*

> *I have disclosed many times to medical professionals, for various—usually genetically based—reasons, and usually it is met with "Oh, good, we don't have to worry about genetic issues being passed from you to your son then," and we move right along …*

Cherie

> *I've never been directly asked, though I get the [question] "So are you the mom or grand—" and they trail off with an apologetic yet inquiring look. Then I tell them everything because I'm so very proud of the journey I have taken. But more often than not, I offer the info before anyone has a chance to ask.*

Lynn

> *I have never been asked if I used an egg donor. Then again, I am very vocal about my little miracle ladies and my journey to parenthood. I share my story often.*

Stacey

> *While I've been asked if I used IVF, no one has ever asked if I used donor eggs. IVF usually comes up when discussing fertility with someone just starting to explore their options.*

In those scenarios, I've always disclosed. I'd be doing them a disservice otherwise.

Marna

I remember distinctly one time when I was between dye jobs—lots of gray and white hair among the color—and I had Nick with me. I think he was three or four at the time. We were meeting my husband for lunch. As we were preparing to sit down at our table, the hostess said, "What a beautiful grandson you have." My husband and I looked at each other and blurted out simultaneously, "This is our son!" We must have been incredibly emphatic in our response because we got an immediate apology and a very awkward remark about how you never know these days, people create their families differently, etc. I thought we were done with the conversation until the hostess said, "Oh, did you adopt this baby?" I again looked at my husband, and he knew what was coming, so he just rolled his eyes, scooped up Nick, and headed to the restroom. I then turned my attention to the hostess, who was probably in her mid-thirties, and I just told her straight out that I was an infertility patient and my son was a product of egg donation. And did she know what that meant? I asked. She did not, and it was one of the first times, other than in my job, that I not only educated another individual about egg donation but also advocated for myself. She ended up telling me that she thought what I did was a very beautiful thing. But I gotta tell ya, it was a little awkward and annoying to be referred to as my son's grandmother.

Pregnant at Last

Emotionally, pregnancy can be very complex. Adding the layer of donor egg to the equation often stirs up many different emotions and invites lots of questions.

Regardless of the means of conception, pregnancy can be very challenging emotionally. This creature inside of you may feel like an alien, very separate from you. You might be feeling extremely anxious. It's normal and natural to feel extraordinarily preoccupied and self-absorbed with your body. It's normal to be very aware of every little sensation, pain, twinge, taste, or smell that you might be experiencing. Morning sickness and fatigue may be ruling your life. Part of you may want to shout your news from the rooftops to anyone who will listen. The other part of you may be feeling more isolated than ever and want to keep this news a secret until physically it is no longer a secret. Maybe you have suffered repeated loss, and the idea of once again telling others that you are pregnant is just too much to bear.

For many women, pregnancy after infertility places them in limbo. They no longer feel they belong in the infertility world, but nor do they feel like they belong in the fertility world. Often, adding the DE component can isolate further.

I feel like there's an alien inside me. Is this normal?

Carole

> *Most people expecting a child, whether carried by the intended mom or by a surrogate, fantasize about what the child will look like. If the baby was conceived with the egg and sperm of the intended parents, they inevitably will imagine a child with his nose and her smile, his musical talent and her science brain, her red hair and his perfect teeth. When donor eggs are involved, especially if there is no adult photograph of the donor available, half of that fantasized equation is missing, as was the case for me. I*

tried to imagine my husband's face with ... whom? Whose nose or eyes or whatever was I to shmoosh together in my mind to imagine my growing baby?

The year before I became pregnant, the movie Alien *came out. Most people have seen this movie, but for those who have not, the movie ends with an alien coming out of Sigourney Weaver's abdomen. Basically, she'd been gestating an alien. And that is what I imagined, but the weirdest part is that it wasn't at all scary. The baby seemed alien, but not monstrous or terrifying. And I have discovered in the decades since, in doing this work professionally, that the feeling of carrying an alien is very common when we cannot picture the physical features of our child.*

Jean

With both pregnancies I was very scared! I was worried the whole time that something was going to go wrong and I would lose the baby. This feeling didn't really end until [the babies] were about six months old, maybe even longer for Karalee. Sometimes I still find myself holding my breath and waiting for the shoe to drop. I did feel like there was an alien in me ... both times, but no more so than what any pregnant woman feels, I think. I have been in love with Karalee and Hawkson my whole life.

Susie

I never felt like I was giving birth to an alien or stranger. I was rare in the fact that I never really mourned my genes. DE wasn't such a hard decision for me. I actually never felt sad about giving up my genes or removed from the process. Instead of a loss, it was a gain, as in I wasn't losing anything; I was gaining a chance to have my much-wanted baby. I was in love with that baby when I saw them shoot the embryos into my uterus on transfer day. I walked out of that clinic knowing that (potential) baby was mine.

Michele

I have an almost-ten-month-old via DE. While I was cycling, I was obsessed with the whole DE aspect of getting pregnant. I'm pretty sure I read everything ever written about DE. I think things started to change at the first ultrasound. From then on, the DE part started to fade. It would pop up still, but I was more focused on being pregnant and getting ready. I was definitely mostly scared of the unknown. Would I bond with the baby? What if he/she look[ed] exactly like the donor? Questions that couldn't be answered until I actually gave birth. That was sometimes stressful. However, I got some very simple, great advice from a therapist who is very educated about infertility and DE, who said, "How about you stop worrying about all the what-ifs and just let yourself fall in love with this baby?" Something clicked for me. We decided to find out the gender, we named her, we bought a matching family Christmas stocking, and we included this baby in our family before she was even born. I have to say that really helped me. By the time she was born, she was already so much a part of our family that a lot of fear had disappeared.

Cherie

I don't think I was ever actually scared. The whole of both pregnancies, I never felt I had an alien or stranger in me. I always felt I had my baby/babies in me. It never occurred to me to feel like the babes were anything other than an extension of myself.

The ultrasounds excited me; the heartbeat calmed me. But it wasn't until I first saw [my first baby's] face and heard her first cries that I immediately fell madly in love.

With the twins, though, I was so sick, and it was hard to find any joy in anything. I knew to expect a rush of mad love as soon as I saw them. That knowledge gave me peace. And the mad love rush came right on time.

The donor egg piece did not affect me at all. I never once felt this was someone else's baby or an alien/stranger.

When it came down to it, I've always known that these little souls are the babies I was always meant to have. They have been destined, mine, a part of me since time beginning.

Am I the real mother if I used an egg donor?

Kitty

In the middle of the second trimester, I began feeling the physical toll of a summer pregnancy. I remember complaining about the pain of my fallen arches, the swelling, [and] the fatigue and then laughing as I told my husband, "If anyone thinks [our donor] has more claim to this baby than I do, they need their bloody head examined!"

I can't stop thinking about the donor: is this normal?

Susie

When I thought about the donor at all, it was in a grateful manner, but I didn't really think about it a whole lot. Of course, that was probably also because there was so much other stuff going on during my pregnancy that all I really ever thought about was how much I wanted that baby and how scared I was [that] I was going to lose him. I used to lie in bed at night and talk to him, beg him to just stick around long enough to give me a chance to be his mommy.

I'm still thankful every day that he stuck around and let me be his mMommy.

Early Pregnancy

Am I in good enough shape physically for this?

Marna

I began to throw up repeatedly seven days after I received a positive blood test for pregnancy. It was debilitating. Nothing but Cherry Coke Slurpees from 7-Eleven and plain bean and cheese tacos from a local fast-food chain would stay down. My poor husband became a regular at those two places during the first three months of my pregnancy. I thought I was going to die some days. I also bled profusely. There were many times during these bleeding episodes that I was sure the doctor was going to tell me, "I am sorry, but your baby has died." I bled for twenty-five weeks. And then one day, the bleeding just stopped as quickly as it began. I delivered a full-term pregnancy, and if you can believe it, I needed to be induced.

My pregnancy was not fun. I always felt like the other shoe was going to drop. If I could've rented an ultrasound machine at home, I would have. I felt incredibly isolated and alone. Because I started out my pregnancy overweight, no one noticed my pregnancy until I was seven months along. Then everyone was shocked that I, of all people, actually succeeded at having a baby. Sadly, I felt very ashamed.

Testing in Pregnancy

There are several kinds of tests during pregnancy. Some screen for birth defects via blood test and/or ultrasound. A screening isn't a definitive diagnosis, but if you get a positive result in a screening, your health care provider will discuss your options for a diagnostic test to confirm the diagnosis.

When you're pregnant via egg donation, chances are your donor is much younger than you are. It's important to be honest with your health care providers about this because if you are over thirty-five and pregnant with your own eggs, the chances of having a baby with Down syndrome are much higher than if you are over thirty-five and pregnant with a twenty-seven-year-old woman's eggs. If you lie about it, you will get a much scarier and incorrect result.

If I'm using an egg donor, do I really need all those tests?

Pregnancy can be a time of great excitement! Yet for some, it's riddled with worry. We may worry about a lot of things.

The majority of pregnancies are uncomplicated, and most babies are born healthy. It's normal that you might worry that your baby will be born with a health problem. Be sure to ask a lot of questions and be a good advocate for yourself and your growing baby. And by all means, be sure to give your doctor all pertinent information, including how your child was conceived. This will affect tests that are recommended and the interpretation of those tests. You will most likely not need any more tests than had you conceived a child with your own eggs.

The worry is killing me—what can I do to cope?

You are most likely already pretty good at coping with bad news. Assuming you are infertile, you've coped with not producing enough eggs, not producing good enough eggs, and/or not making any embryos and with ultimately realizing that egg donation is your best path. You also may have had other kinds of adversity in your life. Rarely do we get to a certain age without having experienced losses through death or divorce, disappointments in career or in love relationships, or medical issues that affect our quality of life. Infertility might be the first thing that has challenged your coping skills, or it might be just the latest in a long line of challenges life has thrown at you.

The question, then, is how have you dealt with bad news thus far? Rarely can we thrive during tough times without community to love and support us. Whether that community is the one best friend with whom you can share and cry or an entire neighborhood or religious community, we all do better when we know people love and care for us and will listen. They may not understand what egg donation is, but they can understand that we are in pain. We need to teach people how to support us; we need to choose our support system wisely. We need to reach out and let people know we need them. Sometimes the worst place to remain is in our own heads, isolating ourselves out of shame or embarrassment or because we are convinced no one will understand. They will if we help them understand.

If you have received bad news about your pregnancy and your baby, find a community of people who have experienced something similar. Whatever you have learned, there is an online or in-person group of people who have been through it and can help you—and who want to help you. Do not think you can do this alone! Reach out. It is healing to talk to someone who really gets it.

Another way to cope when crises occur in our lives is to take care of ourselves, which is usually one of the hardest things to do when we feel beaten down, depressed, or hopeless. Taking care of ourselves means doing things to nourish and replenish ourselves so that we are not running on empty. It is important to do the things we love—manicures, massages, coffee with a friend, a day trip or vacation, calling the friend with whom you've been meaning to touch base. Maybe what helps you is going for a run, or maybe it is going out for a nice meal. Perhaps a walk on the beach helps you to feel whole again. Do it. Make time for it. It is hard to make good decisions and maintain equilibrium when we are depleted.

Many people find it extremely healing to give to others when they are feeling most needy themselves. Active volunteers routinely report that they receive more from giving than they feel others receive from them. Find something you feel passionate about, and give back to others less fortunate than you. Some tragedies are so great that we must simply work through them through therapy and community and time. But many setbacks and disappointments can be lessened through a practice of gratitude. It is hard to feel gratitude when we have experienced great loss, but frequently, reaching out and helping those with great need can fill our spirit with joy and replenish our hope.

It is also important to nurture our partner if we are in a relationship. Infertility can suck the life out of a relationship, as we talk constantly about what the next step will be and cry over the last disappointing cycle. It is extremely helpful to try to maintain the pieces of your union that brought you together in the first place. Although it always feels like time is of the essence, it's helpful to take breaks from talking about family-building, even for a few days at a time. Remember that there used to be more in your life than this; try to regain some of it. Try to focus on your partner; ask your partner how his or her day was, and really listen to the answer. Spend relaxing and fun time together every few weeks.

Of course, it is also important to share your feelings with your partner. If you've received sad or scary news, it is not going to go away just because you employ some of these strategies. Share your fear and grief or whatever your feelings may be about what happened, and make room to really listen to what your partner feels, even if his or her feelings are quite different from your own.

Meditation can be a very effective tool for relaxing. Even if you have never tried it before, and you are sure that it just isn't for you, guided meditation exercises are extremely easy and effective. Many downloadable apps are now available to guide you through exercises that quiet your mind and your body and prepare you for the day ahead or for sleep. Some popular apps are Calm, Meditation Studio, Breathe2Relax, and Insight Timer. Any process that helps you to feel better is the right one for you.

Take things one day at a time. The expression "for now" is crucial when you are walking through the steps of reproductive medicine and pregnancy. "For now, I know my beta level is strong." "For now, the ultrasound is showing the heartbeat." "For now, the doctor says everything looks good." Live in the moments of positivity. Know that if something changes, you have the strength and the resources to cope. Focus only on what you can control. Your actions, your thoughts, and your relationships are what are within your grasp. Everything else has to wait.

Finally, create a long-term plan, with your partner if you are in a relationship. It is helpful to know what the long haul might look like. Perhaps childfree living is an option for you; maybe it is time to talk about embryo donation or adoption. You don't have to make any final decisions, but if parenthood is definitely your goal, knowing there are other ways to get there can take away some of the panic you may feel.

Transition from Infertility Patient to OB Patient

Because we have invested so much in reaching the goal of pregnancy, we might feel like we need to have regular weekly contact with our doctors, the same kind of contact we had during our DE IVF cycle. Often a woman's physician says something like "You may have had to move mountains to get pregnant, but now you are like every other pregnant woman on the planet." For many women, this is quite frustrating. They might wonder why their ob-gyn is not treating this pregnancy like a big deal.

Marna

I clearly remember, after yet another episode of bleeding, that a very well-meaning RE, who happened to see me because my regular RE was out of town, told me that I basically was going to have to suck it up and put on my big-girl panties because I shouldn't expect to see him every single week during my pregnancy just because I was experiencing a little bleeding. I was upset, scared, and furious. I turned toward him and said, "With all due respect, with my spending as much money as I have at your clinic to get pregnant, you will stand by my side and hold my hand while I push my child out of my vagina if I ask you to." The very next day, I was released to a perinatologist who truly got my fear and anxiety. This was pregnancy number ten for me, and I still had no baby in my arms yet. Having contact with the clinic every two weeks gave me peace of mind.

Kitty

At almost nineteen weeks, I had the anatomy scan. Everything was perfect with our baby, but something told me that the sonographer's friendly offer to do a 3-D ultrasound meant something was wrong.

I looked at my daughter's face. It had no fat, so she looked very adult. I wasn't expecting her to look like me or my family of origin, but it was still surprising to see just how unlike me she looked. That was the moment when my brain overwrote all the images of my imaginary children with the one I'd hold in my arms in a few months' time.

I clutched the ultrasound picture while I was given the bad news I'd anticipated: I had placenta previa—where the placenta covers the cervix, blocking the baby's way out—so I'd have to deliver via cesarean. I wept all afternoon. It was another major expectation I'd have to adjust on my journey to parenthood, [and] after everything I'd been through, it seemed bitterly unfair that I wouldn't be able to give birth the way I wanted. I indulged my tears but then determined to make my daughter's birth special, no matter what. I focused on the fact that my wonderful OB would be the person delivering her. That continuity of her care was a boon, and I reasoned that delivering my daughter in a controlled environment would take a lot of the fear out.

Carole

Luckily, the pregnancy was very uneventful. No complications. No nausea. No bleeding. How blessed I was to have my one and only pregnancy be so wonderful.

At the twenty-week ultrasound, they said Daniel's head was very large and explained the various (unimportant to catastrophic) things that could mean. Though many aspects of a pregnancy with donor eggs may seem unrelated to egg donation itself, some issues relate to pregnancy after infertility. There is the panic that there might never be another pregnancy. The wondering if a problem could somehow be related to the donor herself. The worry that we may be deficient in more ways than we already knew. So this experience, which would be frightening for any expectant parent, had the additional layers that exist for donor-conceived families.

Our brains have an uncanny ability to adapt. Particularly, we adapt to that which becomes repetitive in our lives. This is part of the reason it is so hard to change behavior patterns or reverse long-established dynamics in relationships.

Our attempts to become pregnant usually have been fraught with failure and disappointment. First, attempts to stimulate our own ovaries may have resulted in a disappointing yield of eggs. Or we may have had an early pregnancy loss. Or we even might have tried a few different donors before a cycle went the way we hoped. Or perhaps we are single and tried for years to find a partner with whom we could create a family, and now we are approaching single parenthood with at least one gamete donor needed.

After these kinds of losses and/or difficulties, it is not at all surprising that we become negative, expecting another failure, another disappointment. Through our struggles, our brains have been trained to expect this result, and in many ways it would be foolish to expect otherwise. Those who can remain optimistic are fortunate, and both are perfectly acceptable responses.

The narratives that have been shared with us certainly confirm that reticence, caution with one's heart, and guarded optimism are common and not to be judged.

Pregnancy after Forty: A Note from a Reproductive Endocrinologist

Dr. Said Daneshmand is a reproductive endocrinologist at San Diego Fertility Center. He also serves on PVED's advisory board and often answers questions about the egg donation process. Here's what he had to say about pregnancy after forty:

> With advanced reproductive technologies, more and more women over the age of forty are conceiving and having babies. While the majority of women in this age group have healthy pregnancies, it is important to note that whatever can go wrong in pregnancy goes wrong at a higher rate in the forties and beyond. Although a woman at age forty who is in good physical shape can have the same risks during pregnancy as a woman a

decade younger, the overall rates of complications do rise with advancing age.

For example, the risks of both preeclampsia and gestational diabetes are increased after age forty. The risk of gestational diabetes in particular increases from 3 percent below age forty to 7 percent and higher in the forties. Preeclampsia can be a serious concern and involves complications surrounding high blood pressure during pregnancy. If the blood pressure is uncontrolled and starts affecting organs such as the kidney, an emergent delivery has to be performed, even if the fetus is preterm.

A good rule of thumb to follow is that the healthier the woman prior to the onset of pregnancy, the lesser the risk of these complications. Exercise, healthy diet, and vigilant follow-up with the pregnancy specialist are essential ingredients in maximizing the chance of a healthy delivery. The pregnancy specialist can also assess the future risks by evaluating the intended mother prior to pregnancy and recommending changes in lifestyle that can truly mitigate complication rates.

Other complications that are encountered at a higher frequency in the forties include placental abnormalities such as placenta previa and also cardiac abnormalities such as cardiomyopathy. As we get older, our vascular system also gets older and becomes less pliant: so if you have a little high blood pressure and increased cholesterol before pregnancy, those problems can magnify in intensity during pregnancy. Pregnancy adds strain to your organs, much like climbing Mount McKinley adds strain to your heart and lungs. The condition of your health pre-pregnancy is the most important determinant of the risks of these types of complications during pregnancy.

In regards to delivery, the chance of having a cesarean is also dependent on age and is increased in the forties. In many cases, an urgent delivery is needed to preserve the health of the mother and fetus, and a C-section becomes the fastest route to delivery. Recovery from a C-section can be harder than recovery from a vaginal delivery. Some conditions in the forties are also associated with more risk during and after delivery, such as post-delivery hemorrhage. Women who are diagnosed with gestational diabetes have a much higher risk of having full-blown diabetes after delivery. Other placental abnormalities include intrauterine growth restriction, which essentially means that the doctor becomes worried that the fetus is not growing appropriately and that delivery and support outside the uterus would be the best option to maximize the health of the fetus.

Many of the complications we have discussed can also directly affect the fetus: gestational diabetes increases the risk of congenital malformations, and conditions that require early delivery can then cause complications for the newborn.

Overall, the risk of miscarriage is not significantly increased in women in their forties who are using donor eggs; the risk of miscarriage is most dependent on the presence of chromosomal abnormalities, which is in turn dependent on the age of the person contributing the eggs.

Miscarriage aside, it is still important for the medical team to know if your pregnancy is a result of donor eggs.

This is important because the risks of chromosomal abnormalities such as Down syndrome are also dependent on the age of the person who contributed the egg. Women who are older than thirty-five have an increased risk of chromosomal and genetic abnormalities and thus will need more intensive monitoring and testing during pregnancy. Advances in screening technologies, such as cell-free DNA analysis, allow doctors to screen for chromosomal abnormalities such as Down syndrome as early as ten weeks of gestation, with a noninvasive blood test.

Now that I have scared you with these risks, I also have some good news: paying close attention to your health by continuing regular exercise activity and adhering to a healthy diet does truly decrease the risks of all the complications I mentioned. Before becoming pregnant, set a goal for yourself and then initiate a plan to reach that goal. Your health and the health of your baby are of paramount importance, and this goal-setting will inspire you to achieve a good state of health, which in turn will lead to a healthy mom and baby. You can and will do it!

Here is one woman's story about her own pregnancy when she was over forty years old:

Michelle*

[My] first pregnancy was stupid-easy. Worked until the day before my son was born. No issues, reasonable weight gain, no problems at all. I wore stilettos to work every day with no swelling and no discomfort. I found some relatively cute and work-appropriate maternity clothes and generally felt good. Second pregnancy was twins and not quite the

same. I had a ton of swelling and ended up in dowdy and frumpy shoes (a total bummer for a shoe-a-holic). I was working in a very casual office this time around, and I lived in the same dumpy, frumpy maternity clothes and felt kind of miserable about myself. While I didn't have any health issues, the stress of a twin pregnancy, with the worry about something going wrong, really made it a more uncomfortable experience.

Delivery

The highly anticipated day that we have longed for is here at last—finally. For many, the wait has been a few years; for others, it's been several years, maybe a decade. It's the day the child we have fantasized about for so long finally arrives into the world and into our arms.

Most women have a fantasy about how they are going to give birth. Some women romanticize their delivery and envision a completely unmedicated birth with soft lights and relaxing music, with their partner holding their hand and breathing right along with them as they labor. Part of the fantasy is that when the moment of delivery occurs, a beautiful, healthy, robust baby pops out with two giant pushes and is promptly plopped on top of Mom's tummy.

That's not always the way it happens. Sometimes, complications develop along the way, or labor stalls. In these and other instances, a cesarean might be recommended.

Carole

Ultimately, it was time for my baby to come out. Concerns about head size had diminished—yes, he had a big head but not enough that it portended any pathology. And his father had a really big head, so it made sense. But I was forty weeks pregnant, and nothing was happening. Braxton Hicks, yes, but no real contractions and no indications

Daniel wanted to get out. I used to say, "Once they put him in there, he did not want to come out." So we waited, and finally, at forty-two weeks I was induced.

Seventeen hours later, at 12:23 in the morning, I had an emergency cesarean because of failure to progress. After four hours of pushing, that big head just would not drop into the birth canal enough to be pushed out. Although this happens to many women, I was pretty sure I was pushing wrong. How can you really know what that is supposed to feel like if you've never been through childbirth before? So I assumed that, just like how my ovaries didn't work, there was some primary deficiency in me that did not know exactly how to push a baby out. I didn't yet know it was related to his head size.

No matter how we anticipate our birthing experience will be or how much control we would like to think we have during our labor and delivery, sometimes the best-laid plans go awry. When that happens, it's understandable to feel upset, frustrated, disappointed, or even angry.

Fantasy and expectation can be our worst enemies. It's not uncommon for women who have conceived after long and arduous journeys to feel like they deserve an uncomplicated delivery. For many women who are finally pregnant through egg or embryo donation, the delivery is the time when they hope they can prove that their bodies really do work. It may be that they need an uncomplicated delivery to feel "normal." If they end up having their baby through cesarean, or if they are unable to breastfeed, these developments can be experienced as additional traumas to be resolved, on top of the loss of genetic connection.

The good news is that once a child is here, we usually gain the perspective that the ultimate outcome is more important than the method of how the baby got here. Moms and dads are so busy feeding and loving their babies, being exhausted, and learning how to be parents that a disappointing delivery becomes less important and begins to fade with time.

Can a cesarean birth be special?

Kitty

> *I'd had my heart set on a midwife-led delivery in my hospital's birthing center, so [I] was devastated to learn, at only nineteen weeks, [that] I'd need to deliver my daughter via planned cesarean. I felt cheated out of yet another experience that most moms take for granted. By the time the day of her birth rolled around, I was ready. I'd researched cesarean births and decided however my daughter made her way into the world, it would be magical. As my mum—who delivered me with an epidural, my ten-pound brother without any pain relief, and my sister via elective cesarean—said: "No matter how a baby is born, it's all pretty ghastly." I surmised that once you have your baby in your arms, it doesn't matter how they were born.*

What if my baby has to go to the NICU?

Here Carole describes her experience having an emergency cesarean after a long labor.

Carole

> *So cesarean it was. Out he came. Except instead of the long-awaited moment when they put the baby on your chest for the first time, they held him up above the surgery sheet and said to me, "Here's your baby; he's having a little trouble breathing right now, so we are going to take him in the other room to take care of him and you can see him later." And off they whisked my son. My first spoken words after his arrival? "You mean there really was a baby in there?" So insidious was my disbelief. I can't imagine now what I really expected, but there it was. In the shock from the*

trauma of surgery, my true fear emerged. Was there really a human being growing in there?

These things happen. The "perfect" birth story is rare. Some are more dramatic than others; sometimes lives of babies and mothers are at stake. I was very lucky. Daniel apparently had inhaled something—maybe meconium, maybe fluid—in utero, and it had gotten into his lungs. They briefly intubated him and put him in the NICU (the neonatal intensive care unit), where he was monitored for three days. Although it ultimately turned out that he was the healthiest and biggest baby in there, among all the preemies and really ill babies, when I finally woke up in my room after surgery, there was no baby with me. And I remember so clearly, twenty-nine years later, that I said to no one in particular, through postpartum tears, "You mean, after everything I went through to have him, I still don't have a baby with me?"

And there it was again. I did feel deprived. Maybe it just felt like insult added to injury to go through a GIFT surgery and the loss of genes and a traumatic birth experience to now not even have those precious early days with my son. I was wheeled in a wheelchair to see and hold him during the three days he stayed in the NICU, but then I would go back to my room without him.

My story is filled with incredibly good fortune. I had an easy pregnancy that ultimately proved that although my ovaries were dead, the rest of me worked just fine. I am grateful for the experience that allowed me to become a member of that woman tribe of birthers. But it was not without the challenges that had additional meaning for me as an infertile woman. There was the certainty I would give birth to an alien, not being able to imagine the child I would have, and the worst part of ultimately not having my son with me after birth. But I was so lucky. He ultimately was very healthy and able to come home at five days old, but the initial emptiness of my arms definitely recalled the losses that had brought us together in the first place.

Bonding

Is this baby going to love me?

Kitty

Certainly, in the early days of new motherhood—when you don't even have time to stop and think, What the hell just happened?*—being able to feed my daughter in the way I [had] hoped was very empowering. If I had any lingering doubts about what makes a mom, they evaporated pretty early on. If I wasn't her mother, who the hell was?*

V. is now two and it's my arms she wants when she's upset. It's my hug she wants when she wakes up in the night. My donor helped create this beautiful little girl, but if V. could understand the genetic component, I know she'd easily pick me out of a lineup as Mom.

Am I going to love this baby?

Alice*

My overriding feeling was relief. I definitely bonded with my baby during pregnancy, but I always knew that at any time, anything could happen. When the doctor took my daughter out of me (I had a C-section due to [placenta] previa), the nurse said, "She's beautiful," and I asked, "Wait, is she alive?" Despite this, I felt very connected right away. Our donor was anonymous, but I am thankful to her every day.

Jean

From the moment I saw Karalee, I no longer existed. A mother was born. With Hawkson, it somehow happened all over again (though I did have a secondary thought and wondered where all that blood he was covered in came from when I first saw him).

Toni*

[I experienced] an overwhelming feeling of relief, and I cried. I cried for the four and a half years it took to have her. But she was whisked away to the NICU, and I remember [that] the first time I saw her in the NICU, I cried again (love hormones), but there was never a doubt in my mind that she was mine.

Joan

Right after my sons were born—meaning in the first hours—I felt a bit disconnected, like I was watching a movie of myself interacting with them. This experience was probably more due to the fact that I was very ill and on a lot of medications than due to anything DE-related.

Within a couple of days, as I began to recover, I felt protective and loving and interested in learning about these two new people who had come into my life.

Will I fall in love with my baby right away?

Maybe. Maybe not. Some parents fall instantly in love with their babies, and others don't. Most relationships take time to build. If you have carried your baby and nourished it for ten months, there is a possibility that you have developed many feelings for your child. But you still may not feel in love. The most important thing to remember is that all the vastly different experiences we have in becoming parents happen to all parents. Deliveries go well, or they don't; moms can breastfeed, or they can't. Moms *want* to breastfeed, or they don't. Parents feel instant love, or they don't, and none of these experiences are dictated by genetic connection or even gestational connection. There are parents by surrogacy and adoption who are immediately in love with their child although they did not carry that baby in their bodies, and there are other parents who take one look at a child and say, "Who the heck does this child belong to?" That feeling is felt all the time by moms who conceived easily with their own egg and popped a kid out with no problem; even in those circumstances, the baby may seem quite unfamiliar.

Babies and children attach to those who nurture them. When a child is fed, held, talked to, sung to, rocked, and kissed, the child will attach. Babies know who their parents are, or at least they know whom they can trust to attend to their needs. They definitely do not think of parents as strangers simply because there is no genetic link. Chromosomal connection has nothing to do with love and commitment and good parenting. You are not a stranger to your child just because you don't share genes. To them, you are their mom or dad. You are their world. They need you. They most likely understand what makes "real parents" long before you do.

Kitty

When V. was placed next to my cheek, it wasn't a surge of blind unconditional love that I felt. I didn't cry, the way I'd always imagined I would. I took in her features and murmured in her ear. Her face softened from a pucker to a contented pout. I still couldn't believe I was a mom (V. is a toddler, and I still can't!), but I knew right then that I would go through every last bit of miscarriage pain and infertility grief all over again to have this baby. In short, I would die for her, without question.

Jenn

I did fall in love immediately. After all those fears, we had no trouble bonding. We had some bumps in the road, though. At one point she had a very hard time nursing, and in my exhaustion and flood of hormones, I thought maybe it had something to do with DE, like she wasn't accepting me. We quickly discovered she had a milk protein allergy, and once I stopped eating dairy, she was fine. Her belly hurt when she nursed, and it had nothing to do with bonding. I think that DE moms are probably extra-sensitive when there is an issue, and our minds go straight to DE when the truth is [the issue] has nothing to do with it. From then on, we've had a wonderful nursing experience, and I feel so silly for thinking that in retrospect.

Right now I am completely in love with this little girl and can't imagine life without her, but fears still creep in. I'm worried about how people will react when we start disclosing more openly and [about] the inevitable stupid stuff they will say. I'm worried [about] how my daughter will feel about the DE aspect. A different set of "unknowns," I guess. I do think that with every day that passes, I become more and more her mother. I think that is [the case] with any baby, [whether they arrive via] OE, DE, or adoption. Every mother has to get to know her baby, recognize the different cries, and learn to be what that baby needs. I remind myself that by the time my daughter does really start understanding her conception, we will be so connected that it won't be nearly as scary. In the end, this baby was worth every worry, every shot, every pill, every tear. I'm so glad she's here.

Susie

My pregnancy had been so high-risk and so fraught, and I'd had so many previous losses, that I was scared. The entire pregnancy, I was convinced that it just wasn't going to work, because it never had before. After almost thirty-six hours of labor, I had an emergency C-section. I heard my OB say, "There he is," but I didn't hear him cry. My first thought was "See? It didn't work."

As soon as I heard him cry, though, before I even saw him, I felt connected. I was foggy; I was losing a lot of blood, but I didn't realize that at the time. They whisked him away, and I told my husband, "Go with him, go with him! I'm fine. Don't let him out of your sight." After all that time, I needed to make sure he was okay and not out of our sight.

After they got me taken care of, they brought him to me in recovery. He stayed with me until we were discharged. The only time he went to the nursery was for the daily weight and temperature check, and my husband went with him. It really was love at first sight.

Michelle

With my older guy, I definitely felt that immediate connection. What I had a hard time with was feeling like someone was going to come along and take him back because he wasn't really "mine." I remember freaking out when I was being wheeled out of the hospital. The poor [orderly] spoke very broken English, so she was trying to smile and say everything was okay, but I didn't have the words to explain to her what was going on.

With the twins, they were so tiny (just under five pounds each) that they seemed kind of alien and unreal. I felt an immediate obligation to them but not that same connection [that I had felt with my oldest child]. I think the amount of time and energy taken by twins is what was unexpected. There were never enough hands or enough time or enough energy.

Jean

It's difficult to say if DE affects my feelings, since I know nothing else. My guess is that it does. I think I probably love my children more fiercely because I fought so hard for them.

Joanne*

I was apprehensive about what it would mean to have the baby. I was disconnected from the reality of what it would actually mean to be responsible for children.

Kitty

I look at my new circle of mom friends with their kids—all genetic—and know this: whatever residual grief I have about my journey, I am no less a mom to my girl than they are to their children. It really doesn't matter how V. got here. I'm just glad she's here.

Marna

I was apprehensive about meeting Nick. I wasn't sure what to expect. I know I didn't have that experience that many mothers have, sobbing with joy over the birth of their child. I was crying all right—I was exhausted. I was relieved. And the realization hit me that I was finally a mother. He was okay. I was okay. We were a family. Finally.

They placed this beautiful little bundle in my arms and said, "Congratulations, here's your son." My husband was smiling from ear to ear, with this big old grin on his face. I remember clutching my child and looking around in my morphine haze, just waiting for the nursing staff to tell me there had been some mistake and this really wasn't my baby. It took a few days for reality to kick in and for me to understand that he really was mine and nobody was coming to take him away.

What are the "baby blues"?

Mood changes can happen to any woman who gives birth, regardless of how she conceived or delivered. Hormones are fluctuating wildly; surgery is a trauma to the body; new parents are usually exhausted while everyone adjusts and tries to sleep. It all can take a toll.

Perinatal mood and anxiety disorders include depression, anxiety, panic, obsessive-compulsive disorder, and bipolar disorder that occur during pregnancy or the postpartum period. Men also can experience emotional difficulty before or after a baby is born. Postpartum blues are common. Sometimes when we are overwhelmed and tired and hormones are surging, we can feel down. We expect these feelings to pass in a few weeks, maybe a few months at most. But if feelings persist, and you feel so overwhelmed that you can't cope, or if you want to walk away, or if you want to hurt your children or yourself, or if you have a preexisting depression or anxiety that predisposes you to postpartum mood issues, *seek help immediately*. Although some of what you are feeling may be exacerbated by residual infertility feelings, it doesn't matter. Many women experience these things, and a professional can help you sort it out. An excellent reference is Postpartum Support International (www. postpartum.net). If you are struggling mightily as a new mom, regardless of how many children you already have, reach out and know that you deserve to feel good and that you have nothing to feel guilty about; you are not the only one to experience this, and there is help available. And most importantly, whether you became a mom easily or through great effort, you need not suffer postpartum.

There is no doubt that if a mother is unable to breastfeed, or if her baby is kept in the NICU, the issues of infertility can be triggered and make a woman feel deficient. For many women, breastfeeding may be one of the ways they end up feeling competent and fully and completely like a mother. Breastfeeding sometimes feels like the one thing only a mother can do for her baby and the thing that binds her to her child in a way that nothing else can.

Kitty

> *Being able to breastfeed my daughter was, for me, incredibly healing. Such validation gave me a lot of confidence in my ability to parent, even if I hadn't passed on my genes.*

Carole

> *Finally, I was given the opportunity to try to breastfeed, and again, like many women, I experienced challenges with him not wanting to latch on. The shoving of the breast into his mouth by the nurses didn't help my lack of confidence. I felt like it was one more thing I could not do right.*

> *Once we all got home, Daniel breastfed just fine. We were actually pretty good at it, until he was four months old, cut his first tooth, chomped down on me, and I thought maybe we had had enough. Plus, I had an eleven-month-old baby who also wanted to crawl onto my lap and be with me, and breastfeeding was an additional challenge we all did not need.*

Some women feel profoundly disappointed if they are unable to breastfeed, and sometimes this is to their own detriment. If a woman needs to be on certain medications such as antidepressants but is refusing to take them because she is breastfeeding, she may be depriving herself of feeling whole and healthy in the service of feeding her baby. While noble, this is unhelpful thinking. Babies need healthy and happy mothers. Although breast milk is a wonderful way for babies to get nourishment in their early months, it is counteracted if breastfeeding is just not the right thing for that family at that time. Families can address feelings about breastfeeding that arise from donor egg and infertility issues by gaining perspective and focusing on what is truly important at this time for both mother and child. These feelings also can be addressed through consultation with a mental health professional familiar with family-building issues; this professional can help revisit unresolved issues of infertility that may now be rearing up again. As mentioned previously, participating in a community of new moms who have delivered and are feeding their babies in all different ways can be very healing. Gaining support in your knowledge that you are the one and only mom, that you got your baby here, and that you have the rest of your lives together to build and nurture your relationship can offer great perspective and help to heal any disappointment you may feel.

Final Thoughts

Congratulations! By the time you've reached this milestone, one adventure is coming to a close, and another is just beginning! Your baby's arrival may be just around the corner, or you may have already given birth!

But we want to leave you with these seven simple words:

Your baby is going to love you.

Yep! That's it. Game over.

From the moment this incredible, amazing, lovely little being pops out of either your body or a gestational surrogate's, he or she is going to love you to the moon and back. We know you might be nervous or scared—after all, this little sweetheart is essentially a stranger—but don't forget that you don't have to coax or cajole this kid to love you.

It's just what babies do from the very first day they draw their very first breath—they love you unconditionally.

Trust us when we tell you that babies don't care how they got here. They aren't going to care if theirs was a water birth, a vaginal birth with an epidural, or a birth via cesarean.

Babies don't care if they share your genes or if they look like their dad, their siblings, or their aunts, uncles, grandma, or grandpa, or even you!

They aren't going to care if you breastfeed or bottle-feed. They aren't going to care whether you use cloth or disposable diapers. They aren't going to care if your maternity clothes were hand-me-downs from your friends, their aunts, or a garage sale.

They aren't going to care if they have the newest crib, baby equipment, toys, or clothes. They are truly not going to care if the nursery is ready or not.

They aren't going to care how much weight you gained during your pregnancy, whether you are choosing to stay home or go back to work, or even what you've chosen to name them. (They might hate you later for their name, but that's another chapter for another parenting book!)

The point is simply this: your baby is going to love and adore you because *you* are their mommy.

And yes, the after-your-baby-is-born part is crazy with joy, tears, sleep deprivation, and exhaustion, and there will be some nights when you will think, *What have I done? I don't know what to do! Am I going to break this kid?*

You are going to make mistakes. You are going to have some days when you forget to shower or do not even have time to wash your face. There will be many nights when you will stay up almost all night just watching your little angel sleep. You will spend as many nights praying to whomever that your baby will sleep for more than an hour at a time.

So you may be carrying around worries:

> *Will my baby love me? Will I love my baby? Who says I love pregnancy? I hate pregnancy! My back hurts, I can't see my feet, and I have exactly two pairs of pants and one tent dress that still fit. I really did glow! I have to pee thirty-five*

*times a day. I can't wait to meet my son or daughter. Can
I really do this? Am I going to be a good mom?*

But take a deep breath, and fear not! We know you're tired. But we
know that in that delicious moment when your baby is finally in your
arms, you will know that every single difficult step has been worth it.
Every. Single. Difficult. Step.

Chapter 4

WHAT DO YOU WISH YOU HAD KNOWN?

Adapt what is useful, reject what is useless, and add what is specifically your own.

—Bruce Lee

Those of you who are thinking about or soon starting a DE IVF cycle might not know some of the questions to ask. So grab your favorite beverage, settle in, and enjoy advice from those who are parenting via egg donation.

The IVF process is completely different for each person. No two women will respond physically, emotionally, or spiritually the same in any given cycle. It is all very individual. When your eggs are not the ones being retrieved—because you're using a donor—there is an added layer of uncertainty.

Embarking on a DE IVF cycle can be incredibly confusing, overwhelming, and even a little terrifying. When intended parents pause and reflect about the process and all of the moving pieces that are required to make a DE cycle successful, they may find themselves overthinking or even second-guessing their decisions.

You know the old saying "If I knew then what I know now," don't you? Those of us who have already traveled this road and are now parenting can tell you most assuredly that hindsight really is twenty-twenty.

If Only I Knew Then What I Know Now

For many people, egg donation is uncharted territory. It can be overwhelming to consider everything, from the costs to the complex medical decisions for ensuring a successful cycle to wondering about what level of contact to have with the donor. But there are other things that intended parents sometimes don't stop to think about until they are on the other side, parenting. So we asked families created via egg donation, "What do you wish you had known?" Here's what they shared.

Irene* was thirty-four at the time of her first DE IVF cycle with a gestational surrogate.

> *I wish I had known that there was opportunity for an open donor. I didn't know they existed, and my clinic didn't inform me that I had a choice. I wish I had known that many donors are willing to be identified and are just going with the clinic's programs by staying anonymous.*

Irene*

> *I wish I knew [then] how much I would want to meet the donor. Don't laugh, [but] I want to be her Facebook friend. I don't want to be a close friend, but I want to be able to follow her, message her with a question if I have one, share pictures of the kids, and see her grow up over time. I don't understand why my husband doesn't care to meet her.*

> *I fantasize about meeting my donor. Would I like her? Would she like me? Would she like my kids? Would she be proud about the people they are becoming? I want to thank*

her for giving me the best thing anyone will ever give me. Does she understand how she changed my life?

I wish I had known that babies look like babies when they are born. They don't look like any[one], so seeing your baby for the first time and not feeling they look like you is normal. It's a time of intense grief and joy when they are born, and I wish I had been psychologically prepared for it. Family members say, "Oh, he/she looks so much like ..." and that stings and just reinforces that you don't have that connection.

When a woman uses a gestational carrier and an egg donor, she is what Diane Ehrensaft calls "the birth nobody."[1] The husband is the birth father, the carrier is the gestational mother and patient, and the intended mother is the birth nobody, completely left out of the whole process. The feeling of loneliness and isolation runs deep.

I wish I knew [then] that the loss of genes is a lifelong loss, but it gets better over time.

I wish I [had] understood that even if I had used my own genes, these little people [would have] develop[ed] into their own selves. They may or may not be like us. We have the fantasy that a genetic child will be a "mini me," like what we like, be good at what we are good at, and of course, not have any of our faults.

Irene shares sentiments felt by many parents via egg donation. The common denominator that we hear over and over again is the wish that the intended mother would've had the opportunity to meet her egg donor. Irene also talks about the isolation and loneliness of what she experienced in needing a gestational surrogate. Although the loss of genes involves a grieving process that must be experienced fully for closure, it is also something that we have the ability to move on from. We must recognize that the children we have, regardless of their genes, are going to become their own unique, individual people.

Jenn, who was forty at the time of her DE pregnancy, so wisely says that she wishes she had known that not everyone is a candidate for IVF. She wishes she had been more thoroughly educated regarding her fertility.

Jenn

> I wish I had known that not everyone is a candidate for IVF. Before I was diagnosed with DOR (which I didn't know even existed), I just assumed [that] if I had trouble getting pregnant, I would do IVF, and that would be the solution. When I got the call that donor eggs would be my only option, I didn't even really know what donor eggs were! I felt very let down by my primary care doctor, midwife, and other medical professionals who did not tell me about the realities of fertility. Everyone [had] told me [that] since I had already had a child, I would be fine. I feel like I was so misinformed and didn't even realize what questions I should be asking. I thought everyone could try IUI and IVF. I never thought that option would not be possible for me. I still have a lot of anger at medical professionals who should have warned me and informed me. I definitely would have made different decisions earlier on and had more options if I [had] had the correct information. I am now pregnant with the help of an egg donor, and although I am so excited and grateful, I still feel let down by my doctors.

Still others, like Natasha,* who is forty-two and at the start of her first donor egg cycle, are still trying.

Natasha*

I wish I had known that donor eggs aren't a miracle cure. It's true that success rates with DE are among the best of all the fertility options, but it's not a 100 percent guarantee. Failing with DE was quite a shock.

One of the loveliest, most heartfelt and poignant things that we hear from the parents of these amazing children via egg donation is how surprised they are at how much they love their children.

Shelley*

I wish I had known that using donor eggs would have no effect on how I felt about my children. I struggled with this choice for so very long, wasting very valuable time. I worried [about] how I would feel—would I feel like their mother?—right until the day I delivered. What a waste of my time and energy to feel this way! I love my children more than anything. I am their mother. I am so grateful to the donor who allowed my children to come into this world. I wish I had known that accepting help from others does not change your destiny of motherhood.

Tracy, a mother via adoption and embryo donation, shares with us how important being educated about her body and her fertility is and would have been:

Tracy

If I had known what a good ovarian response was, I probably would have given up retrieving my own eggs after the first try. Or if I had known how a period is supposed to feel or how normal sex should feel, I would have gone to the doctor sooner and identified my endometriosis earlier. If I had a choice and could go back and change anything?

I wouldn't. If any of those IUIs and IVFs had worked, I wouldn't have moved on to adoption and would not have my beautiful daughter or a relationship with her very special birth mother. And through our daughter, I made a new friend who was also infertile, and if it wasn't for her, I wouldn't have pursued embryo donation, and I wouldn't have a second, perfect daughter. So knowing would have changed everything, and I'm happy with how things are now.

Melissa* wishes she had known during her journey that everything would be okay, that she would have three beautiful children, and that in the end she wouldn't regret anything.

Melissa

I was thirty-nine when my son was born and forty when my twins were born. I wish I had known throughout my journey that it would all be okay and I would have three beautiful babies when all was said and done. Some days I'm still a little sad about the loss of my genes. No one besides my husband and one online friend that I later met in person know about [my] DE, so I don't talk about it, and most days I completely forget. (My children will get to know their story, and they will choose who and when they will tell.) Most people think my boys look like me, and sometimes I think that my older son looks a lot like me when I was his age. My husband and I laugh about it ... and usually cough it up to epigenetics. I also did not see my donor as an adult and only saw one photo of her as a child, but none of my children look like the photo of her I remember.

I wish I would have known [that] after all the wasted time, money, and heartache, in the end it would not be a waste at all. In the end I don't regret a single thing and am so thankful for being able to take the path I took.

Information Sharing and "Disclosure"

Many intended moms who originally choose an "anonymous" egg donor later wish that their egg donor was a known donor. Many have told us that after their child was born, their insecurities about their role in their child's life either waned or disappeared, and now they wish they had a way to contact their donor for the sake of their child.

Carmen*

[I wish I had known] the importance of establishing a means of contacting my egg donor directly—even if contact and identity remain anonymous. The ability to reach out to my donor, even though I currently have no reason to contact her, gives me enormous peace of mind for the psychological and physiological future well-being of my son.

Michelle

I wish I had known about the benefits of disclosure for a DE child and that there are options to the type of relationship you have with a donor. When we were counseled about DE at our clinic, the staff only told us about their in-house, anonymous program. At the time, we had no plans to disclose. I asked whether donors ever wish to be known and was told [that] young women only want to be anonymous. Shame on me for not doing my research and learning there were other options. Since joining PVED, we have completely changed our mind[s] and have disclosed to family and close friends. Ultimately, I love our DE child with all my heart, but I do worry that the fact [that] we used an anonymous donor, whom she will likely never get to meet, will cause her emotional pain.

🔊 *As we discuss in chapter 9, "Let's Talk about Egg Donation," we avoid the term "disclosure" because the word means that something is secret and then revealed in a moment's time. We never want this topic to be a secret but rather want it to be something that is always part of the family conversation.*

The landscape of "anonymous" egg donation has changed drastically over the past ten years, and although there are still clinics and agencies that run strictly anonymous egg donation programs, we are seeing more and more parents sharing information with their children about their genetic origins—even if the parents originally selected an anonymous donor.

At present, about half of the programs in the United States have options for known or directed egg donation cycles. And with the help of other resources, such as the Donor Sibling Registry, having continued contact with an egg donor in a neutral setting is becoming easier.

Shelley

[I wish I'd known] that keeping the use of an egg donor private from your kids [would be] so much more complicated than it sounds beforehand! You will save yourself a lot of future aggravation if you just accept the fact that disclosure is a simpler solution. I'm not saying you have to shout it from the rooftops, but please save yourself the headache of having your kids find out in a manner where you are not in control of the disclosure or at an age when they might harbor resentment toward you for not telling them earlier.

In this day and age, where health care is geared toward genes so strongly, kids need the most accurate information they can have to protect their own health. What are you going to do when your child is twenty-five and your agency calls you to let you know that the donor has been diagnosed with ovarian cancer, and your daughter needs to see a doctor immediately to discuss prophylactic removal of her own breasts and ovaries? How are you going to explain that to your kid? It's much more complicated in real life than it sounds when you are cycling!

Or what if you die and your kids are cleaning up your house and find your cycle paperwork? You won't even get a chance to address the questions that they may have.

When we die, there are no secrets, so why keep something from your child that they have an inherent right to know? At the end of the day, if your child discovers that you've lied about something as basic as their genes, they will wonder what else you have chosen to lie to them about their entire life.

Choosing a Clinic

One of the most important decisions you will make when growing your family through egg or embryo donation is where to go for treatment. Ideally, you will select a clinic where you feel respected and cared for by a physician (or team of physicians) who has your best interests in mind. The relationship that you develop with your physician and their staff is incredibly important. As you research clinics, look for a doctor who is compassionate and, above all, willing to partner with you during your treatment. We can't encourage you enough to search for a practice that you feel comfortable with. You can go to the best clinic in the world from a success-rate standpoint, but if you don't feel good about where you are and how you are being treated, that can make for a more stressful experience.

Following is a list of helpful hints to aid you in your clinic selection.

Clinics come in all shapes and sizes. Keep in mind that no two treatment programs are alike; each clinic has its own set of statistics (success rates), protocols, and procedures. As consumers, we want to get the most value for our money—after all, no matter how much we might come to love our reproductive endocrinologists, clinics are running a business. Because donor egg IVF is expensive and not always covered by insurance, it's important to be educated about the process and to have a list of questions to ask your physician and the clinic's business office and insurance specialist, so that you can make an informed decision.

There are large mega clinics run like factories, small boutique clinics, and everything in between. Don't think that going to the most expensive clinic will automatically get you a positive pregnancy test. That's not the way it works. No matter how cool your RE is or how warm and fuzzy you feel about the staff, the clinic is a business.

Many clinics do not accept insurance, but some do. Learn what your insurance does and does not cover. You may live in a state with mandated infertility coverage. But even if you are not, double-check your insurance again to see what your insurance will and will not cover. But don't choose a clinic just because they accept your medical insurance. That's not the right reason to choose a clinic to work with. Make sure you do your homework, and learn the inner and outer workings of your clinic of choice.

Learn about success rates—but remember that success rates are only a starting point for choosing a clinic. Published success rates are generally two years old. That means if you're seeking treatment in the U.S. in 2019, the United States Centers for Disease Control (CDC)[2] will have clinics' success rates for 2017. Start by looking for a clinic success rate directly on the clinic's website. If you can't find a success rate easily on the website, move on, because that clinic is really not worth your energy or time. Compare success rates from the CDC site—which, again, will be from two years earlier—and clinics' current success rates. If a clinic is doing well, the number of cycles will have increased, and the success rates also will have increased. Even if that increase is small, it's the upward trend that you're looking for. Clinics should list all of their success rates by treatment, age, and number of embryos transferred, and their frozen embryo transfer success rate should be listed separately from fresh transfers.

Pay attention to the number of single-embryo transfers (eSETs) performed, and pay attention to the number of double-embryo transfers. Then *compare*. Yes, we know that there is something appealing about having twins after infertility, but clinics on the cutting edge of technology do more single-embryo transfers. It's safer and healthier (for you *and* the baby) to have one baby at a time. One healthy baby is better than two babies who don't make it or are born prematurely with health issues.

Do not be afraid to travel. Unless you live in the middle of nowhere, you probably have several fertility clinics to choose from. That's why we say that not all fertility clinics are created alike. All clinics with high success rates have great programs where the intended parents can fly in, meet with the doctor, have all of the tests needed, and are sent back home to have all of the monitoring done locally in their city. When it's retrieval or transfer day, the intended parents fly back out to the clinic, undergo the embryo transfer, spend the night, and then head home to patiently await the results of the pregnancy test.

Think of your consultation appointment as your physician's interview *with you*. When you find a clinic that meets your criteria, schedule an appointment for a consultation. This is like a job interview—and you are hiring a team of people whom you're going to pay between $35,000 and $45,000 to have a baby. You owe it to yourself, your partner, and your future child(ren) to select wisely. This isn't like buying a house or a car that you can trade in or resell later—this is the rest of your life. You really want to get it right the first time. When conducting research, check out the RE to make sure he or she is board-certified in reproductive endocrinology and infertility. Because you're seeing a specialist and you want the very best, do your due diligence.

There are a few other things that may not seem like a big deal, but in the grand scheme of things, they all add up to create a great package.

➤ Is the clinic responsive when you call? Do the staff return messages promptly? Or are you waiting days, weeks maybe even a month to have your questions answered? Lack of communication is incredibly frustrating.
➤ Is the clinic open seven days a week?
➤ Does the clinic conduct scans, blood tests, retrievals, and embryo transfers seven days a week?
➤ How accessible is the clinic after hours and on holidays? Does it have an answering service?
➤ Does the staff answer email in a timely fashion?
➤ What is the financial department like? Does the clinic provide a printed cost sheet for all procedures—from egg retrieval through the embryo transfer—or are the cost sheets a maze of confusion?
➤ Does the clinic offer a money-back guarantee? Is the clinic part of a shared risk program?
➤ What about lab costs? Ultrasound costs? It's important that you know the costs ahead of time so that there are no surprises along the way. Don't forget to ask about ultrasound costs, lab costs, costs for extra office visits, and the cost of after-hours calls if needed.
➤ Does the clinic empower you, cheer you on, and appear to be hopeful and encouraging?

The bottom line is that you have to be your own advocate. This is a partnership. This is not just your doctor telling you what to do and you blindly following the treatment plan. You must be educated about what you are embarking on. You know your body better than your doctor does. Trust your gut—if it doesn't feel good, ask questions or change something.

Nobody but you is going to advocate for you, so know there is no such thing as a dumb question. Arm yourself with as much information as you can, ask lots of questions, and take detailed notes during every appointment. If you don't understand something, pick up the phone or email your clinic until you do understand. Do not be afraid to speak up. And if you come across a treatment plan or a study that you'd like to know more about, just ask.

This may all seem time-consuming and overwhelming, but just remember that you are in the driver's seat. The clinic is a service provider designed to meet *your* needs. You, the patient, have the very last say in your treatment—this is *your* body! And above all, keep your eye on the prize: a baby!

Stacey

I wish I had initially known [that] traveling for IVF was so common. Financially, we only had one shot at DE. It didn't occur to me to seek out the very best clinic no matter the geographic location. We started with the local clinic that had the best DE live birth rate. As I went through the process and learned more, it became apparent that patients travel for treatment routinely. After three donors fell through for various reasons, we reevaluated how we wanted to proceed. We decided to go with the clinic with the best live birth rate whose staff we gelled with. We wanted to give ourselves the best chance for success.

Christine

I wish I had known that all clinics that provide DE IVF cycles are not created equal. We would not have wasted time, money, and emotions on a clinic with very poor success rates and would have gone straight to the best clinic we could afford.

I wish I had known that my insurance was going to pay for it. I could have afforded a much better clinic with a much higher success rate. In the end, it all worked out, and I'm a momma! So really, I wish I had known it was going to work so I didn't have to worry so much.

Leslie*

> *We recommend that you learn as much as you can about the clinics you're considering. If you can, talk to current or former patients. Do your homework, research, ask questions, and know that it's really okay to travel.*

Seeing Photos of the Donor

Eden*

I wouldn't trade my babies for anything. They are the babies I was meant to have. But I wish I had not seen adult pictures of my donor. I keep thinking of her when people are trying to pick out characteristics of me and my husband. (We did not tell anyone our DE story.) But I would have not been convinced when we were picking a donor that I shouldn't see adult photos. So I guess I wish it had not been a choice.

One of the first questions we might ask Eden is why it bothers her that other people are attempting to pick out her and her husband's characteristics in their child. That is very normal and typical for people to do. However, this shows you that there are different things that affect each person differently, and for some women, seeing an adult photo of the egg donor can be bothersome later. Some say they don't like the donor taking up their headspace, and some women want as much information as possible.

We have seen that Eden's view is shared by only a minority of parents. Most wish they had seen photos and even wish they had the ability to have contact. Eden might feel better if she'd had help working through her grief.

Kitty

> It was only after I was pregnant that I learned that [our] not seeing photos was a decision made by some clinics. I was horrified! Why would I not want to see photos of my donor? I have a vivid imagination, so for me, not having information is a lot more scary than not knowing what my donor looks like.

Donor Selection

Vicki*

> I wish I had known about options and [the] possible importance of using a Jewish donor so that my children's ethnicity would never be in question. I'm glad I didn't know how controversial DE could be, the wide variety of opinions, and [the] many negative attitudes. I also wish I had given more thought to donor anonymity, realizing now that my kids may want more info than I have to give them and they may have a very hard time coming up with anything if they decide to go searching for genetic connections to the donor.

Ethnicity, religious views, and cultural backgrounds can be very important in the donor selection process. We discussed this in more detail in chapter 2, "Selecting Your Egg Donor." Third-party reproduction is more commonplace and widely accepted now than it was ten years ago. However, we still work daily to educate the masses about egg donation, embryo donation, and gestational surrogacy. Time and again, we hear from parents who originally selected anonymous donors and who now wish they had a known donor. They recognize that as their children grow up, they may want more information about their genes.

The Baby You're Meant to Have Is the Baby You're Meant to Have

Kitty

How your child was conceived has no bearing on your relationship. After your child is here, those become smaller details. I couldn't have known before how little it matters to me that my baby doesn't share my DNA. I mean, it's strange to have a kid who looks nothing like me, but this kid is all mine. She's two, but I've felt this way since I was pregnant.

Robin*

I wish that I had known that the donor aspect makes zero difference in how I feel about my children. There's never been any question in my mind that these little girls are all mine. I'm thankful that someone donated an egg to give me a start to becoming a mom again, but after that, it's all me. I am so in love with my two that we're planning [another baby] soon. My sons from my prior marriage adore their sisters.

Amy

[I wish I had known] that for as much as I stressed about the what-ifs of the decision and the procedures, birthing

and parenting would come naturally. It was the best decision I ever made.

Marna

I wish I had known that the genetic piece to all of this just doesn't matter. When he was born and they placed this perfect little person in my arms, all I could think about was that he was truly here, and I did this. I had this whole "You make me feel like a natural woman" thing going on! But seriously—it would have saved me a lot of angst, worry, and heartache because at the end of the day the baby you're meant to have is the baby you're meant to have. And I couldn't be more happy, joyous, or fulfilled with the birth of my son and watching him grow up into the young man he is today.

Susie

I wish I had known that it doesn't matter. I didn't need to worry so much about picking the "perfect" donor because whichever donor I picked would be the perfect one, resulting in the children I'm supposed to have.

As Carole always says, "love, not genes, makes a family," and donor-conceived kids really are okay. We worry about so many things when we navigate the uncharted waters of egg donation and embryo donation: Will our kids grow up to hate us? Will they really love us? How do we tell them how they were conceived and where they came from? What will people within or outside of our family think?

Most angry kids, regardless of how they arrive into a family, will say those dreaded words "I hate you!" or "I wish you weren't my mother!" Just think back to when you were a teenager! At some point, your child is going to hate you—but it will have nothing to do with how your child was conceived and everything to do with the fact that he or she is a *kid.*

The experiences of donor-conceived individuals vary greatly. The voices of donor-conceived persons are teaching us more and more that some of them also experience grief at the loss of genetic relatedness. Some care more than others, but just because we as parents feel that the connection to our children is unaffected by lack of a genetic connection doesn't mean that our children may not experience periods of distress over the lack of information or absence of connection to genetic relatives. We need to do our processing before we have our families, and then we can support our children through whatever their feelings may be.

On Being Educated about Our Bodies

Rose*

When we finally went to an RE ... I wish my OB had sent us to a specialist much sooner.

Dana

What I wish I would have known about the DE process before going through it is that many people would still not understand the need to take these steps to be parents, believing instead that those who couldn't have children [without assistance] should do without. I often remark, "Is it also that those with diabetes should then be allowed to die because their pancreas doesn't work anymore?" People are limited in their ability to reason, it seems.

Frances

I wish I had known that I would end up here so I could have skipped four years of heartache between the ages of thirty-four and thirty-eight. They tell you that you're so young—keep trying. I'm much happier on the other side, genes or not.

Cristin

> *I'd like to say that I wish I knew back in my early twenties that I'd lose my egg supply in my thirties to endometriosis. But had I known and had I frozen my own eggs, I would not have the children I have today. And I would never trade P and T for a genetic link.*
>
> *I wish I'd known that three 5-day blasts would be more than enough for us to cycle with. Mid-cycle, during the fertilization reports, I was in a panic that we wouldn't have enough embryos. However, quality over quantity. The two we transferred were the only two we needed.*

It's easy to fall into the *should've-would've-could've* line of thinking—please don't do that to yourself! Many intended parents come to this process not really knowing anything about fertility, ovarian reserves, and hormone levels. Really, who would? When we are younger, fertility is not something we spend a lot of time thinking about—if anything, we think about how to avoid getting pregnant. We anticipate that we are going to find partners, have sex, and quickly get pregnant the old-fashioned way. However, the truth is that getting pregnant and staying that way takes effort, and if we are older or have any sort of endocrine or ovarian issues, that makes the process that much harder.

We Wouldn't Change a Thing

Penelope*

> *I know without a doubt that DE is the* best *thing to ever happen to our family! I feel like every tear, every failed cycle, and every heartache led us to two of the most perfect miracles. Honestly, I feel like we went into this process with our eyes wide open; all of our questions and concerns were answered before we proceeded with our embryo transfer.*

Delilah*

I actually don't wish I had known anything because [additional information] might have changed what I did or when I did it—even finding the same donor at a different time would have given us different eggs—and thus changed the outcome. I'm so happy with my two little boys and so glad that things turned out how they have turned out!

Brooke*

I am thrilled at my new [extended] "family"—by which I mean the genetic connections of my daughter ... her genetic siblings and their mothers. We have become like cousins who share photos and stories and laugh over the genetic similarities. I was pretty sure, like 99 percent, that a non-genetic child would feel identical to a genetic one, and I was right. Now I am 100 percent sure. I mean, you can't wish you knew you would have success eventually. You keep trying, [and] you will have a baby if you want a baby, if you don't rule out options.

If I had to pick one thing, which, again, I already learned the hard way, [it would be] that all the pain you go through to have children is always worth it once the child is here.

Sandy*

I wish we had realized that thirty-four could be the edge of the fertility cliff and not been so laid-back about not worrying until I started approaching forty. But even then, who's to say that my eggs were any better at that time?

Alison*

Mainly, I wish it had not taken so long to become parents. I wish I was younger. It sometimes hurts a little that everyone sees a resemblance to my husband mainly, though that could have happened with my own eggs. But I wouldn't have my wonderful son if things had gone any other way!

Bella*

The only thing I regret is not telling my family. I wish I had been braver and told them that they could @#$%&! themselves if they "disapproved" of how I chose to have my family.

Hope*

I thought DE IVF [would be] more or less a slam dunk. I didn't expect it to take three tries. Hence, it was also more expensive than we initially anticipated, both emotionally and financially. Part of me wishes I'd started sooner, but I also believe in divine timing. Everything happens when it's meant to happen.

April*

One challenge has been my regret [about] not using a known donor. Once my boys were growing up, I began to see my choices [through] their eyes and not my own. I began to feel that they have a right to know their donor and meet her. This is still something I struggle with from time to time.

I feel that I have dealt with the challenges in healthy ways. I knew I would love my children beyond measure, and I do. I guess a bit of me is surprised that I feel as close (if not even a bit closer) to my twins as I do with my genetic child. They are such miracles. The other night I was watching them play and just felt a surge of gratitude for who they are as people. I knew that had anything been different, they would not be my children. There was definitely that belief that we were meant to be together in this lifetime. Sometimes when I feel this way I say a little thank-you to our donor in my heart.

Lindsey

I was [as] prepared as I could be for the challenges. I haven't been really surprised by anything, but I wish I had known how strong the connection would be between my daughter and me. I was really terrified that the lack of genetic connection would impact our relationship. The minute I found out we had five embryos growing, they were mine. There was nobody else in the picture as their mother except for me. I cheered them on as they grew.

Josephine*

I think being totally open and honest helped both of us feel okay with everything. Actually, when K was first born, it used to bother me when my in-laws would talk about what attributes she received from their side—because my parents could not do this. But I got over that with time and talking about it with my husband.

Diana

I guess what's surprised me the most is how simultaneously monumental and unimportant the fact of DE is in our life. On one hand, I think about my daughter's origins and the donor much more often than I thought I would. I intended to do this [conceive with a donor egg] and then edit that part of the story out of my mind and my thinking. That hasn't happened. On the other hand, it hasn't impacted one iota how much I love this little girl. In fact, I love her about a thousand times more than I ever dreamed I would. She's so much more than I ever hoped for. It's unimportant in the sense that I just don't care how I got her. I wouldn't trade her for an OE child if I could. She's perfect.

Helpful Tips from Parents via Egg Donation

We asked people who are now parenting after egg donation, "What do you wish you had known?" The answers are unique, brilliant, similar, different, funny, sad, happy, and angry. Here are some of their responses:

Time is of the essence. The general consensus is that parents wish they hadn't waited or put off childbearing. They wish they had been better-informed or educated earlier by their doctor and had not listened to their well-meaning friends who said, "Celebrities are having babies at fifty, so don't worry about it."

The $15,000 Ivy League donor does *not* create better eggs than the $5,000 community college donor. That's not the way biology works. Many intended parents have spent a lot of money on an egg donor only for their first cycle to be a complete bust. Then once they have selected a donor by factoring in the donor's reproductive health, they've taken home a baby nine months later—a baby whom they love to the moon and back.

It doesn't matter that their donor had blonde hair and they do not, that their donor was short and they are tall, or that her eyes were brown, and theirs are blue. At the end of the day, the baby they were meant to have is the baby they were meant to have. Even those who say they never believed in fate or destiny say this about their children.

The majority of intended parents wish they had met their donor. Lots of intended mothers say they began their egg donation cycle anonymously, only to research their donors later. Parents often look for the donor on the internet, hoping to make some sort of connection. Embarking on an anonymous egg donation cycle is a very common regret. And the reasons are understandable—many intended mothers feel insecure about their place and the role they will fulfill in their children's lives.

"No one could have prepared me for how painful losing my genetic connection would be." Sadly, this is a matter where you can't really understand how the loss is going to feel or what it's going to be like until you experience it firsthand. Coming to terms with genetic link loss is a process. Some intended parents sail right through, not looking back from the day they receive their diagnosis, but for the majority of others, it's a process, an often painful one.

"How do I tell my child?" Lots of parents feel awkward and scared about telling their children they were conceived via egg donation. They worry about how their children will react. They wish they would have begun the conversation with their children when they were toddlers. If their children now are older, they often don't know what to do and worry about anger and rejection. Our mantras have always been "Tell them early and often" and "If you don't make it weird, they won't make it weird."

"Can you help us? Our child has begun to call the donor a weird nickname. What should we call our donor?" I always tell parents via egg donation that their donor is usually referred to as the egg donor, the helper, or the genetic contributor or simply by her name. I also share with intended parents that it's pretty normal for kids to come up with names for things or people—both for people they've met and for people they haven't. I also share with parents that my son referred to his egg donor as Nel (short for Nice Egg Lady) for many years.

"My clinic didn't tell me that I could have independent legal representation and a legal agreement between myself and my egg donor." Some clinics are still using old, outdated forms of legal consent and agreement between the clinic and the intended parents. Every single egg donation cycle, anonymous or not, should involve outside legal representation for the egg donor and the intended parents, which includes a legal agreement drafted by a reproductive attorney.

Intended parents from around the globe all say the same thing: "I only wish I would've known that having a baby via egg donation would have no effect on how I feel about my children." So here's the thing: we love our kids. That's the bottom line. It doesn't matter whether or not we share DNA—they are our children. They may make us crazy and give us gray hair, but we love them so much that sometimes we forget to breathe. And over the fifteen years I've been working with intended parents worldwide, I've never come across a parent who wants to give their kid back. That's just not the way it works.

"How come nobody told me about the Donor Sibling Registry and the fact that our egg donor could have other offspring out there, since we are her third donation?" I hear this every single day. I'm not sure why there's a disconnect between agencies, clinics, and those egg donors who are repeat donors. An egg donor is almost always asked to donate again if her donation produced offspring. Every single agency and clinic should encourage the egg donor to register with the Donor Sibling Registry. It just makes sense.

The reality of third-party reproduction is that it's a billion-dollar business. Over the years, thousands of intended parents have shared with me that they wish they had found PVED sooner—because we would've saved them a lot of money. It's easy to feel pressured to select the wrong clinic. Your friend may have gone to a certain clinic because she had a different diagnosis, but then you select that clinic because she went there. Or you may go to the clinic closest to you even though the success rates are terrible because you think traveling will be an inconvenience. Then there are those who have selected clinics because of their low cost, but they end up going back three or four times with no success. By the time they contact PVED, they've spent upwards of $100,000 and still have no baby. Lots of intended parents tell me every day that no one could have prepared them for the sticker shock and cost factor.

When I tell intended parents that in reality, they are in the driver's seat and the fertility clinic and egg donor agency are service providers, they almost always gasp. For some reason many intended parents feel like they are working for the fertility clinic, the egg donor, the egg donor agency, or the reproductive attorney. The reality is they are working for you. You sign many checks along the way in creating your family, and all the checks you sign support those people who are working for you to help you have your baby.

Lots of parents don't think about remaining embryos or what they're going to do with them when they've completed their family. Ninety-nine percent of the calls I get about embryo donation start out with this sort of explanation: "When we were beginning this process, I didn't even stop to think about what I would do with remaining embryos. I was so focused on trying to get pregnant and have a baby that remaining embryos were the farthest thing from my mind." It's never too early to think about what is comfortable for you in regard to remaining embryos when you have completed your family-building. Many parents want to pay it forward and donate embryos to other families who are trying to become parents, whereas others donate remaining embryos to science. Some have their embryos destroyed once their families are complete, and some do a "compassionate transfer"—wherein embryos are transferred during a stage of the menstrual cycle when pregnancy cannot take place. And finally, there are a few families who will continue to pay storage for the rest of their lives and have those embryos buried or cremated with them upon their death.

Most importantly, every parent via egg donation tells me they wouldn't change a thing. Many say that all the trials and tribulations were worth it to have their children—and they would do it all over again because their children are perfect. This is truly a journey not for the faint of heart. It will stretch your mind and emotions in ways you can't imagine, but in the end, every painful shot, pill, hot flash, ultrasound, and blood draw—all of it will be worth it once your baby is in your arms.

That's a promise.

Chapter 5

FEELINGS TOWARD THE DONOR

Let us be grateful to the people who make us happy; they
are the charming gardeners who make our souls blossom.

—Marcel Proust

It's very common to have all different kinds of feelings about the women we select to help us become mothers and fathers. We are using their genes in order to have a baby because, for whatever reason, we can't with our own. Our feelings can vary wildly—sometimes we feel maternal and protective toward our egg donor; sometimes we feel like a big sister, friend, or aunt; and sometimes we feel nothing at all. At other times we can feel insecure, unsure, or even sad.

More often than not, we have feelings of gratitude and kindness toward the young women whose genes we use to build our families. We hear a lot of parents express gratitude.

Mary*

Our donor started out "anonymous" but ended up being
known. She is truly one of the kindest, most beautiful and
interesting souls I've ever met. I'm so glad to know people

like her exist and feel privileged that she is part of our
family origin story.

Even if they didn't have the opportunity to meet their donor, many intended parents feel a connection to her. For many, there was just something that jumped out at them from the donor's profile—such as a parent and donor having attended the same university, having similar career paths, liking the same kinds of music, food, or books, or sharing similar political views. Sometimes, the egg donor may look like a member of an intended parent's family or resemble the intended mother in some way.

Some intended parents worry about how their donor is tolerating all of the injections and medications that are prescribed, or they are concerned that their donor may feel overwhelmed by the process. They may worry about whether she was okay during the retrieval. Many intended mothers say they feel protective, almost maternal, toward their donor during the cycle.

Those intended parents who actually meet their donor and have a known cycle almost always say that once the voice and face-to-face connections occur, they feel an even deeper connection with her. She no longer is just a number that a clinic or agency has given her—she has a name that goes with her face. They now have heard her voice. They've heard her story. In many cases they've shared a cup of coffee or meal. The egg donor has heard the intended parents' story as well. Often, there's a lot of hugging and almost always a lot of giving thanks.

And there are those parents who feel thankful they are receiving genetic material from an egg donor to help them create or grow their family but who have no real feelings about their selected donor—and that's okay too.

Almost everyone on both sides of the equation is thankful. The egg donor is thankful that she's able to help someone who otherwise might never have a child, and the intended parents are forever thankful and grateful to their donor. Usually, the parties go their separate ways, and life goes on just like it's supposed to.

Many parents don't really think about the egg donor after they've had their baby—they are too busy in the trenches of parenting and raising children to really stop and give any of this much thought. However, some moms do think about the egg donor at different times for myriad reasons.

When the donor was anonymous, it may be more difficult to think about her in concrete terms. "Anonymous" means without name or without identity, but of course, everyone has a name and an identity; we just might not know what her name is. If parents saw a photograph before choosing a donor, it may be easier to picture her, and if it is easier to conjure her image, parents may think about her more often. It is neither good nor bad to think about a donor.

Started Out Anonymous but Then Became Known

Stacey

Our donor was unknown, but prior to our cycle, [she] became known to me through a funny set of circumstances. It was an unusual situation to have what was considered a known donor that I didn't really know. We bonded pretty quickly, but I was still guarded. We went hand-in-hand through the cycle. As we grew closer, I still questioned how much I wanted her involved in our family. I didn't know what to expect because I'd never been through it before. So I just felt my way through, day by day.

After our son was born, our donor just became part of the family. There was some awkwardness initially, but that went away pretty quickly. She assumed the auntie role, and I welcomed it. She is the sister I always wished I had. I can't imagine my life without her or the amazing gift she gave us. The more I got to know her and experience her wonderfulness, the more grateful I was that our son would have one more person in his life that loves him so dearly—actually, two. Her teenage son adores our son. He totally gets the donor thing. He's even schooled adults about it. So we hit the jackpot, in my opinion.

Carole

Until my son was seven years old, the donor was completely unknown to us. Truly, it was more like she was invisible. At the time of donation, she was a patient going through IVF, so we did not have a photograph or history about her. My son looked exactly like his father, so I used to joke that there really was no egg and that they had simply cloned his dad's sperm. It's hard to imagine someone you never met, someone who for you has no history, no name, no face, and no personality. I wanted to, but I had nothing to work with, especially since my son looked so much like his dad's side of the family. So I did think about her, but not really her; I just wondered about the missing part of him.

Marna

At first I was curious about her. It bothered me that I didn't know her name. It was a completely anonymous cycle with no picture; our doctor helped us select her. In the beginning I thought about her quite a lot, and I hoped she was happy. I knew she lived in the same geographical area as me, and sometimes when I went into the city, I wondered if I was going to see a young woman who resembled my son.

As my son grew older, he began asking questions about his egg donor, and I thought about her more. In 2012 she became known to us, and meeting her made her very real. She had a name. She had a voice. My son met her. She has become someone very special to us. Suffice to say, we are all incredibly thankful for her because without her we wouldn't have our son. It's pretty simple—she now has a name, and we love her very much.

Anonymous and Stayed Anonymous

Joan

Our egg donor was anonymous. To the extent that I feel anything toward her, I am simply grateful for her contribution to our wonderful sons coming into the world ... although I know a lot about her from her donor profile, I don't truly know her. I do think of her at least a few times a week, with gratitude.

Jessie

Our donor was anonymous, and I really don't feel anything towards her and don't really think about her at all now. At the time I was going through the process, I thought about her a lot, and I am very grateful for everything she has done for me.

Jenn

I feel nothing but good things towards [my donor]. I feel gratitude. I want her to have a wonderful life. I see a little bit of her in my daughter, and I'm okay with that. I have no bad feelings towards her. [Without her] I wouldn't have this beautiful, sweet, smart, perfect little girl. I am so lucky to be her mom, and I adore every inch of her. I wouldn't change a thing.

Rabbi Rachel Brown

Our donor was anonymous. I will be forever grateful to her, for without her I wouldn't have my amazing son.

One of our tasks in creating a family with the help of donors is to help our kids see the difference between what is a family-building issue and what is a regular growing-up issue. It can be challenging because parents rarely know. Thus, we see that parents often don't think about the donor unless something goes wrong or something unexpected occurs. If there is a developmental milestone that is a bit delayed or a medical issue, parents will often wonder if the donor is responsible. Of course, anomalies occur all the time in the general population, but we tend to wonder about what we or our donor(s) may not have known about their medical history and whether that may be contributing to whatever our child is going through. Ultimately, our children are their own people, and we are called to parent the children we have in front of us, whether or not we know how they got their little personalities, quirks, brilliance, or medical issues.

Robin

We had already gone through one donor unsuccessfully before we chose this one. It was strictly anonymous, picked from the donor pool by my RE. I was forty-three for my first pregnancy and forty-six for my last one. The feelings that I have for her are complex. I'm thankful that she decided to donate, but on the positive side that's it. I remember the anguish that I felt having embryos left over and not knowing what was the best route to take with them. It really got me thinking of how someone could donate not knowing who would wind up with [her eggs], not knowing how they would be treated if they became babies. And I feel that most anonymous donors donate for the financial benefit.

Feelings about donating embryos may change after one has had a child, which is why it is so important that parents wait until their families are complete to make decisions about embryo donation. Seeing an embryo before transfer is very different from knowing that frozen embryos could be just like your son Johnny, who is funny and spunky, or your daughter Jenny, who is contemplative and affectionate. After parenthood, the idea that embryos become real people takes shape, and parents may think differently about the embryos and often about the donor herself. Before cycling, the donor may be thought of as simply a collection of cells needed to bring a longed-for baby into one's life. Or she may be a headshot found on a matching site. After parenthood, parents may think more about who she is, what her life is about, what she is like, and whether one's child is "like" her.

Debra*

We had an anonymous donor (double donors actually), and I really don't think about them as individual people at all. I'm very thankful that they contributed to the creation of our beautiful daughter, but that's all I really think about them—abstract contributions to the uniqueness of my daughter ... well, except when I wonder about which one of them must have been a late teether, which leads me to wonder what other medical history might have been nice to know.

Jamie*

Grateful we live in a time where egg donation is possible. I'm grateful for my donor's gift. I have no other feelings for her.

Norma*

> *I know almost nothing about her. I am, of course, grateful for what she did, but I don't think about her. I hope she is happy.*

Frances

> *I thought of her often during pregnancy and for a few months after. Now I think about her every couple of months. I am either wondering about a trait my son has or thankful she helped make this happen. Most of all, I hope that she does have her own children one day so she can appreciate the magnitude of her gift to our family.*

Ruth

> *I'm very thankful for her, but I really don't think about her at all.*

Sandy

> *Ours was a shared cycle, meaning the donor was also doing IVF. I think about her once in a while, all good thoughts, and hope she was as lucky as I was.*

Many donors are anonymous but indicate in many different ways that they would be willing to be contacted in the future. Sometimes this means they are willing to be contacted if medical information is needed; sometimes they are willing to be contacted and identified by the offspring at the age of majority. Many donors, if asked, will register with the Donor Sibling Registry so that offspring or family may locate them in the future.

Beverly*

> *[The donor was] anonymous but "willing to be known,"*
> *whatever that really means. Would like to discuss this*
> *further at some point. Sperm banks seem so cut-and-dried*
> *and transparent about this, but our egg donor agency was*
> *not. We used donor sperm too and are involved with our*
> *donor siblings, so the egg donor feels much more of a mystery*
> *to us and kind of inaccessible.*

Beverly is correct to question what the language "willing to be known" means because often the matching programs or clinics do not carefully clarify the kinds of donor contact available. Still, a willingness to be known is most likely in the best interests of all concerned, given what we know about the curiosity many donor offspring have about genetic origins.

Beverly

> *We feel so grateful to her and [are] happy that we picked*
> *her—our third choice after the first two didn't work out.*
> *When the cycle coordinator at our clinic met her (and she*
> *had met at least one, maybe both, of the others), she said,*
> *"She's the one," and we believe she was right. We think she*
> *lives in the suburbs, but that's all we know, except [what*
> *we know] from the profile and from the donor coordinator,*
> *who said she was bubbly and fun and sweet. We think our*
> *kids are beautiful souls and just so lovely, and we attribute*
> *a lot of that to her.*

Beverly's comment that she believes her donor was "the one" reflects the beliefs of many who ascribe to theories of fate and destiny. The child you have is the child you were meant to have. Most people will say they cannot imagine being parents to any other child and would not ever want any other child. Over and over, parents via egg donation will exclaim,

"If you told me today that my ovaries are working and I could have a genetically related child instead of the children I have, I would absolutely decline the offer!" Of course. These are our children, and like any other parents, we can't imagine any others, nor would we want any others.

Directed Donation (Donor was known to the family prior to the cycle)

Jean (whose donor was her niece)

I love her with my whole heart! She's my first "daughter." My children adore their Aunt Kadie. Karalee says she's moving to Raleigh to get a job (like Aunt Kadie just did). I think about her every day. I think of the gift she gave us often, and my heart swells more if that's possible. There are no weird feelings or uncomfortableness because that's not who we are or ever have been. She and her (husband) are close to trying for their own babies, and I just can't wait for my babies to have these close little cousins!

Elaine*

We knew our egg donor, as she was related to friends of ours. I think about her all of the time. She is my angel, my gift from God, who in turn gave me the gift of motherhood, selflessly donating eggs to us as a gift. I especially think and cry about her every Mother's Day. I thanked her on Mother's Day one year, and she replied simply, "Everyone deserves to be a mother." Truly an angel. I can never express how much gratitude I have towards her ... I love her.

Lisa

[Our donor was a] known donor. She was a friend of my husband's from his work. We met for a dinner when I was

going to try one more OE (own egg) IVF, which never happened. At the time, I felt very weird and asked her why would she do this for someone she barely knew. She simply wanted to help us have a family, and her eggs were going to waste. She is kind of a go-getter type-A person who I got to know better through this. I did go through feelings of inadequacy and fear. I was so afraid she would change her mind and back out. My desire to have a child outweighed everything. After the first successful cycle we really didn't talk anymore, and she kept in touch with Facebook. She said she felt a bit weird and wanted to step back. I respected that. My husband still spoke with her at work and gave her (home-buying) advice. My husband bought her a dog. We all went over to her house. I did leave feeling weird. We got invited back a few weeks later for a housewarming party, and I felt more comfortable. I went to the retrieval and watched on the screen while they took the eggs out. Coolest thing ever. The whole experience really was. I think of her every few weeks. We are so busy; I get caught up in our awesome life she gave us.

Lisa's experience reminds us of the importance of including mental health professionals in the process of egg donation, whether a donor is known or not known, selected from an agency or from a clinic. It is a wonderful gift to children to be able to identify the people with whom they share genes, so known donation can be extraordinary in many ways. These arrangements are filled with love and generosity. At the same time, a mental health professional can assist the donor in determining whether she is someone who can do this and not be psychologically harmed. It is normal for a woman to think about the offspring she helped to bring into the world. How much and how she thinks about those offspring makes the difference between whether this will be gratifying and fulfilling for the woman or uncomfortable and regrettable. We want her to feel connected but not maternal. We want her to feel proud of her contribution yet not take ownership. We want her to be able to see the family and the offspring without feeling like she has lost a child.

Creating new forms of kinship is complicated, and we would expect that at times it can feel awkward. Working through any awkward feelings can be well worth the effort in exchange for taking the mystery out of the process of having someone else's genetic material help you become a parent.

Semi-Anonymous (No ongoing contact but had some contact before the cycle and exchanged some identifying information at that time)

Marie

> *I talked to my donor on the phone, then met her during her retrieval. She looked amazingly similar to me, and I am in contact with another family (in Germany) that she donated to. I look at my twins often and am amazed at how the one who looks like her egg donor "diblings" looks less like me than the one who looks like her sperm donor "diblings." I actually have access to her Facebook, so I check in on her sometimes. I want my girls to have access to her if they so choose when they're older.*

Cherie

> *I think of my donor quite often—daily, in fact. And always in a positive way. I know she planned to be married about six months after our cycle. My thank-you gift to her [for donating] was a bottle of Dom Pérignon for that reason. In my mind, she and her fiancé/new husband drank/ toasted with it to their new lives. I envision her having a loving and happy marriage, always smiling. I suppose that's because she gave me so much love for my life.*

Sometimes I wonder if I should "save" an embryo for her on the off-chance she has a hard time conceiving. Then I can return the favor she granted me.

Kitty

It's a total cliché, but I feel immense gratitude towards our donor. There's not a day that goes by that I don't think about her fondly. When we chose our donor, we wanted someone who was comfortable with ongoing contact, so we hired a lawyer to draw up a bespoke contract, instead of just using the clinic's boilerplate contract for standard anonymous donations. [Our donor] and I exchanged a couple of emails, and although she said she was happy to meet us, communication fizzled out at her end. I am really disappointed by that. I had hoped that the three of us would be able to meet before egg retrieval, so we could have a photo to show the child(ren) she helped create.

I have to respect her choice. Maybe one day she'll change her mind … or maybe she won't. Either way, we are raising our daughter so she knows about her genetic origins. As she grows older, she will learn there is a very special woman out there who helped bring her into the world—and, in her own words, for no other reason than she wanted someone like me to experience the joy of parenthood.

Being the mom of a toddler is hard work. It's the hardest thing I've ever done, and there is still the added layer of pregnancy loss and infertility grief. But overall, I am at peace because everything led me to having this amazing little girl in our lives. In that respect, I wouldn't change a damn thing.

Annie was on the PVED forum when she read about one of the members meeting the donor who had helped produce a now twelve-year-old son. That meeting led to the donor's integration into their family, as a member of the family. Annie talks about the impact this had on her thoughts about the donor's contribution versus what it means to be a mother.

Annie*

> *We had an unknown donor. To be honest, I guess I am still figuring out how to feel about her. Of course, I am eternally grateful to her, but now I wish I could meet her to underscore the fact that she is simply the egg donor and I am the mama! I feel like I am constantly battling the sadness that my own eggs were "too old" … it was really so helpful to see the photo of the egg donor with the PVED member's son. Somehow it helped me to see this relationship more clearly, like "Of course, that isn't his mom! The mom is!"*

Stephanie*

> *I think of my donor often. I feel as though I have a loved one out there who I haven't met yet. She gave me the most wonderful gift in the world. I couldn't have asked for two more beautiful, happy, healthy, sweet babies! I want to share my happiness with my donor … I want to tell her I love her. I just can't explain how much my twins have enriched my life, my marriage, and my heart! She was open to a known relationship, but time factors made us go with unknown. I so deeply regret this now.*

Lynn

> *I feel immense gratitude and appreciation for the gift my donor bestowed upon me. I met her for lunch once before the transfer. I studied her physical traits and mannerisms and etched them in my mind to compare them with my girls later. She had a calm and sweet energy. We had a lot in common in terms of spiritual beliefs, and we are both left-handed. I thought about her a lot when I was pregnant and the girls were babies. I rarely think about her now. I'm sure when the girls get older and more curious about their identity, she will come up more often.*

Amanda*

> *Our second attempt was embryo donation with people who were originally perfect strangers halfway across the world. We have an open donation relationship and have gotten to know each other over the years. We have met a couple of times, and we still live across the globe from each other. We're not family and technically not friends, but the nature of our relationship makes us an important and special part of each other's lives. The bond is indescribable. I'm deeply grateful for their selfless generosity in donating their precious embryos to us. I can only imagine the strength and courage it took to come to their decision to donate a part of themselves to perfect strangers. It humbles my husband and I to know that our son is a result of their selfless decision. He's the most amazing gift from God and man that we've ever received, and this experience has given me hope for the future in this crazy world of ours.*

Some of us may think about our donors frequently, and some not at all. Most parents feel gratitude when they think about the people who made it possible for them to become parents.

We have seen here that it seems easier to think about the donor when a fair amount of information is shared. If we know her name, have a photograph, and think of her as a real person, that may facilitate our ability to hold her in our heads and hearts. No matter how much information we may have or how known or not known she may be, we were not just given eggs. We were given the beginnings of life, which will be passed on for generations.

Infertility does not stop when we become parents. Our grandchildren will be the product of the gifts we were given. Forever after, we will be linked through a new form of kinship to those who imbued our children with aspects of who they will become. Hopefully, this will allow us to feel mostly positively about the person or people who made it possible.

Chapter 6

LETTING GO, MOVING ON

An excess of sorrow is as foolish as profuse laughter; while, on the other hand, not to mourn at all is insensibility.

—Seneca

The sadness we feel over the loss of our genetic offspring is grief. But unlike the grief we feel when a real person dies, infertility grief means saying goodbye to someone who was never really here. When there is an actual death, we have ritual around it. Sometimes we have funerals and wakes and make social calls. We go to church or temple, and we often light candles. But when we are told that we need genes from someone else in order to conceive—when we need to confront that our child may not look like us, be like us, laugh like our grandparent, or have our partner's intelligence—no one brings us a casserole, and no one says they are sorry for our loss. There is no name to give to a person whom we never got to meet, even though we feel like a real person has passed. We feel that way because the person has been so real to us for so long, even if we didn't realize it.

Carole

> *My maternal grandfather's name was Sam Brown; he had*
> *no middle name. He was born in New York City on May*
> *21, 1896. He was an appliance salesman all of his life, even*
> *during the Depression, when no one had money to buy the*
> *refrigerators or televisions he was selling. I was his favorite*
> *grandchild, or so he made me feel. He had been married*
> *to my grandmother for fifty years when he keeled over and*
> *died from a heart attack on May 27, 1968. I was fourteen,*
> *and although I was not a little kid anymore, I was too*
> *traumatized to attend his funeral. He is buried in Mount*
> *Sinai Cemetery in Los Angeles, and every few months or so*
> *for the last forty-five years, my mother and I have visited*
> *the grave sites of my grandparents, leaving a pebble on their*
> *headstones, as is the custom in the Jewish tradition.*

Name. Birth date. Marriage. Children. Occupation. Date of death. Cause of death. A life lived and a life lost. That's the way it is supposed to work. But losing a dream is different from losing a person. Losing someone we never met but have carried with us in our heart and our imagination means there is no birth date, no death date, no headstone, no history, and no life well lived. No memorial, no funeral, no ritual to help us say goodbye.

Marna

> *I belong to a Native American Indian tribe. When I had*
> *my son, I approached the tribe to see about having him*
> *registered with my tribe. I was very transparent and honest*
> *about his conception and the egg donor piece. The tribe*
> *was very kind and left it up to me to decide if that was*
> *something I wanted to do. After thinking about it for a very*
> *long time, I decided that I would not have him registered*
> *with my tribe because he truly is not a Native American*

*Indian. He's English, Norwegian, Italian, and Irish. That's
his ancestry. Will I still share my Native roots with him,
pass down stories from my family, and talk to him about
the Indian tribe I identify with? Absolutely. But the reality
is he's not Native American. And he never will be. And that
part was difficult for me to let go of.*

The inability to become a parent when and how we want is, for most people, an extremely stressful experience. Sometimes it can be devastating. Many people grow up expecting that someday they will choose a partner, get pregnant, and become a parent. When that doesn't happen, the losses start mounting.

We lose time. We lose a sense of control. We lose trust in our bodies. We lose the ability to stay in sync with our peers who are transitioning into the parenting stage of their lives. We are deprived of a feeling of moving forward, and we feel stuck. We stay in jobs too long because of health insurance benefits or flexibility, we postpone large purchases, and we don't book certain vacations because we might be pregnant at the time we planned to go.

Added to all of these losses is the very real loss we experience when we are ultimately unable to have a child that is genetically related to us or to our partner. Through all the months and years of trying to conceive, we have had so much time to fantasize about who our children will look like or remind us of. Many people imagine in some detail that the child will have their partner's nose or grandmother's laugh or a special talent that runs in the family. Quite often, we picture a child of a certain age, parent and child engaged in some activity together. Most of us imagine dressing our kids in cute outfits, playing our favorite sports with them, or simply reading a bedtime story. We ascribe to our fantasy children the belief that they will be good in math or weak in science, because those qualities match us, our partners, or our relatives. We keep trying to bring that child into the world, and we can't.

Marna

It took seventeen years before I had my first and only living child. And throughout this entire process, my experience was that nobody knew really anything helpful to say to me. By the time I embarked on the journey to try to conceive through egg donation, I think I might have done almost anything in order conceive and carry a baby to term.

Delilah

There was huge grief for me. My family has great genes (healthy, long-lived, kind, smart, good-looking people), and it really hurt to think I would be losing that connection. My husband was sad about it too. He didn't want to be much involved in the donor search—he left that to me, and then we discussed the ones I'd tentatively found. I spent almost a year searching for an uncannily good match in a donor who was also proven and finally found one … there were several we were interested in, and once I saw that there were a lot of good donors, it felt better.

Kristin

It was and it wasn't a difficult decision. I was devastated at first to know that the only way I could have a child is through someone else and someone I do not know. I always dreamed of the traits that my future children would get from me, and that was all thrown out the window in an instant, and I had absolutely no control over it. But on the other hand, we want a healthy child, and we know that through a donor we can make that happen. Our end goal is to be parents.

Marna says:

> I think it's important to stop and think about the intended fathers in this equation. We focus so much on intended mothers, and often we forget about intended fathers. I think it's quite natural to do that because the fathers often don't have to mourn the loss of their genes. But what they do have to cope with is the fact that although their partners are having their baby, they had originally embarked on having a baby with their partner's genes. Many intended fathers have said to me over the years that selecting an egg donor was quite difficult because nobody could hold a candle to their wives or partners; they were with these women for a reason.

John

> *I didn't want to create a life with another woman. I wanted my wife's genetic child for all the reasons I love her. But in the end, the mother she is to our daughters are proof that we did indeed create a child together, just not with her DNA.*

Josephine

> *At first I did not want to do DE. Adoption was my plan B. It really bothered me to think about "carrying another woman's baby." Through the process, my feelings slowly changed. It took several years.*

Jenn had a daughter before receiving a secondary infertility diagnosis.

Jenn

> *When I was diagnosed with DOR (secondary infertility) three years ago, it felt like the end of the world. When my*

RE told me the only way I'd have another child is by donor egg, I actually said, "Nope. There is no way I'm doing that. That's crazy." That statement seems ridiculous to me now, but when you are first told you need to use donor eggs, it is scary as hell. It is lonely and overwhelming, and the whole process seems kind of bizarre and sci-fi. We've all been there, right?

One thing that really helped was hearing all the stories from those who had gone through it and were on the other side. All of them loved their babies, and I've never heard anyone say they regret using donor eggs. That was huge for me. I found comfort and inspiration in these stories.

Once I understood what it really is to use a donor egg, my mindset totally changed. I went into the process not looking to replace myself, but to replace my eggs. There is a big *difference in thought there. I never felt like I was being taken out of the picture, but rather [felt] that something extra was being added. I wasn't replacing me; I was replacing my crappy eggs with healthy eggs. My daughter has a mother and a donor, and those two things exist separately and independently from each other.*

I've had many struggles throughout this journey, but one thing I know for sure is that DNA is something, but it's not everything. Our baby is here because of our love and our intentions for her to exist. Our kind and generous donor gave us a healthy microscopic cell that helped us create a human being. Our donor was absolutely necessary, but I've never felt like her role in my child's conception has ever diminished my role as a mother.

So now that I've gotten to know and love and care for this little girl for over a year, I can tell you that being her mom is exactly like being a mom to my OE daughter. Sure, there is this extra thing about her conception, that we will always be honest about and always be thankful for, but loving her and raising her is exactly as it would be if we had used my own egg. A few weeks ago, my daughter was sick, and all she wanted was me. She would actually push my husband away. At one point she was literally clinging to me for comfort, and I said to my husband (in a tired and exasperated voice), "Remember when I was pregnant and worried that we wouldn't bond?" And we both laughed! Three years ago, when I got that awful phone call about my DOR, I could never have imagined laughing about what we've been through. And here I was, just a regular everyday exhausted mom with a cranky baby.

And just for the record, the only time I think about my daughters in terms of OE versus DE is on PVED, for clarification purposes only. In real life, I just have two little girls I adore.

Like Jenn, Diana had one child from her own egg but was unable to conceive again.

Diana

I hear tales of those rational few who get the diagnosis, dust themselves off, and then promptly turn to DE, but I wasn't one of those women. I had to mourn the loss of my dream first, to let go of the idea of another genetic child. I think that's a critical part of this process, and there's no way to fast-track it. After I'd mourned and really accepted that without DE, there would be no more children, I was then able to direct my attention to a new dream.

And I think that's another important point: a DE child is not a consolation; a DE child is a different journey altogether. My DE child is not my second choice; she's a different choice, not lesser, just different from what I originally intended. It's not like I was going to buy an Audi A6, [and] it wasn't available, so I decided to get an A4; it's more like I got a Harley instead. Completely different ride.

Hope

At forty-four years of age, I would now need a donor egg to conceive. I cried from the depths of my soul. As the only living child of my parents, I wanted so badly to provide them a grandchild who shared their genes. The very idea of using a donor egg made me recoil with horror. It was too much for me to accept at the time …

Danielle*

It was … a difficult decision because I had to really give up any hope of seeing my mother's smile, my grandfather's eyes, my cheeks and hair. I had to mourn my genes even though they were never that important. They are important even if we think they aren't. I looked on the bright side: the child would also not inherit all the genetic maladies I have.

Not everyone experiences the sense of grief and loss described here. A few, such as Jayne, feel disappointed if their child does not receive the positive attributes for which a donor was chosen.

Jayne

I have a nearly five-year-old OE daughter and a just-turned-two-year-old DE daughter. I've honestly never mourned the loss of my genes with [my] DE daughter, perhaps because I already have an OE daughter. Yes, I worry about the complexity of having a daughter who is not genetically related to me and what that might mean for her, but I'm not upset for myself that we don't share genes.

Yet I think I'm disappointed—not disappointed in my DE daughter but disappointed for her because it doesn't appear that she has inherited any of those things that I admired in the donor and thought were so much better than what my gene pool had to offer. In my mind I had already played out conversations I would have to have with my OE daughter, where I would be apologizing that she didn't get the beautiful/clever/interesting gene pool of the donor. And now I'm realizing that perhaps my genes weren't that second class after all, as my OE daughter is every bit as beautiful and clever as [my] DE daughter.

Jayne idealized the donor, perhaps to make it feel more acceptable to need someone else's genes. Sometimes we decide it is better that we are using a donor because we can replace the genes that we do not want to pass along. Whether we are concerned about mental illness or addiction or being extremely short, selecting a donor can allow us to compensate and find the positive in choosing someone in whom we think we can screen out our "bad genes."

Jayne

Anyway, I think I put the donor up on a very unrealistic pedestal and in doing so created some silly expectations about things I thought I would see in my daughter. I realize I may be a bit of an outlier here in looking for donor qualities in my child when most people here may prefer the opposite (not to see too much donor in their child).

Kitty thinks about the donor in a different way:

Kitty

> *My donor and I look so alike that my clinic's egg donor coordinator gasped when she first met me. I expected to see a real mix of my husband and donor in my daughter, but she mostly looks like her dad's side of the family. That said, I regularly see flashes of our donor, and it doesn't bother me in the slightest—I actually really like seeing the wonderful woman I chose to replace my genes. It's the most obvious way in which I see my influence. I am pleased that my daughter has my donor's beautiful large blue eyes instead of my small deep-set brown ones.*

It's actually healthy to think about the donor and look for her qualities in one's child. It is our task as parents to love all of our child, not just the parts that remind us of ourselves or our partner. Without the women who gave us their DNA, we would not have our children, the children we cherish and adore. Appreciating and seeing donors' qualities in our children may be a reminder of our loss, but it doesn't have to be. Our loss led to our gain. Embracing the entirety of our children and not just specific attributes is our gift to them, ourselves, and the contributors we honor. If this is painful, it tells us that we have work left to do to mourn the loss of our idealized child.

Saying Goodbye to the Child You Will Never Know

Stephen J. Forman, hematology oncologist at the City of Hope in Los Angeles, reflects on loss and the "myth" of closure in his article "Cancer Insights: The Myth of Closure."[3] "Going on with life is not the same as gaining closure," he writes. Of course, we move on, but that doesn't mean we never again think about someone we lost. And for us, that someone is a fantasy.

We don't have a way of maintaining the memory of someone we never met. There is no public ritual, no place to honor them, and no way of paying our last respects. We have only the memory of a person we created in our imagination.

Most people will say that they frequently think about someone they have lost. Some say they think about that person every day. And why not? Those whom we have loved and lost don't go away; they never leave our hearts. But it's different with reproductive loss. The real child we end up cherishing takes the place of a child we only imagined.

An exercise that was originally created for those who have experienced miscarriage has been adapted to help those who have lost a genetic offspring say goodbye to that imagined child. Many have found it extraordinarily helpful in clearing a space for the children they will have, because there isn't enough room in our homes or our hearts to hold the ghost of the child we thought we would have and the children we will eventually parent.

The idea is to bring our fantasized children to life in order to say hello before saying goodbye. This is often counterintuitive to some, who think that the less they think about their imagined child, the better. On the contrary, we want to go ahead and "birth" that child through a creative process in order to say goodbye.

Most people bring the child to life by writing a letter. This is, in essence, a letter to the child you will never know. This could be your first or fourth child. It could be a child you terminated at an earlier time. It could be a child who is like your partner, a child you will not have because your partner is infertile.

Some people actually name these children in the letter, usually using a name they will never use for an actual child they do parent. Many imagine a child of a specific age, fantasizing that Dad would be playing ball with her or Mom would be singing lullabies. Some people imagine an infant, whereas others picture sending a kindergartner off to school. Regardless, this is a letter to that person, however imagined.

In this letter, we might tell the child who we thought they would be and what we thought we'd do together (even though we will definitely do those things with any child we parent). We might tell the child that we thought he would have his grandfather's sense of humor or that she would have her aunt's curly hair. Then we need to tell this imagined child that we need to let them go to make room for another child to come into our hearts.

This is a very sad and hard thing to do. Everyone cries when it is described to them, and everyone cries when they write the letter.

The invisibility of reproductive loss often adds to the pain of it. We don't have those rituals that help us say goodbye to someone who has died. So now the task is to create a ritual with the letter. We usually don't keep dead bodies in our home, so we have to let go of this letter we have created.

The ritual can be absolutely anything that has meaning to you. Many people go to the beach and read the letter to the seagulls and the dolphins, then rip it up and throw it into the water. The eternal and ephemeral quality of the ocean is very healing, and watching our letter get carried out by the tide can be cathartic. Some people bury the letter in the sand, knowing it will get carried out to sea. Others hike to their favorite mountain and bury the letter under their favorite shade tree; some simply burn the letter in a fireplace. Many people say goodbye by planting a favorite tree or bush in their yard; they watch this plant flourish through the years as a symbol of that which was lost but which has now made space for something beautiful. The act of digging a hole in the ground is funereal, and many feel that in doing so they have finally said goodbye. Those who have religious or spiritual beliefs also may go to church and say a prayer, light a candle, or go to synagogue, accompanying the other ways to ritualize a loss with an activity they find comforting and meaningful.

Though it is certainly not a panacea, most people find that this exercise helps to move them just a bit further toward resolution of genetic loss. This doesn't mean you will never again think about some imagined child, but it does mean that you have said goodbye in a way not previously experienced. Genetic loss very often does feel like a death in the family, and deaths in a family require concrete recognition of the loss.

It is very helpful to do this exercise in conjunction with support from a mental health professional who has expertise in fertility and family-building issues. Having a place to go where you can share how the exercise was experienced, what was said in the letter, and what ritual was chosen completes the process and lends to the feeling of resolution.

Elaine

Learning that I was incapable of conceiving a child using my own eggs was, in a word, devastating. I was thirty-one years old at the time and was in no way prepared to hear that I would never be capable of having my own genetic child. After four failed IUIs and four failed IVF cycles using my own eggs and one miscarriage, my gut was telling me [that] my doctor was right and that using a donor was the next step. Still, "it's time to move on" were the hardest words I've ever had to hear.

My grief was very raw and deep. I was angry, embarrassed, lonely, depressed, and jealous of every fertile person I came in contact with. I withdrew from many of my friends, especially those with children. Given that many of my friends were of childbearing age and were starting/expanding their families all around me, I felt extremely isolated and alone. Some of my friends had even experienced infertility and had already gone through treatment, resulting in successful pregnancies. But no one knew what it was like to experience so many failures and to no longer have the option of having a genetic child of their own. I felt like I was on an island of grief all by myself. Not even my husband could fully understand the devastation I was experiencing. Of course, he had to watch me fall apart, but he wasn't losing a piece of himself the way that I was. With all of this said, the ultimate sadness I experienced came from the idea of possibly never becoming a mother. While simultaneously grieving, I wasted no time in beginning my search for a donor. The same day I was told we needed to move on to donor eggs was the very same day I joined PVED. Not having children was not an option for me, so I needed to figure out how to be okay with losing the genetic connection to any children I might have.

It was more painful than I am able to fully articulate. Once we started on our journey to get pregnant with donor eggs, my difficulty with infertility did not end. It ultimately took us three different egg donors, six additional IVF cycles, and yet another miscarriage before we were ultimately successful. It was hard for me to decipher where the heartache from so many failed attempts stopped and the pain of needing the help of [a] donor started. Our three-and-a-half-year journey of nonstop fertility treatments was simply the hardest, most heartbreaking time of my life.

The sense of isolation is powerful. Regardless of the knowledge that thousands of families have been created through egg donation, many men and women feel like they are completely alone. It is important to reach out and find community. When Marna conceived her son Nick via egg donation, she felt incredibly isolated and alone. Her husband didn't process egg donation the same way she did. Marna didn't really know anyone personally with whom she could talk or share anything about this process. A small email list she subscribed to was literally her lifeline during her cycle and pregnancy with her son. The support she received from those women whom she had never met was invaluable. During her pregnancy, Marna had the epiphany that if she succeeded in giving birth, she was going to give back in some way. Because she was determined that no one should ever have to go through what she did alone, PVED was born. Certainly, PVED is one source of support, as are organizations such as Resolve and Path2Parenthood. (See the Resources section for more information.)

Support groups can be helpful as well. Talking to others who are experiencing similar feelings is usually very healing. Here is what Elaine did to help process her genetic link loss:

Elaine

> *I met some lifelong friends through PVED that helped*
> *me to keep standing. Connecting with women from this*
> *group has been life-changing. I also opened up to a few*
> *close (fertile) friends for support in my day-to-day life. In*
> *all honesty, I was so focused on trying to become a mom by*
> *whatever means possible that there wasn't much emotional*
> *space to truly process my feelings of loss.*

Creating a family with the help of others' DNA presents lifelong differences, and residual feelings of loss can creep up and tap us on the shoulder when we least expect it. Many parents find themselves revisiting old feelings, although the feelings are so different than they were before they became parents. Again, Elaine describes it this way:

Elaine

> *I do still struggle every single day. I have nine-month-old*
> *twins whom I love dearly. Given the choice, I would choose*
> *those two precious babies to be mine a thousand times over.*
> *Still, when I look at them, I'd be lying if [I said] a part of*
> *me didn't feel "less than" because I couldn't conceive them*
> *using my own genetic material—less of a woman, less of*
> *a wife, less of a mother. It's something that I know I need*
> *to work on. This is the journey I was given, and while I'm*
> *beyond grateful that it led me to where I am today, I have*
> *a lot more self-healing to do in order to be the best mom*
> *I can be. Right now, I struggle with not being "enough,"*
> *but I'll be damned if my children ever feel that way for a*
> *second, so there's definitely more work to be done!*

The reminders are just that: reminders. There are moments when we say to ourselves, *Oh yeah, I don't have children who resemble me or who share my genes.* But there are many things we won't have in life, yet we don't live in that sadness forever. Grief does not stay a knife in the heart as it did so many long years ago before you had children. Now it will simply be a little tap on your shoulder, but it won't hurt anymore. The pain definitely fades with parenting, with the building of relationships with our children, and with knowing how much they need us, their parent. In truth, the pain goes away completely, even if there are still occasional reminders, not unlike missing someone whom you once held dear but who is no longer here.

> *Mourning can go on for years and years. It doesn't end after a year, that's a false fantasy. It usually ends when people realize that they can live again, that they can concentrate their energies on their lives as a whole, and not on their hurt, and guilt and pain.*

> —Elisabeth Kübler-Ross

Chapter 7

LGBTQ FAMILIES

All I can tell you is this: Some hearts break from grief, some from joy. Some even break from love. But hearts break because they are too small to contain the gifts life gives us. Your task will be to let your heart grow large enough not to break.

—Catherine M. Wilsonson

The process of becoming a parent can be challenging, lengthy, expensive, and overwhelming, and the longing to devote one's life to a child does not discriminate. The feeling of wanting to hear a child say, "Daddy, come hold me" or "Mommy, I love you" is most certainly not limited by gender identification or sexual orientation.

Becoming a mom or dad when that process involves doctors, surrogates, egg donors, agencies, medicine, shots, and lots of money can be extremely stressful and time-consuming. But we live in a time when same-sex couples and LGBTQ individuals have already forged paths to parenthood. Laws are in place in some states to ease the process; where they are not, surrogacy may not be legal at all, or the system may not be friendly to such arrangements. Fortunately, there are many organizations, resources, and attorneys that specialize in collaborative reproduction specifically geared to the LGBTQ population, and these groups and people can help guide the way. (See the Resources section.)

Here are a few stories from parents who became dads via egg donation and a gestational carrier.

Kevin and Dennis

Kevin and Dennis had been together for ten years when they decided to bring a child into their lives. In 1992, there were very few, if any, same-sex couples who had created a child through egg donation and surrogacy. Kevin describes how the status of gay men and women at that time made it such that few ever imagined they could become parents. Only in the last ten years has it become more commonplace for gay men to become dads through egg donation and surrogacy. Many more lesbians chose to become parents through sperm donation in the past, but even then, the numbers were fewer until fairly recently.

Kevin tells us:

> We realized only on reflection that we both had always wanted to be parents, but because of the of the societal pressure and shame of being gay, we had suppressed that desire until it was deeply hidden and felt impossible. We were shaken into action when three different friends, separately in one week, suggested that we be parents because we had such a wonderful relationship. That awakened our parenting desires, and we started the journey to parenthood.

Like many of us, Kevin and Dennis wanted, if at all possible, to have a child who was genetically related to both of them. Dennis's sister offered to be an egg donor, which of course meant that Kevin's sperm would be used. Then they needed a surrogate.

There is a risk that a woman may donate eggs to help a family have children but then not be able to conceive her own children in the future. This is a risk for any donor, but with family donors, the psychological risk can be greater, since the donor might end up watching the child she helped to create grow up while being unable to reproduce herself.

> 🔊 *Regardless of how we choose to create our families, the process is almost always somewhat complicated. As we see in Kevin and Dennis's situation, they, like any other couple, desired to have a child who was genetically related to both of them. The idea of losing that genetic connection is often overwhelming. When we attempt to navigate the uncharted waters of egg donation and surrogacy, it's important to think about all of the individuals involved, as beautifully done by Dennis and Kevin. One of the loveliest parts of this equation is that their little girl grew up in a family where she knew her genetic history, which included the two loving women who helped her into the world.*

Kevin and Dennis asked Kevin's cousin Sandy to carry for them, and she agreed. Even though they were family, and even though they really had no template to follow, they knew contracts were necessary to legalize the arrangements between them. They went to a reproductive attorney, and together they figured out how to do this. This was a time when almost all surrogacy was still "traditional" surrogacy (as opposed to IVF with a gestational carrier), meaning a woman would be inseminated and become pregnant with a child who was genetically related to her but who was never intended to be her child to parent. (Although there were few problems with traditional surrogacy, it would eventually be understood that the legal and psychological risks were greater if a surrogate became pregnant with her own eggs, even if she never intended to parent that child.)

In gestational carrier arrangements, the carrier's egg is not used for conception; it is either the egg of the intended mother or the egg of a donor. Egg donation was just becoming a known entity when Kevin and Dennis got started in the 1990s. Although the first child in the world born through egg donation was born in 1984, the process was still not as widespread as it has become in recent years. This process was so unusual at the time that Kevin and Dennis had to locate and then convince a doctor who was willing to do IVF for them. Once they accomplished this, it was still not an easy path. In contrast to today, when single-embryo transfers have become the recommended standard of care, multiple embryos were transferred:

Kevin

> *Our first transfer we put in four. It was a time (1992) when the science of IVF was not as exacting. That transfer did not take. So we took the remaining frozen six embryos and transferred all of those. Those did not take either. So we went for another egg retrieval and got six embryos and transferred all of those! From those, we got one … [our daughter whom we] named Chelsea.*

Today it is very rare for more than one or two donor egg embryos to be transferred because IVF success rates have so vastly improved in the last twenty years. And how lucky that they persevered, that Dennis's sister was willing to do a second egg retrieval, that they made so many embryos, and that eventually one out of all those embryos transferred to Sandy's uterus and became their daughter, Chelsea, now twenty-four years old.

Dennis told us he never felt grief or sadness that Chelsea was not from his sperm, but Chelsea was still genetically related to him through his sister. This may have mitigated some of the feelings other men may have when they have children through an unrelated egg donor. Kevin told us, "From the moment Dennis held Chelsea for the first time, he was smitten. There was no hint of feeling [like he was] not the full father to his daughter."

They subsequently went to court and had Dennis's name put on the birth certificate so that they were both legal parents. Today this is no longer necessary in certain "surrogacy-friendly" states such as California. In those states, an order is issued by the court prior to the birth so that the intended parents are the legal parents from the beginning. Of course, you will have legal representation to help you through this process when the time comes.

We asked Kevin and Dennis about the relationship the family now has with Chelsea's aunt, the woman who contributed the egg. They all work together in the family business. Dennis's sister now has two children of her own, whom Chelsea thinks of only as her cousins. Neither Chelsea nor her two cousins think of themselves as half siblings.

From the moment of her birth, Dennis has been Daddy, and Kevin has been Dad.

Even though it was very unusual for same-sex couples to have children through egg donation and surrogacy, mental health professionals already knew a great deal about teaching parents how to talk to kids about these ways of creating a family. Early in the process, Dennis and Kevin saw a psychologist who gave them advice to "answer honestly and simply to every question."

Kevin

> We were told not to over-explain. When Chelsea was three, she asked, "Where did I come from?" I said, "A tummy." She said, "Whose?" And I said, "Sandy's." She said, "Did she give me away?" And I replied, "Oh no! You need a boy and a girl to have a baby. So Sandy loved us so much she said she would help us. So we took you and put you inside of her until you were ready to come out, and then we got to take you home." She said, "Well, that's good, because I always wanted a Daddy and a Dad anyway." When she was almost ten, she asked about who donated the egg, and we told her [it was] her Auntie Helene. She was beyond thrilled. She said she fit right in between both her Dad and Daddy and was so grateful. She always considered her Auntie Helene just that—her auntie. She never felt like she was her mom, although they are very close. She always just called her Auntie Helene.

As will be described in chapter 9, the recommended approach for helping kids understand how you created your family is to begin at the beginning, when a child is an infant, and then *practice, practice, practice* until you have the story comfortably rolling off your tongue. Kevin and Dennis waited until Chelsea asked whose egg had been used to conceive her, and that seemed to work just fine for them. Many kids may be curious about that much earlier. Other families are more comfortable when all those details are integrated into the story all at once, with the information woven into the fabric of family life, including the identity of the special helper who made it all possible.

Over twenty years later, the story for Rich and Tommy was very different. Many had gone before them, laws were in place, agencies had been created, and medical technology had improved.

Rich and Tommy

Rich and Tommy are a married couple living in California. Tommy always knew he wanted to become a parent, but Rich's desire did not emerge until he was in his thirties. But "truly," Rich told us, that desire blossomed "once [he] met Tommy."

Like many families who want to add to their family, Rich and Tommy considered adoption. However, the risk of a birth mother changing her mind was a huge deterrent. In addition, they both "had a very strong pull toward having a genetically related child."

In 2008, a system had been set in place that had not yet existed for Kevin and Dennis. Tommy and Rich chose both the egg donor and the surrogate from agencies. They initially signed up with one agency but could not find the donor they were looking for, so they switched agencies and then found her "fairly quickly."

Because they had a donor who was not related to either of them, they needed to decide whose sperm would be used in the IVF cycle. Since both of them desired to be a genetic parent, they both fertilized the donor's eggs.

Rich

> *We both contributed sperm and were content to work with whatever viable embryos we had. For our first transfer, which was ultimately not successful, we transferred one of Rich's embryos and two of Tommy's embryos, and we had nothing left to freeze.* (Just seven short years later, it would be more typical to transfer only one or two embryos because the success rates of IVF improved so much.) *This transfer did not work, so we took the same donor through another cycle, and both contributed again, and [we] had two viable embryos each to work with ... However, all were considered to be low-quality. So at that time we transferred all four embryos (something we know would not happen these days, but then we also did not do PGS [preimplantation genetic screening] then and would do that now and lower the risk and not transfer so many). We ended up with fraternal (genetic half sibling) twins, one from each of us.*

Transferring two embryos in this way, with each father's sperm used to create one, has become a controversial practice. Many mental health professionals as well as some organizations such as Men Having Babies are concerned that the psychological risks to the intended parents and the resulting children outweigh the benefits of having twins from each dad. Aside from the risks associated with twins, other issues arise in a pregnancy from mixed genetic origins.

Marna says:

> I am always amazed when I hear stories from parents about when they knew it was the right time to have a baby. As Rich shared with us, it was when he met Tommy that his desire to have a child blossomed. In women, the impetus is often that loud and annoying

biological clock that often ticks louder and louder as the years go by. It doesn't matter who you are or what age you are; when you know it's the right time, you know it's the right time.

Tommy and Rich were fortunate that their cycle worked and they ended up with fraternal half siblings. As the boys have grown, both Rich and Tommy have begun to see genetic qualities in their twins that have made the two men believe that Rich is genetically linked to one twin and Tommy to the other. The two dads have never had any DNA testing on the twins to confirm their thoughts about this. They are just thankful to have two beautiful boys, and as of now, they do not believe their genes matter; they are just a very happy family.

Many same-sex dads who are married or partnered have one child genetically linked to one dad and then wait a year or two and repeat the process again in the hopes of trying for a second child that will be genetically linked to the other dad.

The organization Men Having Babies says the following in its "Best Practices" section of *A Framework for Ethical Surrogacy for Intended Parents*:[4]

Transferring more than one embryo is sometimes desired by IPs for reasons such as maximizing the likelihood of a pregnancy, the desire to have twins, or the desire to implant an embryo from each partner. However, it is important to acknowledge the significant health risks associated with multiple pregnancy for both the carrier and future babies. Beyond the health risks, it should be taken into consideration that a multiple embryo pregnancy tends to be more painful and disruptive to the surrogate and her family. We recommend that parents and surrogates seek professional medical advice regarding these risks before deciding on a multiple embryo transfer. In any regard it should be noted that the transfer of more than two embryos should almost always be avoided, barring specific medical conditions and explicit professional advice. In these rare cases, a contingency plan should be devised for embryo reduction in case of the high-risk pregnancy that may result.

The document goes on to address a practice in which the intended parents contract with more than one carrier at a time. This is done to avoid the aforementioned risks of a multiple pregnancy when individuals still want to have more than one child at a time. The medical risks here are mitigated by having two singleton pregnancies; however, the increased psychological risks to the children and to the gestational carriers again outweigh the benefits, and the practice is not recommended. The *Framework* document goes on to say,

Some IPs consider embarking on two surrogacy journeys in parallel or close proximity, whether in order to have more than one child while avoiding the risks of multiple embryos pregnancy, or in order to maximize the chances for at least one successful pregnancy. We advise that IPs and surrogates exercise caution, openly discuss and fully consider the potential emotional and practical complexities of such arrangements prior to the match. Establishing and managing a supportive relationship with one surrogate and her family is a considerable challenge already, and managing two such relationships in parallel could be significantly harder still. One or both of them may very well perceive it as disrespectful and impersonal.

Most people who want a physician to transfer embryos from different origins say that they don't care which embryo takes and will eventually be their child and that they will know "whose it is" as soon as it is born. If this is true, one dad could contribute sperm first, and then the couple could have a second child later with the other man's sperm. Of course, surrogacy can be very expensive, and there are certainly practical reasons to want to do it only once.

Marna says:

> Of course, dads care about their genes. It's understandable and common to want to be genetically related to your child. Coping with the loss of our genes is often hard. That's why I think it's imperative to have your favorite therapist on speed dial to talk about these kinds of things before embarking on bringing a child into the world, regardless of how loud your biological clock is ticking.

The reality of pregnancy is such that unfortunately not everything always goes perfectly. Sometimes an anomaly is found in the fetus, and parents may have to make the excruciating decision to terminate the life of an unhealthy baby. Sometimes pregnancies start out as twin pregnancies, but one vanishes early. Sadly, there are many ways intended parents and gestational carriers may experience reproductive loss. And although thankfully it is very rare, a tragedy may occur at birth or afterward. All of these scenarios are horrendous to experience in any case, but imagine the couple who have two babies growing, each conceived with sperm from each dad. It would only be human nature to wonder which father was genetically related to the twin who was lost, terminated, or stillborn or who was born with a serious problem. In addition, a DNA test would be required to determine which twin was genetically related to whom.

Although most people insist they will know "whose is whose," the reality is they don't truly know unless this information is known pre-transfer and the embryos are of different genders.

Although genes are not important for creating family, they are still most definitely important. And the fact that couples are choosing this option proves how important genetic relatedness may be for some people. If it were not so important, it would be easier to let go of the genetic connection and wait, even if that meant the second partner might never have a child genetically related to him. This involves the same grief and loss we have discussed previously—the grief that comes when a woman realizes that she will be mothering a child conceived through egg donation, that she must give up the fantasy of the imagined and longed-for child and embrace a new and different child who will not be from her genes. Just as the desire to parent does not discriminate, neither does grief. Gay dads may feel differently about egg donation than an infertile woman, but the parallel arises if they discover that they are unable to have a genetic offspring who shares their genes. It can be so helpful to explore how it will feel if one partner has a genetic offspring and the other does not.

Telling the Family Building Story

As we discuss in chapter 9, the recommendation is to tell children early and often about how they came to be. Children are never too young to hear their story. Many parents think it might be a waste of time to begin sharing information with their baby because their baby won't get it. The reason we advocate telling even babies about how they were conceived and came into the world is the benefit to their parents. If we begin to share the story with our infant, we will have ample time to practice. By the time our child is old enough to put the pieces together and understand even a little, we will have told the story so many times that it will just flow off the tip of our tongues easily, without any awkwardness whatsoever. You want your child to always know this information, rather than be able to look back and tell you that they remember your telling them on a specific day that they were conceived with an egg donor. That's why it's important to tell them early and often.

Rich and Tommy started to talk to their sons at about age three:

Rich

Our children know that there are all kinds of families: some with one parent, some with two, and some with two dads, two moms, and a mom and a dad. We started that conversation at age three, and it has been a concept they've grown up with as a non-issue. They also know they were carried by a surrogate—a conversation we also started with them at age three because we explained that a mommy had to carry a baby … but since we were two dads, we needed help, and our friend Joyce helped us.

We have not had the discussion about an egg donor yet. In all of our conversations, we let them guide us—if they have questions, we answer truthfully and in simple concepts they can understand. When they are ready to ask about genes, we will have the donor conversation. We've read a couple of books to them about this, but we don't think they [the books] made a big impact because we'd already explained everything to them, and they seemed to understand the concepts. We do think, however, that the books helped reinforce what we had told them.

Kevin and Dennis and Tommy and Rich all talk about letting the child guide them. This is a very respectful way to navigate the discussions. But we hasten to add that children don't always ask the questions about the things we may want to talk about when children are very young. Children generally won't ask, "Daddy, did you have a gestational carrier to have me?" or "Who is my egg donor?" They will ask, "Where's my mommy?" or "Who is my daddy?" Tommy and Rich had the right idea about starting early. Between the ages of three and five is when children begin to realize that babies come out of women's bodies, so they will begin to be curious at that point about which woman's body they might have come out of.

Tommy

> *We email with our surrogate maybe once or twice a year*
> *and share pictures of our families with each other.*

This is a great way for kids to picture where exactly they were and grew before they were with Papa and Daddy. Being able to see photos of the carrier pregnant with them makes the abstract concrete. And hearing parents speak lovingly and respectfully about the carrier confirms that they were conceived in love and were well taken care of before they were even born!

The egg donation piece is a little harder to bring up, but come up it will. Rich and Tommy's boys are seven, and they have not yet talked about this part of their process, but they will. At some point, probably pretty soon, the kids will realize it takes a part from a man and a part from a woman to make the beginnings of a person. They may begin to assume that part from a woman came from Joyce, and the dads will begin to clarify all of that. They can start to talk about which parts of each boy might have come from each dad and which parts might have come from the woman who gave them the other piece they needed—the egg, ovum, cell, or whatever they decide to call it.

Nicole and Colleen

> *I had a hard time letting go of having a genetic connection*
> *to my kid, which surprised me because I already had one*

biological child. Some of that for me was caught up in racial identity.

Nicole and Colleen give us an additional perspective about being in a same-sex relationship and having children via egg donation.

Their first child is now five years old and was conceived through IVF using Nicole's eggs and the donated sperm of a friend. Nicole carried the child. But when they sought to add to their family a few years later, two more rounds of IVF failed. When Nicole said she was not willing to try again with her eggs, Colleen—then her partner, now her spouse—agreed to use her eggs. Nicole again carried the pregnancy and their twins are now two years old.

Colleen told us she had not been interested in being pregnant and really did not care at all about having a genetic offspring. So it had been an easy decision the first time around for Nicole to use her eggs. They describe not having any grief issues because Colleen didn't ever feel the desire to have a genetic offspring. However, Nicole was very distraught when the two IVFs using her eggs failed, which really surprised her. She said:

Nicole

> *It was more difficult than I expected given that it was my partner's eggs [that we would be using instead] and not a stranger's. I had a hard time letting go of having a genetic connection to my kid, which surprised me because I already had one biological child. Some of that for me was caught up in racial identity. I am mixed (black/white), my partner is white, and I wondered what it would be like to navigate that with the kids.*

The twin pregnancy was extremely hard. Nicole said she "was huge." "I couldn't put on my own socks after thirty-two weeks. I had preeclampsia, so I was induced at thirty-seven weeks." Despite the psychological challenges she felt about not using her own eggs and despite a very challenging pregnancy, Nicole "loved them right away." She said, "I never thought about them not being my genetic offspring."

Navigating the conversations with the outside world is interesting because they are a mixed-race family. This seems to dominate their lives much more than being a family with two moms does. They describe the sperm donor as a "dad." This is certainly not often or usually the case, even when the sperm donor is a friend. Often the donor may be like a special uncle or special friend, but in this case it was determined before IVF that the donor wanted to be and would be their dad. If a sperm donor is engaging in a fatherly role with a child, he is indeed a dad. However, if the sperm donor is not acting as a father to the child, the word "dad" is not recommended. "Donor" or "helper" is much more descriptive, and these terms do not create a situation where a child may feel like they have a father who is not involved in their life as a dad and where the child may thereby feel abandoned by him.

Nicole and Colleen are open about how they had their children. Although they have not yet started conversations with the kids about egg or sperm donation, they have been extremely open with others. And they have read the children the book *What Makes a Baby*.

Nicole

> *If someone says they look like me, I say, "Thanks, but they don't." And I tell them they were conceived with my partner's eggs. Because we're a couple, people think it's really "cool" that we did it that way.*

Though Nicole was initially quite distraught about the loss of additional genetically related children, that is not the case now:

Nicole

> *I don't care at all. I love them equally ... I'm intrigued by different things about them. My older daughter, who is my genetic offspring, looks a lot like me and has some*

*mannerisms that are inherited through my family that
I think is kind of cool. I do struggle a bit with how to
handle their different racial/ethnic backgrounds. They have
the same donor/dad, who is mixed black and white, as
am I, so the kids are all technically mixed. But my older
daughter looks clearly more so, whereas the twins are much
fairer-complected, with blondish hair. My in-laws are very
Irish-American-identified, and I struggle a bit with how
that fits in for my older daughter and how to explain the
family tree to all of them when that time comes.*

In addition, Colleen said she is fascinated about the similarities she shares with the twins. "Our daughter looks just like the donor," she said, and she is surprised by how interesting she finds that. Colleen said, "My family loves all our kids the same, but it's cool to see them compare the twins to other people in the family."

Of course. This is normal. Having a genetic link and children who are like us is a normal narcissistic desire that brings most people a degree of pleasure. When we have children who are not like us or don't look like us, there is understandably an initial period of disappointment and loss.

Ultimately, this couple tells us that they would do only one thing differently, knowing what they know now:

Nicole

*I wish we had done the DE cycle sooner and not done the
two first failed IVF rounds. I wish I had known how little
I would care about having a genetic connection to them.*

Of course, hindsight always seems clearer than foresight. They did what they needed to do to get to the exact right family. Had Nicole not tried those two cycles, she might have had regret. And Nicole acknowledges that she might feel differently if she had not already had a child who shares her genes.

Marna says:

> When I listen to the fears of intended parents regarding family-building, many tell me they worry about genetic link loss, others tell me they worry about navigating different racial/ethnic backgrounds or about creating an interfaith family, and others tell me they are fearful about being mistaken for their children's grandparents. But at the end of the day, the common denominator is that they just want to become parents, and all the worries are worth it, regardless of how hard it might be to achieve that goal. One of the fondest memories I have is talking with same-sex intended mothers who were Caucasian. They wanted to add to their family and had received embryos from a couple who were Asian and Caucasian. Both intended mothers were going to undergo an embryo transfer with these embryos. The other siblings in the family had been adopted from Guatemala and China, and the family had also adopted twin girls who are African American. They were very happy when they described their Thanksgiving table as the International House of Pancakes. It's just all about love, not genes.

Megan

> *I'm more sensitive to "different" family origins and structures. I try and educate (passively) whenever I can about DE.*

Megan gives us a different perspective on the experience of parents who identify as LGBTQ. Megan is a lesbian and became a mom as a single woman. Her daughter was born to her via embryo donation, and Megan carried the pregnancy.

As the desire to be a mom took hold, Megan took a "Maybe Baby" class through Rainbow Families when she was thirty-eight. She started trying to conceive via IUIs with anonymous donor sperm.

Megan

> *My lab test results were terrible. I looked into adoption but felt that controlling prenatal care was so important (and adoption so hard!), so I moved on to egg donation. Because I was already in an adoption frame of mind, DE and later donor embryo were never really an issue for me.*

Great effort is needed to become a parent through the many options available. Megan experienced two chemical pregnancies and a miscarriage before she finally gave birth to her daughter, now twenty months old.

> *It was very important that my kid have the opportunity to know as much about the donors as possible.*

She was ultimately connected to the donors and creators of the embryos through PVED. Megan's story reminds us that when we have children through egg and embryo donation, we are not just becoming parents; we are forming new forms of kinship in which families are now connected to each other in new and different ways—whether or not they ever meet or know each other personally.

The embryos were donated to Megan by a husband and wife and their known egg donor. Megan is in regular contact with the couple who donated the embryos, as well as with the original egg donor and the egg donor's mother. This will allow her to give her daughter the information needed to form a true and complete genetic identity. When someone comments on how her daughter may be similar or different to her, she says she doesn't really respond.

> *I say thank you if it's a compliment. I feel like this is the one area that I'm uncomfortable navigating. I am completely*

open about my daughter's origins, but it is still difficult to talk about it casually.

She added that she has not really started having conversations with her daughter about their family-building story.

I had planned to—early and often—but I just haven't. I think getting some children's books on the subject will help.

As we have seen over and over again, new parents are frequently very surprised by the constant comments about their children's physical characteristics and their similarities and differences to the parents and by how it feels when those comments are made. Preparation really helps. Talking to others who have walked that path before you can be so helpful.

Ultimately, the fact that Megan is a lesbian is irrelevant to her role as a mom. She has a child who came to her through a unique gift. She will have to explain to her child—and occasionally others—how she became a mom and to whom her daughter is connected. Like all single moms by choice, she occasionally also will be confronted with the "Where's her daddy?" question. This she has in common with all single parents by choice, gay or not.

Erin

Erin is transgender. As a single person, Erin carried and delivered their[5] son, who was conceived with donor eggs and donor sperm. Adjusting to the probing inquiries of those they randomly meet each day has proven to be much more challenging than Erin ever imagined.

I don't think it occurred to me how much incorrect terminology would be used and how much it would bother me. I've been asked if I know who his father is when what they're actually asking is whether I used a known or unknown donor.

I've had people ask about the donors but refer to them as the "parents"—as in "Do you have pictures of his parents?"

One person made a comment that hit me pretty hard, which was "It's incredible how much he looks like you. It's like he could be your real son!" I said, "He is my real son," and didn't even call them any names. I also wasn't aware how frequently strangers comment on your baby's features and whether they got them from you.

Indeed, we are frequently called upon either to be educators about positive family-building language or to evade and dodge questions that are unknowingly hurtful. You may be a very open person, comfortable with such responses as "Actually, he is my real son" or "I am his real mother," or you may be a more private person who prefers to get out of the grocery store without being the ambassador for alternative family-building. Remembering that our children are always listening and watching, we may want to arm ourselves with that repertoire of responses that all parents need—regardless of our gender identification. You may simply say, "That is my child's private information, but thank you for your interest," or you could say, "Yes, isn't my son beautiful? He looks exactly like himself!"

Sometimes the simplest and best response to questions about your family's appearance is "Why do you ask?" It provides the person asking the question the opportunity to realize they may be intruding. We don't really have to share information we don't feel like sharing in that moment. And this response means you can make a quick getaway if you choose.

But regardless of what you say to others, the feeling you have inside if people comment on dissimilarity is what is important—because that is what you will be communicating to your child. Feelings of grief and loss are often re-stimulated when a child doesn't look like you. This is not a reason to choose a donor you think will help you produce a clone; it is a reason to do the work to resolve whatever loss issues remain that cause a stab when you recognize difference. We address many ways this work can be done in chapter 9, "Let's Talk about Egg Donation," as well as chapter 6, "Letting Go, Moving On." Our hope is that once you get to the parenting part, you will be armed and ready to respond to your children and others about the unique way you became a family and to feel wonderful about the choices that finally brought you all together.

Having a child with the help of an egg donor adds an extra layer to parenting. Having a child through both egg and sperm donation adds a whole additional layer to your family creation story. Then if you are a parent who is also gay or transgender or queer, you have so many things to share with your child, and you are confronted constantly by curious minds, most likely everywhere you go. Ultimately, your family is a family like all others—exhausted and exhilarated, loving and compassionate, sometimes struggling to keep your heads above the water, but a family nonetheless.

Chapter 8

SINGLE PARENTING: HAVING IT ALL (SORT OF)

It takes a village to raise a child.

—African proverb

Maria Shriver said, "Having kids—the responsibility of rearing good, kind, ethical, responsible human beings—is the biggest job anyone can embark on."

She's not kidding. Every day, parents do the impossible. We take care of our children before taking care of ourselves. Day after day, our kids are our first, last, and main priority.

Marna says:

> When I think of mothers and what we do, I am simply awestruck. The strength and fortitude we possess and exhibit every single day is amazing. But there is another group of women who outshine most of us moms. I think of them as warriors, courageous champions, loving generals, strength personified, down-to-earth heroes, nurturing advocates.

It can be tiring to care for children when you are part of a two-parent household. Single parents are on duty 24/7 without reprieve. Add to that the challenge of being a one-income household and knowing that if you or your child gets sick, or if you lose your job, it's still all on you. And you alone are responsible for every decision made regarding your kids; this can be both a curse and a blessing!

Of course, there are still people who believe that the classic two-parent heterosexual family is the best environment in which to raise children. Single parents by choice—regardless of their sexual orientation or gender identification—can find themselves defending their choice to have children without a partner.

Yet single parenting is on the rise as technology has made it possible to have children later in life. Most single parents by choice are older and more educated and have higher incomes than moms who became single parents by chance.

Despite the wisdom that comes with being in one's thirties or forties, and despite the fact that these single mothers may have decent incomes, they still face many challenges. We asked some to tell us about their experiences of being single moms via egg and embryo donation. Some spoke about the challenges of single parenting through egg donation, but most parents simply spoke about the difficulty of single parenting regardless of whether their children came from their own or donor eggs.

Molly*

> *If you are making the decision to be a single mom by choice, get tough. Don't let others tell you that you're "doing it wrong" or you could be "doing it better"—this is your life, not theirs, and your choices are your own.*

One of the most important attributes a solo parent can have is that of being a community builder. Introverts (men and women alike) who tend to isolate often struggle more mightily than those who reach out. All parents need support, but single parents often need to seek out the support that a partner might otherwise provide. Single Mothers by

Choice and Choice Moms are two national organizations in the United States that provide information, support, networking, and referrals to men and women choosing to parent without a partner.

Building community allows you to talk with others in the same boat. It provides people to talk to who also are struggling with how to answer questions from their children and others. It's helpful to hear how others are handling the challenges you may face. Creating a network of support also allows cooperative childcare arrangements; families frequently trade babysitting so that the single mom or dad can get away and have some adult time or can go to work when a child is sick. That's why we encourage all of our single parents by choice to get lots of support, so that they can create their own community. If you were not already a planner and a networker before becoming a parent, now is the time to get organized and become one.

Lynn

> *You have to be a certain kind of person—[you have to be] organized, you have to have the ability to get shit done. No drama—you just have to plow through, no whining.*

Louisa*

> *It's exhausting. Your plate is bigger than a Las Vegas buffet.*

Parenting children in a two-parent home can be challenging. However, parenting as a single person is even more daunting.

Cienna* shared with us that her relationship ended because she wanted kids and her partner did not. It was after she decided to become a single mom that she learned she had fertility issues. Ultimately, she used donor eggs to create her family. Like many women, she struggles with the lack of genetic connection, but she has the added complicated layer of having no dad in the picture.

Cienna

> *It's hard that there is no genetic relation. I sometimes don't know what to say when people say, "She looks just like you" because I wonder how that could be ... [One time] someone said to my folks that she looked like my brother!*

> *I'm very open about the use of a sperm donor but tend to keep the egg donor [part] to myself. It's hard that I'm not able to be as open with that ... If I'm being completely honest, I don't want anyone, ever, saying, "So who is their mom?"*

Regardless of whether you're partnered or single, letting go of that genetic connection can be difficult and is the common denominator among most parents via egg or embryo donation. But there is a double loss when you're a single mom using donor eggs.

Molly* thinks that one of the most important aspects of being a single mom is being flexible and prepared to make career and parenting decisions on your own. Although she has no regrets and wouldn't change a thing, she sometimes feels guilty that she has to juggle her time—something she never has enough of—every single day. She is also candid about her lack of social life.

Molly

> *Even thinking about dating is a joke. There is a lot of guilt. My adult interaction is a play date. But I love my children, and I wouldn't change a thing.*

Miranda* was forty when she had her first child and forty-four when she had her second. Her infertility journey was filled with many peaks and valleys. After two years, five IVFs, and multiple losses, Miranda had a child with her own genes. When she started trying to conceive her second child at the age of forty-three, she did four more IVF cycles with her own eggs, but she knew that success was unlikely, so she moved on to egg donation. It was difficult for Miranda to come to terms with using donor eggs. She chose egg donation over adoption because she wanted to choose the genes and control the pregnancy.

Miranda

> *Single parenting is incredibly lonely and isolating, regardless of whether donor eggs or your own eggs are used.*

We asked other moms what they found most challenging about single parenting through egg donation:

Lynn

> *I have guilt about not spending quality time with each of them, as I have two; it's a twin thing, I think. And I have a hard time asking for help.*

Kathleen*

> *If I actually thought about all the pressure that's on me, it would actually put me in a home. Plowing through is so much easier than sitting and wallowing. I willingly made the choice to be a single parent; I chose not to be a victim.*

Mindy

> *It's hard telling others I've chosen to do this on my own, but it's a challenge I feel prepared for. But when I tell them I wasn't successful until I used someone else's eggs, the reaction is always surprise. It's almost as if most people can grasp the concept of doing it alone, but when they hear what extremes I took to get there, they react as if maybe God, [the] universe, Mother Nature, [or] whatever your belief was trying to tell me something and that maybe*

I went too far. No one has said this so far, except the unintended insensitive joke that I should have just gone out to a bar. So far everyone has been very supportive. But I'm also not quite ready to tell everyone. I plan to tell coworkers and extended family very soon, and I am expecting mostly good reactions.

Leslie

When my baby was first born, missing the genetic connection was emotionally hard, especially because friends and family don't know and make comments about how the baby looks like so-and-so.

Loretta*

I'm glad I didn't know how hard it would be ahead of time.

Lynn shared that it's frustrating trying to relate to all the other moms twenty years her junior.

Lynn

So here I am, the first day of kindergarten, waiting to pick up my twins. I am fifty. There's a woman next to me with a full face of makeup and flaunting a tube top. She's incredibly endowed. I wasn't fascinated with her boobs as much as I was sizing her up as a woman in my age range. Yes, I thought, another mom that isn't twenty years my junior. As the little boy approaches, he says, "Hi, Mimi." "Mimi" isn't "Mommy," so I ask her, "Are you his mom?" She said, "No, I am his grandmother. He calls me Mimi because I don't want to be called Grandma. I'm only forty-eight." AHHH! I wanted to bury my head in the sand.

Families who have children created from the mom's own eggs as well as children from donor eggs have various concerns and observations. Some worry about how each child will feel as time goes on; many told us they feel no difference in the experience of parenting children with different origins. Some expressed the grief that comes from genetic loss.

Miranda

It does make me sad sometimes when I talk about one kid being from my own egg and one from donor eggs. (It comes up as part of their stories, which they have always known). I am waiting for the point in time when what that really means occurs to them and when one of them, because they are kids, talks about who my "real kid" is.

Roberta*

My youngest is only twenty-two months, but I have not found parenting my DE child any different than parenting my OE child. I worry a little about how she will feel about being a DE child, but I hope to make it a normal and positive part of our life.

Shannon

It will be interesting to see, as I have one child from my own egg, and the one I am now pregnant with was conceived with a donor's egg. My first child strongly resembles her sperm donor and doesn't look very much like me but has a lot of my traits. My first child is a little girl, and I almost hope for a little boy, as this new baby will be "different" from his/her big sister, and I wonder if it will be less of a big deal for a boy.

We already know that donor-conceived children do fine in the world. These moms are right to be considering how they will navigate telling their children the stories of their different origins. However, when the stories are told from the beginning, when the questions and curiosities are honored, and when every effort is made to get answers to kids' questions, these families will do just fine. Children can understand that families are created in many different ways. Either way, kids conceived through donor conception will most likely integrate this information into their identity and come out whole and healthy.

Grieving the Family You Will Never Have to Make Space for the Family You Will

If women who have children by egg donation grieve the loss of their fantasized genetic offspring, single parents who have children through donor sperm and donor eggs have an additional layer of grief.

When an unpartnered man or woman makes the decision to parent on their own, they must first say goodbye to the dream they may have had for themselves, which most likely was closer to a 'traditional story'. Few little girls imagine that they will grow up, go to college, get their dream job, and then become a mother by choosing sperm from a cryobank or by asking a friend to provide sperm. So when they ultimately realize that the time has come to move forward without a partner, there is almost always sadness along with the excitement for the future.

As with the loss of a person or imagined person, it is helpful to name this loss specifically. These stories we carry with us are often unconscious, and it may only be upon trauma or crisis that we realize the picture we have been carrying around with us. Writing about or drawing the fantasy picture of the family we won't have can be healing in order to say goodbye and move forward. Just like we do when saying goodbye to our fantasy genetic child, recognizing and naming what we have lost can help move us to the next stage, to feeling healthy and whole.

Discovering that we not only need a sperm donor but also will not have our fantasized genetic child and will need the help of an egg donor adds another layer of grief. Despite what seem like insurmountable odds, many women emerge from this process as strong, determined, empowered, self-confident mothers, deeply devoted to the life they worked so hard to create.

Lynn

I started at forty-two, trying to have a baby with my own eggs. My friend said, "What are you doing? Just use an egg donor!" My doctor didn't mince words; he said, "If you want to have a baby, you need to use a donor." So I did.

I did three rounds with a proven donor, thirty eggs, and I still didn't get pregnant, and [later] I unfortunately experienced a nine-week loss. I then proceeded with a second donor, [which] then worked—it worked so much [that] I was pregnant with triplets and had to undergo a reduction. I had twin girls.

Jolene

[It was] not entirely [a difficult decision]. Being adopted, the hardest part was giving up the idea that I would get to share DNA with my kids, as that was my only chance [to have that genetic connection to someone]; but it was a selfish (not in a bad way) difficulty.

Shannon

It was tough at first. Since it [had been] so easy the first time, and I was seeing some fellow single moms by choice conceive for a second time, I had a hard time believing that I couldn't conceive with my own eggs. Since we have a nontraditional family (being a single mom by choice), I really wanted my daughter to have someone that was essentially exactly like her (created identically).

Mindy

> *I didn't feel a deep need to pass on my genetic material. I told someone [it's like] I'm being a chef. Everyone can buy the same ingredients, but how the chef combines them and cooks them makes it great.*

Debbie

> *In some ways I think this was probably easier for me than [for] others, as by the time I found there was an issue with my fertility, I had already gone past the point of anyone recommending I try with my own eggs (because there were none). So I didn't have to make the choice on when to stop trying with my own eggs and start with DE. My choice was use DE, adopt, foster, or don't be a mum. It was very tough initially, but I knew that not being a mum was not an option for me.*

> *Using DE was the first choice for me because although the child would not genetically be mine, it would have my blood and body growing it. I went through a grieving process initially, with a lot of anger directed at my ex-husband for wasting years of my life, but in the end had to let that go and move on so I could be happy.*

Financial Challenges

The financial burdens of reproductive medicine are immense and are rarely covered by insurance. These costs are clearly staggering even for many two-person households. For single parents the financial challenges are tremendous.

According to the US Department of Agriculture, the cost of raising a child today will exceed $250,000 before a child turns eighteen. This doesn't include the cost of college. When you are the only income earner and need to work, raising a child takes even greater planning, saving, and managing of finances.

Sylvia*

I wish insurance coverage was universal. It was hard to see other women have coverage for it when everything I did was completely out of pocket. I stopped trying with my own eggs and saved money for two years to afford DE IVF. It hurt so much to wait longer after I'd already spent time trying with my own eggs. It also definitely is impacting my thoughts about having a second. If I'd gotten pregnant two to three years ago, I feel certain I'd have gone for a second. Now, at my current age, I'm not so sure.

Lynn

It's hard. It is actually brutal. I don't spend any money on myself; it goes all to the girls. There is a lot of guilt, but money only goes so far.

Shannon

My company restructured shortly after I returned to work from maternity leave with my daughter, and my position was eliminated. I ended up taking a lesser role, earning less money but requiring less travel and offering a flexible work schedule. I rented out my primary residence, moved in with family (planned to rent, but they insisted), and sold a few investment properties to be able to keep the nanny, whom we adore for my daughter, and to be able to fund this effort to build my family. I've easily spent several years' worth of childcare and/or a year or so of college tuition on this endeavor, but [I] ultimately believe that this investment

*was the wisest decision I could have made … for myself,
but especially for my daughter.*

Kathleen

*I left a job making a boatload to be home because it costs
more being away from my children than it does making less
money and being here when they need me.*

Shannon

*If there was some way for insurance to cover more for this
single mom by choice, it would certainly have been nice to
know, as I'm about $70k+ in. It has been painful to see
peers with husbands have multiple IVFs and have them
totally covered by insurance, while I, as a single mom by
choice, have had to pay everything out of pocket. It's really
bothersome. I hope to enjoy some benefits on my taxes from
having spent substantially more than 10 percent of my
income on fertility treatments.*

Information Sharing

Whether you have children with your own eggs or with donor eggs,
the road to single parenting by choice is a bumpy one. The choice to
have a child with the assistance of two gamete donors adds a layer of
complication to the already complex decision to become a parent with
only one donor. Educating yourself about the needs of donor-conceived
children and families, grieving your losses, and being prepared to guide
your children through understanding family-building will help you deal
with the curiosity and questions you will face from your own family and
the community at large.

Questions and Comments by Others

One of the questions most commonly asked of single parents by people out in the world is some version of "Who's the dad?" or "Where's the dad?" The same is true for single dads, who are asked about the mom. When a parent is "missing," people are naturally curious about whether there ever was a father, whether there was a divorce or a parent died, or whether there was a sperm donor involved. It can get tedious to continually answer or dodge such questions, so it is helpful, just as with donor-conceived two-parent families, to have a repertoire of responses to pull out of your back pocket whenever you need one. Here are some suggestions:

> *"We are a family of two. Yep, it's just Johnny and me."*

> *"Families are built in many ways. Technology is miraculous!"*

> *"We don't have a dad [or mom] in our family."*

> *"That's a private matter I prefer not to discuss."*

> *"That is Johnny's information to share as he pleases."*

Or you could be somewhat more explicit and reply:

> *"I had my son through the gift of donors."*

> *"I'm a single mom [or dad] by choice."*

Lynn was forty-four when her twin girls were born. Forthright and positive, Lynn is truly a mover and shaker. What she finds most challenging is "keeping all the balls in the air." Lynn also finds explaining her family's dynamics at school frustrating. Her daughters are very aware of how they were conceived, but other people don't seem to get it at all.

Lynn

[Other parents ask] a lot of dumb questions about why no dad, and then they are amazed when they hear the real story—they are often dumbfounded! One mom said, "Wow, you have balls for doing this on purpose on your own!"

Molly shared that she and her kids get asked, "Where's your dad?" or "Why don't you have a dad?" Not only do her daughter's classmates ask those kinds of questions, but well-meaning parents have asked as well. Such questions aren't always comfortable to answer, and regardless of how the situation is explained, some people still don't get it.

Creating such a collection of answers to the "who's the dad?" questions to use on the spot will help you avoid being caught off guard and have to make an answer up each time. Your responses will vary depending on who is asking, where you are at that moment, how much sleep you had the night before, and how old your child is at the time.

Ultimately, your child will become empowered to answer these questions himself or herself. One day at school, your daughter may tell a story about her father living in another state, which is perfectly normal and nothing to be alarmed by. But a few years later, when she is in middle school, she may be telling all her peers that her mom used an egg donor and a sperm donor in order to have her. Children watch and listen and copy our behavior, so we don't want to respond to questions with hostility or defensiveness—because that sends a message to our kids that there is something wrong with our family. Normalizing family-building options with our kids happens outside the home as well as inside the home. Remember, you are always entitled to your privacy, but secrets are about shame and embarrassment. You will find the line between the two as your family grows.

Questions and Comments from Your Children

When unpartnered men and women choose to have children, the decision has been made after much consideration. Nevertheless, sometimes the questions from kids and others can be challenging if parents are not at least somewhat prepared to answer them.

Lots of kids ask questions about their fathers or lack of fathers in their lives. It's known in many circles of single moms as the "F-word"—a word that can cause a great deal of angst in many families.

Like all information sharing in donor-conceived families, it's helpful to think about the "Where's the dad?" question before it's even asked. This will give you time to give the subject matter great thought and consider how you might broach this topic in a positive manner with your children and others. You can practice what you might say ahead of time in your head. It's important to allow our children to lead the conversation and talk about the subject as they choose; let them express their feelings and listen to their perspective, thoughts, ideas, and concerns, regardless of what those may be. Feelings don't remain static. They are very fluid. How our kids feel one day about anything can change quickly the next day.

Although the F-word question might be uncomfortable or awkward, it's a great launching point to talk about these important topics with your kids. They will revisit the subject at different times in their lives as they grow up. As parents, the most important thing we can do for kids is just be comfortable with the subject matter and not make it weird. If we make it weird, they may feel like it's weird; if we don't make it weird, they won't feel like it's weird. Being as comfortable as possible with your choice, being able to share information, and giving thoughtful, balanced, and meaningful responses will be incredibly helpful to you and your kids.

Aspects of the family-building story are always the same, no matter which body parts may be missing. You might explain, "It takes a part from a man and a part from a woman to make the beginnings of a baby. Then all babies grow in women's bodies. Mommy was missing the part that comes from a man, so the doctor helped me find that part so you could be my Suzy!"

You can adapt the story to include egg donation by adding, "And Mommy didn't have the part that comes from a woman, so a helper [or Sally, or a nice lady, or a donor] gave me that part so we could be a family!"

Of course, this story will build and grow over time, but the earlier you start, the easier it will be. We've included basic scripts in chapter 9. Many children's books are now available to help you share your family-building story. They make great conversation starters to which you can add or subtract pieces of your own story.

Mindy

> *A mom of twins told me about [a conception storybook she made for] her kids. They are four now, and they love their storybook and have started asking questions. She said she started before they could even comprehend, in the hopes she'd be comfortable by the time they could, and it totally helped her. She shows them the book once a month on the day of their birthday. I like this plan.*

Debbie

> *She is too young to understand it really, but I have been telling her [her] story since she was two months old so I would get comfortable with it. I will tell her about once every two to three weeks, and she will sometimes ask for it. As with all good stories for little girls, it starts with "Once upon a time ..." and ends with [my] telling her that if she wants to know more about the very nice lady and very nice man, then Mummy will share the information she has [about] them; and that once she gets older, if she wants to find out more and maybe contact them, then that is okay. And if she does, then Mummy would like to say thank you to them.*

Having a child through egg donation changes us. We have grieved the loss of the child we thought we might have had, and we have made sometimes painful, often difficult decisions to select replacement DNA. We have become educated about how to talk to our kids and others and how and when to share information.

Doing all of this as a single parent is more challenging in the ways we have described. But ultimately, egg donation is one of many paths to parenthood. Explaining and talking to our kids about having a sperm donor and an egg donor, while making sure we have done our emotional homework first, becomes one thread that runs through our family life. We do homework and set limits; we go to soccer and have teacher conferences; we snuggle up together with a movie or a book; and we share meals and stories about what happens in our daily life. All of this occurs just like in all families, but with an extra layer. Throughout all of our regular family activities, we as parents need to remain aware that our focus is to help our children create a healthy identity, which includes the knowledge of how our family was formed.

Christine

> *[I think of the egg donation piece as] an interesting quirk in my kids. It makes me wonder when they have an interest or habit, where did that come from? And also, when they do something exactly like me, I think,* See, there I am!

Shannon

> *[Egg donation] freed me in the sense that I am watching him to see who he is, rather than expecting him to exhibit qualities of mine.*

> *I think it shows how important it is to me to have a family and to provide my daughter with a sibling. It shows strength and determination.*

As John Lennon said, "life is what happens when you are busy making plans." Life is often not fair, and it's rarely easy or simple. For those of you who are embarking on this particular path of having a family on your own, it's important for you to remember that there are millions of healthy, happy, well-adjusted kids who have grown up in homes with parents who became single parents by choice.

Chapter 9

LET'S TALK ABOUT EGG DONATION

A journey of a thousand miles begins with a single step.

—Lao-tzu

Single or partnered, straight or gay, all parents whose children came to them through donor conception have a story to tell their children. It is a story of wanting very much to be a parent, and it includes missing at least one of the parts that goes into making the beginnings of a person—eggs, sperm, uterus, or even all three. The story includes the gratitude we feel for the person or people who helped us become parents and the ways in which our families will forever be entwined with the people to whom our kids may be genetically related. It is, first, last, and always, a love story.

Talking with our children about conception and navigating the all-too-familiar "Where did I come from?" discussion can become a little awkward and anxiety-provoking even for the most experienced of parents who conceived their children the "old-fashioned" way. When you create your family with the help of an egg donor, there is an added layer of complexity: how do we talk to our children about the way they were conceived?

Regardless of what title we may hold at work or how successful we are in the world—whether we are medical or mental health professionals in this field, or even if we are the kind of people who seem to always have it together—when it comes to talking to our kids about how they were conceived, many of us find ourselves feeling anxious or even terrified.

Many parents find that the conversations about how they formed a family are the most gratifying, poignant, special, and often funny moments they will have in parenting. It is a time when parents and children share something very special: it is the story of love and how everybody came together to make a family.

Most parents find that having these conversations becomes second nature over time as their relationships with and attachments to their children grow. Parents grow to feel so secure in the relationship with their children that they realize this is a bond that cannot be broken by the truth. Family-formation conversations are full of the stuff of all families—some questions can be answered; some comments can cause certain feelings to arise; some interactions need follow-up. But in every case, the message is "We are in this together, and we will figure it out."

The question that we most often hear is "How do I tell them?" This is generally followed by the query "*When* should I tell them?" Last, most people then want to know, "Does the world need to know this? Should I be obligated to tell people in our everyday life? What about my child's pediatrician? His or her teachers?"

By addressing some of the common fears about telling the truth, we hope to take you from an anxious place to a place where you can feel excited and look forward to beginning the story of how you all came to be a family—whether your child is an infant, a toddler, a grade schooler, or even an adolescent. After overcoming your fears, you not only will feel confident about talking to your child but also will feel comfortable deciding how, when, and with whom you want to tell your story.

A Word about "Disclosure"

Many people use the word "disclosure" in reference to talking with children about egg donation. We prefer not to use that word. "Disclosure" means exposure or revelation. It means that something is unknown, and then in an instant it becomes known. This is definitely not what we recommend when we talk about information sharing.

As you will see throughout this chapter, the approach we recommend for helping children understand their donor origins is to weave the information into the fabric of your family life. We suggest that you begin telling your family-building story as early as you feel comfortable and then find ways to chat about it from time to time. In this way, knowledge builds upon itself, and the child won't have to integrate a very complex topic all at once. This is the opposite of disclosure.

> 🗨 *Remember! There is no one single telling. These are lifelong conversations.*

The only time we use the word "disclosure" in this chapter is as it relates to starting conversations about egg donation with adolescents or when we discuss *unintended* disclosure. We make this differentiation because when you tell children that they are donor-conceived for the first time when they are older, it is indeed disclosure because they previously did not know about it. Contrast this with the approach in which children have never known anything different, which is the circumstance in which children feel most comfortable with donor conception.

Language has power, and we have chosen words very carefully in describing this amazing process of sharing the story of how you became a family.

When Do I Begin?

> *"Hey, Mom," Daniel called out. "Can that donor lady come over for dinner tonight? Then she can go home again."*

You never know what kids are going to ask. One minute they are not the least bit interested in knowing anything about the donor; the next, they want to know if her favorite color is purple.

Beginning conversations with your children long before they may fully understand egg donation sets the stage for casual conversations at unexpected times. This allows you to demonstrate for your children that how you created your family is a subject like all others—it does not need the right time or the right place to be discussed. Whenever your child has a thought or a question, your child will know he or she can simply ask you. Although that may seem really terrifying to you at this moment, by the time this actually occurs, you will find you really enjoy talking to your children about the amazing way you found to create your family.

There are no right answers. You don't have to know exactly what to say. Your child is not only looking for answers; your child is looking for engagement, willingness, honesty, and validation that her or his curiosity is something you embrace. The answers we give kids are not nearly as important as how we approach their questions. Children are curious about so many things and certainly say the "darndest things." We encourage our children to ask a lot of questions, and we delight in their adorable questions. "How high is up?" "Where does the sun go when it's nighttime?" "Where was I before I was your little girl?" To children, there is no difference between asking these questions and asking whether the donor liked the color purple or was great at basketball. Our job is to be as comfortable as we can with the way we became parents so that we can talk to our kids as casually about egg donation as we do all their other many questions.

Ten-year-old Daniel was able to ask the question about the donor coming for dinner only because Carole had been talking about this his whole life. In fact, he was only interested in letting his mother know that upon their move into a new home, he was thinking about the woman who he knew played such an important role in their lives, even though she wasn't present. He may not really have wanted her to come to dinner; he may have just wanted Mom to know she had popped into his head.

A primary goal of beginning the stories when children are too young to remember is that when they are asked, as our sons frequently have been, "How old were you when you were told?" their response will be "I have no idea; I've just always known."

> Many parents ask how early is too early. It's never too early. But it's never too late either. If your children are older than seven or eight, don't worry!

How Do I Get Started?

The easiest time to begin having conversations with your kids about donor conception is either when you are pregnant or when they are infants. The next-best time to begin is when they are in preschool. Ideally, it is best to have begun these conversations by the time a child enters kindergarten. If you start when they are babies, you have the opportunity to practice, flub your words, feel awkward or sad, and rework the story before your kids are really cognizant of what you are saying. But how do you get started?

Marna says:

> I began to practice telling Nick the story of his conception when I was pregnant. In fact, when I began my journey, I was bound and determined not to tell my child anything about how he was conceived. I was going to sweep all of the information under the rug, pretend the egg donation part had never happened, and just go on with my life, carrying that secret around with me forever. When I met Carole, she helped me find the right words to say, reduced my anxiety, and helped me to understand that telling my son how he had been conceived not only was one of the healthiest things I could be doing for myself, my child, and my family, but also would be one of the best gifts I could ever give to my son. That absolutely turned out to be true!
>
> The secret to all of this is telling your child early and often. So when I was still pregnant, I told my growing baby:
>
> "Mommy and Daddy wanted to be a mommy and a daddy very much. Mommy and Daddy tried to be a mommy and a daddy for many, many years, and we just

never could have a baby. Mommy went to the doctor, and the doctor told her that Mommy needed eggs to make a special baby and that her special eggs were broken. Mommy was very sad until the doctor told her that they could receive some very special magic eggs from a very special lady. Mommy and Daddy were very happy when they received these very special magic eggs, and out of these magic eggs came *you*!"

We also made up a special little song I'd sing to my son while I was pregnant and for a long time after he was born. Of course, the story changed as he got older and could put the pieces together, but if you ask my son today when he learned about the fact that he was conceived via egg donation, he will tell you most assuredly that he cannot remember when he was told about his conception, but it is something he's always known.

Carole says:

You may not be comfortable with "magic eggs." I always tried to avoid the word "egg" because children are so concrete, and I knew that a child would imagine something he eats for breakfast. When my own mother was pregnant with me, my brother suddenly began to weep at the dinner table. When my mom asked what was wrong, my brother said, "I feel so sorry for that little baby with all that food plopping on its head!" Children don't know that a tummy is not really the same location as a uterus. And they certainly don't know that eggs containing the beginning cells of human life don't come from a chicken. I always used the words "ovum" and "uterus" when speaking with my children about conception. But one day, when Daniel was fourteen and being interviewed for a video about egg donation, he was again asked the question about how and when he had been "told." He said, "My mom always used very technical language with me, like 'ovum' and 'uterus,' and I didn't really understand until when I was in kindergarten, my dad told me it's like a car. A car needs all its parts to run, so if you are missing one of those parts, you need to get a part from somewhere else so everything works."

This makes so much sense in light of how concretely young children think. You certainly never know what is going to help children understand the meanings of complex concepts. This is why we have conversations all of our lives, at different developmental stages, with many opportunities to clarify and enhance. A one-time telling would never suffice!

Another reason for starting to create the family story when children are very young, or before they are even born, is that parents may still have residual feelings of sadness over the loss of their genes. Sometimes when a mom practices her story with her infant, she may feel weepy or even angry that she is not genetically connected to her child. This is all perfectly normal. These feelings are not to be feared but instead should be welcomed as the incredible and complex combination of grief and gratitude, sadness and excitement, a bit of sorrow and a lot of joy. The time before our kids can understand our facial expressions reflecting all of those different feelings is the best time to work out those feelings.

Vicki*

> I didn't want to have to be talking about the donor to my newborn. I was really pissed at the time. But I knew the more I told the story, the less intense those feelings [would become]. I just wanted to be a regular mom, and somehow talking about egg donation made me still feel different. But I realize now that feeling a bit different is okay. I wish I had known then how normal I really do feel. I am

very much a normal mom, with a normal kid, and we are a normal family. I am single; my kid was conceived with donor eggs and donor sperm. She is seven now and understands there are parts that make a baby that we needed from others. I try to answer her questions, but if I can't, I try to understand how she feels about the donors. I want her to feel like she can tell me anything and I won't take it personally. When we are pregnant or the kids are so little, it is hard to trust we will get there; but I know people who didn't start as early as I did, and now they struggle with how to converse about it a bit more than I do. I think it's just all practice. That's what really worked for me.

What we want to do is normalize the way our families were built. In families where donor conception is talked about easily, the way the family was formed is just normal. Many children end up believing that all children come into families the way they did because that's how their family was created.

When parents begin telling the family-building story when children are very young, the story becomes woven into the fabric of their lives. It's not a separate story—it is just *one* of the many stories about their family. Later in their lives, this story may be no different than the story of how they met their spouse or partner or how their parents met or where they grew up. It should have the feel of what we call "pass the peas." Carole describes the night her family was having dinner, and Daniel said, "What was that lady's name again, Mom—and can you pass the peas, please?" And just like that, the question was thrown into a conversation that ranged from how the spelling test had gone to what had happened when Griffin and Riley had a fight on the playground and whether homework had been finished.

In this way, the story of how family members came to be in the family can pop up at various times—it is never a one-time telling. These are conversations that begin when a child is very young and continue throughout the life span of the family. Now in their late twenties, Carole's children are still talking about adoption, egg donation, genes, and connectedness and what makes a family. The dialogue gets funnier and lighter and less frequent as time goes on, but it never completely disappears.

What to Call Her—and Whose Donor Is It Anyway?

If you begin the story when you are pregnant, when your baby first comes home, or in the first few years of your child's life, you have the opportunity to practice the language you prefer. Some people use the word "donor"; others like the word "helper."

Brooke* discovered that the word "helper" was a better term to use with her daughter.

Brooke

> *I had been using the word "donor" with my daughter. Then, when she was age three, we were collecting her old, outgrown toys and clothes to donate to the local homeless shelter, and Lana asked me if we were donating her old stuff like that donor lady donated to us. I realized then that the better term might be "helper." All children understand what it is to be a good helper, but the word "donor" or "donate" has many meanings.*

Some families who know the name of the woman who contributed her genes will simply use her name. This is a lovely way of helping our children begin the process of understanding that they are actually connected to another person in the world and to all the people to whom that woman is linked. They are not just from eggs, which they relate to something scrambled in the morning for breakfast; those parts of the body came from a real person. So if the name is known, by all means, say her name. Some people will create an acronym—Marna's son called her family's donor Nel, which stood for Nice Egg Lady. That worked until her family was united with the previously anonymous donor and established a relationship with her. Now Marna and Nick call her by her name, Jennifer.

When Daniel was about five years old, he asked Carole the name of their donor. She told him she didn't know and asked him what he would like to call her. He thought and thought, looking up at the ceiling as he pondered this very important question, and finally said, "Kelly, like on *Saved by the Bell*," which was his favorite show on TV at the time. So for several years they called her Kelly, until they were able to eventually establish a relationship with her and learned her name was Renee.

Lynn called her family's donor "the egg angel" until their arrangement became non-anonymous, and then they were able to call the donor Ashlee. Cherie* also considers herself a very spiritual person and refers to her donor as an angel. Other families refer to a wonderful woman sent to them by God to make it possible for them to become parents.

Christine and Todd always refer to "the egg donor," whereas Lisa uses the language "your donor" or the "woman who helped us have you" when speaking to her son. Whose donor is it? Does a donor donate genes to the mom or to the child? The truth is that it doesn't matter, as language will change with time.

Joe* and Sam* know their donor personally, so of course they always referred to Nicole* by name when telling their story, knowing their child was going to grow up knowing Nicole as a dear friend in their lives. Diana knows her donor's name, so she always refer to her as the person she is, and the same is true for Kitty and Make and their donor.

Rose* and Aron* always just told the children that they needed one of the parts that makes a baby, so another woman gave Mommy that part so the children could grow inside Angie,* the surrogate who brought their children into their lives.

However one refers to the donor, it is important to remember that the goal is to lay the groundwork for our children to eventually understand that they are connected to another person or people in an important way, even though they will not understand the genetics for many years.

Common Fears

> *A ship in harbor is safe, but that is not what ships are built for.*

> —John A. Shedd

What are these fears that seem so prevalent when we anticipate sharing information? Here are the most common fears we hear expressed about raising children with the truth of donor conception.

"I am afraid my child will reject me."

The fear that a child will reject or not love the non-genetic parent is normal and universal. Somehow, we maintain the myth that love is contingent on genetic relatedness. Nothing could be further from the truth.

Young children love those who take care of them. They love the adults who nurture and teach them, who feed them and tuck them into bed at night. They love the adults who set fair boundaries, who are reasonable and steady, and who are there day after day. They don't know or care about DNA. Even when they understand the meaning of egg donation, children, adolescents, and adults report that the knowledge has never changed how they feel about their parents, except when they are lied to by omission and the fact of donor conception is concealed.

"I am afraid my child will not love me or will be really angry with me once they know the truth."

Children don't stop loving a parent just because they learn they don't share DNA with the parent. Typically, children are angry with their parents only when they find out the truth at an older age, usually in the teen years, once a sense of self-identity has been formed. This is why we encourage parents to start early and often.

Marna says:

I posed the following question to my son Nick: "There are many moms in our community forum who are really worried about telling their kids they were born with the help of an egg donor. They are worried their children will be angry and not love them anymore. Do you have any advice?"

Nick, who was nine at the time, said quite simply, "Mom, there are so many other more important things for me to be pissed at you about besides being born with the help of an egg donor."

This was a record-scratch moment for me. We sat down to hear about all of those "other more important things," and it turned out Nick was angry that I made him go to bed on time. He was also angry that I limited his screen time, didn't allow him to watch PG-13 movies without me, required him to wear a helmet while riding his scooter, and didn't allow him to drink lots and lots of soda pop.

Those were Nick's first-world problems—not the fact that we'd had the help of an egg donor.

Nick's mantra is that you should tell your kids early and often. He concluded, "They have the right to know about the other half of themselves. It's the right thing to do; wouldn't you want to know?"

Carole says:

When Daniel was twelve and was asked the same question, on behalf of the mothers in an online forum who were very fearful of telling children about egg donation, he simply said, "Egg donation is not who I am; it's just how I got here."

"I am afraid that telling them the truth will make things weird or strange between us."

Actually, families have proven that things get weird when children are *not* told the truth. Having the secret in the family creates the big, fat, stinky elephant in the room that no one is speaking about. Talking about how the family was created takes the weirdness out of the relationship. Topics are not dodged or avoided or dreaded. Telling the truth does *not* make things weird or strange.

Twenty-three-year-old Sasha grew up knowing her donor. Knowing the truth definitely did not make things weird in her family. She told us, "My parents were wise enough to always keep that dialogue open, and once it was open, it stayed open for other topics of importance during my youth—sex, relationships, race, and gender issues."

"I am afraid that if my child knows the truth, he or she will go searching for the egg donor."

Many parents fear that if their children are aware that they were conceived with the help of an egg donor, their children will want to look for the donor. This fear may be especially acute in a country such as the United Kingdom, where donor anonymity is lifted when the donor-conceived person turns eighteen.

No one can tell you whether your child will or will not want to seek contact with the donor; what we absolutely can tell you is that if that occurs, it is normal and healthy and in no way a reflection of your child's feelings about you as the parent. In this way, we have learned so much from the adoption world. We know that some adoptees search for a birth family. But all research tells us that when people search for a birth family, they are not looking for parents. They tell us they have parents already. They might be looking for someone who looks like them or has characteristics not shared with anyone else. They may be looking for answers to questions, perhaps for a story, perhaps for medical history. But they aren't looking to replace the parents who raised them.

When people who are donor-conceived seek out the people to whom they are genetically connected, it is *not* a rejection of parents. In fact, if parents are invited to participate and help with the search, that is a compliment. This is a reflection of the trust built between parents and child and the child's confidence that the parent will try to help the child in whatever he or she needs. It is normal for people to be curious about genetic connectedness; it is also normal not to search. In either scenario, the attachment to parents is never in jeopardy, unless the relationship has been strained for other, completely unrelated reasons.

"I am afraid of not being viewed as the real mother."

With regard to the fear that one will not be viewed as the "real mother," we can unequivocally say this: The real mother is the one who mothers. Real fathers are the men who father their children. "To mommy" and "to daddy" are verbs. People contribute eggs or sperm to create children they never parent. Children in families formed in all kinds of ways unanimously tell us that they are and always have been very clear that they have one real mother. (The exceptions to this are families with two mothers, two fathers, or no mother.) Kids may have many questions about who they are, what they inherited, or to whom they are related in different ways, but they are not confused about who their parents are.

Sasha, who grew up knowing her donor, expresses what most donor-conceived people feel: "I always think of my parents as my parents— they're the ones who encouraged me to pursue all of my goals and explore all of my talents. But having a third 'cool aunt' parental figure isn't bad either."

"I want my mother to love all of the grandchildren the same, and if she learns my child was conceived via egg donation, I don't want her to treat my child differently."

Or:

"I don't want my child treated differently from other members of our family."

These fears are frequently misguided. Sometimes the fears that come from our own insecurities are attributed to others. It is really rare for grandparents to reject their grandchildren. Of course, it can happen, but with the exception of certain cultures where genetic relatedness is imperative for family connection, grandparents love their grandchildren. Grandparents sometimes reject an idea, but they rarely reject children. Family members may not like the concept of non-genetic family-building, but it is extremely rare to actually feel differently about a child created that way.

Alternative family-building takes time to get used to. For many of us, it took months or years of therapy and support networks to become comfortable with egg donation. Our family members don't have the benefit of all the information we gather over time as we learn how to grieve our losses or how to talk with kids about donor conception. They don't read the books, go to meetups, talk to therapists, write goodbye letters, or understand how to talk to kids about family-building. Very often, we just drop the news on friends or family and feel disappointed if they have concerns. Time and patience are what it took for many of us to believe that egg donation was the right decision; sometimes family needs the same.

Fears about Sharing with Others

Sometimes the most challenging hurdle is not telling children the truth about donor conception; it is the question of who else needs to know, should know, or can know.

The fear looks a little different when we are considering who should or can know about how we became parents.

"This is my child's story, and my child should be the one to tell it when he or she is old enough."

Some people believe that no one else should know about egg donation until the child knows. This is another theory that comes from our knowledge of adoption, in which respect for a child's story dictates that it be that child alone who tells the story. Respecting the privacy of a person's origins is a worthy and appropriate goal. But this is not realistic. Most infertility patients, especially women, have a need to talk about the trauma they have endured. Most people need support that can come only from talking with intimates about the decisions that lie ahead.

This concept also raises questions about sharing information with people on a need-to-know basis. Your pediatrician needs to know in order to have as accurate a medical history as possible. Your child's teacher may not need to know unless you choose to tell him or her. In some families, the way the family was created is spoken of freely and often with those within and outside of the family. In other families, it is clear that only the immediate family speaks about it, and it is not to be discussed with everyone. Some children will perceive this as a message about a secret to be kept; others will understand that it is precious knowledge about a special way they came to be. Ultimately, it is the motivation for sharing or not that will determine how the style of information sharing is perceived. Is it embarrassment, shame, or fear cloaked in the garb of privacy, or is it truly respect for the autonomy of our children and a wish for them to own their story that makes us try to keep the information so very private? Each family must decide on their own.

"I am afraid that when my children are angry, they will shout, 'You're not my real mother!'"

The fear that children will use egg donation as a vehicle for their anger is a reasonable and realistic fear. Children say all kinds of things out of anger when parents set limits and deny children or adolescents what they want.

Many parents via egg or embryo donation are afraid that their children will one day say to them, "I don't have to listen to you–you're not my real mother!" But who hasn't ever blurted something out in anger? One thing is for sure: when we are armed with responses, and when we know why our kids do or say what they do or say, fear has a way of dissipating or altogether disappearing.

All children say hurtful things when they are angry. And kids are usually that angry when they do not get what they want. Both very young children and adolescents may say, "I hate you—you're the meanest mom in the world!" when Mom will not bend to a child's will. Children both desperately need and rebel against limits. Some kids push limits more than others, but whether it is the young child who can't have a bowl of cookies for breakfast or the teen who is not allowed to go to a party, children will frequently react by trying to hurt their parents. Sometimes children may say, "I don't have to listen to you—you're old!" Or they may say, "I don't have to listen to you—you're short!" Or maybe they will shout, "I wish I lived at Suzi's house—her mom is nice!" In families formed through adoption or assisted reproduction, children will frequently pull the "not my real parent" card to see if it gets the reaction they are looking for.

When a parent responds to this outburst with the calm demeanor of a confident parent, quite clear about the boundary being set, the child is unlikely to use the strategy again. The child may try other ways of getting back at the parent, but it won't be with the "real parent" comment.

Here are some ways to respond to a child of any age who tries to get her or his way by claiming the parent is not a real parent:

> *"You know that if you have questions about how we formed our family, we are happy to answer them, but first you need to get your laundry finished because that's your job right now."*

"We have always said that if you have questions about egg donation or the way we all came together, we are happy to discuss it with you anytime, but right now you need to get back in your room and finishing cleaning it because that is what I asked you to do."

"If you have questions about egg donation or the way you were conceived, I am happy to talk about it, but right now you need to finish your homework."

In other words, real parents discipline, set limits, and don't allow children to do whatever they want, whenever they want. Real parents hold their children's rage, fear, disappointment, sadness, or confusion for them until kids can put pieces together. Real parents through donor conception have the extra job of helping children distinguish between regular growing-up issues and donor issues. This is not always simple, because as parents, we don't always know. But when kids blurt in anger something intended to be hurtful, we guarantee it has absolutely nothing to do with donor conception and everything to do with not getting their way. Most likely they will not try this strategy again if you do not dissolve into a puddle of mush, imploring them to know how much they are loved and wanted and asking how they could say that to you. If you react that way, they will use the "real parent" card every time they don't get their way.

Who Else Should Know?

Once you have committed to having conversations with your children about donor conception, you may be wondering whom else you "should" tell. What happens when strangers in the park or the cashier at the grocery store make inquiries or comments about your family? It is not uncommon for families in which not everyone is genetically related to receive questions such as "Where did they get their blond hair? Does their father have blond hair?" "Gee, you were lucky to get pregnant in your forties. Are they yours?" Or more bluntly, people may simply ask you if you used donor eggs.

We like to think about who "needs to know" as a series of concentric circles. At the center of the circle is your child or children who were conceived with the help of donor conception. They are the most important people who will be best served by knowing the truth of their origins. In the same center circle are any medical professionals who will be treating you or your surrogate during pregnancy and your child after the child is born.

The next circle out from that are the other children in your family, regardless of how they joined your family. Whether your other children came to you through adoption, donor conception, or a previous marriage or were conceived the easy, cheap, and fun way, the family will be healthiest if everyone has the same information about genetic relatedness. Keeping the matter secret can significantly interfere with the functioning of a family. Issues of who knows what can create unhealthy alliances, put pressure on some to keep the secret, and generally create a toxic atmosphere as the secret takes up air in the house.

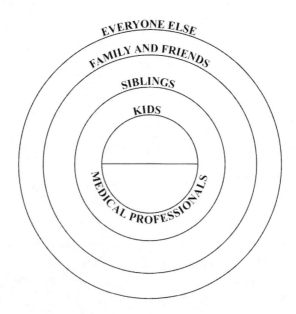

The next circle to be considered is that of friends and family. Some people are generally more private than others. Many people are comfortable talking to anybody about egg donation, and that is really just fine until the children reach a certain age and don't want their mom or dad to ever talk about them at all. Generally speaking, life is much easier if the families of each parent have the same information the child does, but certainly, there are some exceptions to this. If a family member is mentally disabled and unable to handle the information, or a grandparent is perhaps so elderly that they truly would not comprehend assisted reproduction, or if there has been so much estrangement that it would not be appropriate to share, then you may not want to do so. But in most situations, having grandparents, aunts, and uncles in the loop makes life easier.

When it comes to friends, most women want to share the information with close friends. Remember, how you formed your family is private, not a secret, so whomever you decide to share with is fine. Your child won't mind that others know. Your children will mind only if others know but they were not told until much later.

Then there is the question of strangers and others. Our best advice is to have a repertoire of responses in your pocket at all times. There are many ways to answer inquiries or comments without giving private information that you don't feel like sharing or that would be inappropriate to give because your children are old enough to not want you to be talking about them.

Where'd they get their blond/red/black/curly/straight hair (different from yours)?

> *Just lucky, I guess.*
> *Their grandmother was blonde.*
> *No, their father isn't blond; he's gray.* (This is Carole's son's favorite.)
> *Aren't they gorgeous?*

You were so lucky to get pregnant at your age! Are they yours?

> ➤ *Yes, I was very lucky!*
> ➤ *We are very blessed.*
> ➤ *We had lots of help.*
> ➤ *Why do you ask?* (Marna's favorite.)
> ➤ *Yes, they're mine!*

Other responses you can use at a moment's notice:

> ➤ *We're not all genetically related to each other.* (This one raises eyebrows and makes the inquirer wonder what you mean.)
> ➤ *Don't know where the hair color came from. You never know who you're going to get.*
> ➤ *I was blond as a child.*

Once you have your family, you will become very good at responding in different ways at different times. Sometimes you might want to share the whole story, and other times you just want to get out of the supermarket in a hurry. When your community becomes the parents of your child's classmates, these conversations will be very frequent. While watching their kids play, parents share all kinds of information. There may be many times when you befriend the parent of your child's friend and feel comfortable sharing somewhat intimate information. The topic may come up when the other parent shares first. Maybe the other parent's family obviously was built creatively too, and you feel comfortable sharing your story. Other times, you may feel that the person will not become a close friend, and you will keep the information to yourself.

Either way, if you have already been talking about egg donation at home as a family, there are really very few risks. Likely nothing your children hear outside of your home will be different or confusing, and if it is, they can come home and ask you about it. You never have to be afraid that Johnny will blurt out something hurtful to your child because you know you have been discussing family-building, and if your child has questions, she or he will come home to you and tell you what Johnny said. There are no rules about who else needs to know, outside of your family and medical professionals treating your child. Once you have your repertoire of responses, you will feel ready and armed for any comment that comes your way.

But If Kids Think It's No Big Deal, Why Do I Have to Talk about It?

Many people ask, "If kids think being conceived through egg or embryo donation is no big deal, why does it feel like such a big deal to tell them?"

The great paradox of creating a family where kids and parents are not genetically related to each other is that genes are not at all important for love, commitment, family, devotion, or attachment. But genes do, in fact, matter a great deal.

Genes obviously matter tremendously to us as we move through infertility treatments, often trying cycle after cycle to have a child with our own DNA. Egg, sperm, or embryo donation is no one's first choice. Most people grieve the loss of the little child they thought they would have, which is part of the process that we must go through to be fully prepared to embrace a child that is not the narcissistic reflection of ourselves.

Genes most certainly matter in helping us to form a genetic identity. *Where do I come from? To whom do I belong? Where do I fit?* These are questions asked by all humans, even when we don't know we are asking them. We put our identity together from our knowledge of our genetic background and the environment in which we grow up. For most people, those are one and the same or connected. But in donor-conceived families, it takes a bit more effort and information to put together the puzzle of oneself.

Sasha describes the experience like this:

Sasha

When it comes down to it, having an egg donor both biologically made me who I am and figuratively transformed me into who I am.

Genes don't necessarily make a child feel like they belong in the family. Genes have nothing to do with a child knowing that Mom and Dad (or other combinations of parents) are the people who love and nurture them. But that doesn't mean genes are unimportant. If our genes were irrelevant, many of us would not struggle to make the transition to donor conception.

Some parents fear that children's questions about their genetic link signal a lack of connection to the parents. But if this were true, wouldn't that work the other way around as well? If we grieved the loss of a genetically related child, can't our children feel a little grief too? Not all will, but if they do, we can certainly empathize. We felt it too—long before we were the mom or dad to this kid we adore.

> ● *Remember that although some of the fears faced by egg donation families are universal, every family is unique, and therefore so is the telling of how that family came to be.*

What Can You Expect If You Choose Not to Tell Your Child about His Genetic Origins?

Two people can keep a secret as long as two of them are dead.

—Benjamin Franklin

In the Path2Parenthood article "Genes Make People, People Make Families,"[6] Dr. Madeline Feingold describes the ways in which children make sense of their world.

> Children can manage frustrations and confusion as long as parents offer their children explanations for their actions and decisions. When parents provide meaning for their children's experiences, children feel secure. Problems likely arise when children do not understand their situation and parents do not intervene to help them …
>
> When children learn about their donor origins at a young age, they seem to have a more positive experience about their donor conception than those who are told later in life.

Dr. Feingold goes on to say that we also know that "just because people are not told of their donor origins does not mean that they remain unaware. Many donor-conceived people report growing up feeling uncomfortable in their family because they sensed that information was being withheld."

If you believe that you do not ever intend to tell your child the truth about egg donation, it is important to ask yourself *why* you believe this is in your child's best interest. The question to be asked is whether you truly believe this to be private information or whether you really consider it a secret. And do you know the difference?

Secrecy versus Privacy

The terms "secrecy" and "privacy" are frequently used interchangeably, but they do not mean the same thing at all. A secret is always something we are afraid to share because of what others would think of us if they knew it. It is information about which we are ashamed and that makes us afraid of judgment.

There is a big difference between privacy and secrecy. One way to think about this is that privacy is not telling the person in line at the grocery store; secrecy is not telling your hild.

Privacy refers to things in life that are really and truly no one else's business. We use that expression frequently, but too often people say something is "no one's business" out of fear and confusion. Usually, when people use the expression, they are not really talking about private issues. Here are some examples of **private** matters:

➢ How much money you made last year.
➢ How much you paid in taxes.
➢ How often you are sexually intimate with your partner.
➢ Nicknames you have for each other when you crawl into bed each night.
➢ How many alcoholic beverages you drink in a week.
➢ Using the bathroom—which is why we close the door.

Secrets are matters about which we feel some shame, embarrassment, or fear. We can take the preceding items and change something to flip them from private to secret:

➢ Instead of how much money you made last year, the fact that you filed for bankruptcy.
➢ Instead of how much you paid in taxes, the fact that you didn't file your taxes or you cheated on your taxes.
➢ Instead of how often you are sexually intimate with your partner, maybe the fact that you invite your entire block over for group sex each weekend, and that is not something you want people to know.
➢ Instead of how much alcohol you consume in a week, the fact that alcohol has become a problem in your life.

The immediately preceding issues are almost always kept secret because they may be embarrassing or shameful. Issues in families such as substance abuse, alcoholism, spousal or child abuse, or sexual abuse are almost always secrets.

The story of how you built your family is one of very much wanting to become a parent—overcoming obstacles, asking for help, utilizing resources, working hard for a dream, and ultimately achieving parenthood through the love you have for each other. Is this really in the same category as bankruptcy, child abuse, lying, or cheating? Your family-building story is a love story, and although it may be a private matter—meaning that you discern carefully how and when and with whom to share it—it most definitely ought not to be a secret.

Can You Keep Donor Conception a Secret Forever?

The current research shows that when you are honest and open with your child, this places honesty and integrity at the center of your family's relationships in all other areas of life. This also provides children the opportunity to learn the details of their genetic history and to integrate that information as they grow. It allows them to accept their story as part of who they are without any discomfort or distress. This also gives the donor-conceived child his or her true medical history, which can then be given to their physicians, which makes their medical care more accurate.

As the authors of this book, we are committed to the mindset and practice of openness and transparency with all donor-conceived children. However, we understand that some intended parents are limited by religious or cultural restrictions surrounding third-party reproduction. These parents may come from a culture or community where donor conception is strongly disapproved or, in some places, banned. In some cultures and communities, undue hardships may be placed on donor-conceived children and their families. These families often have spent much time questioning whether donor conception is an appropriate method of family-building.

So what would it look like to try to keep the donor conception a secret forever?

To begin with, being the keeper of such a secret is going to be a burden on you and your partner, if you have one. It's going to be extraordinarily challenging, complicated, and hard. Really hard. You will have no one with whom to discuss this except each other.

If you truly intend to keep this a secret for the rest of your life, that means that even in a moment of vulnerability, you will not have the ability to share this with your family, your best friend, your child's physician, your child's teachers, your community, or your clergy. You can't tell your sister or your mother or the woman in the grocery store.

Because the secret must die with you and your partner, it's important that you consider the ramifications of this secret after your death. Experience has told us that secrets about family-building never stay secrets forever. But if you do manage to keep it a secret until your death, your child (hopefully then no longer a child) will almost definitely learn the secret at that time. Many family members learn long-held secrets when they clean out boxes in the garage, go through files, and find medical records or donor profiles. That means that every shred of paper, every receipt, record, and donor profile, and any other information you may have that will lead to your donor egg cycle must be destroyed. The reason for this is very simple—in the event of your death, your child or children will be going through your things. And not *if* but *when* they find this information, they're going to wonder what else their parents lied to them about over the course of their lives. This will undoubtedly cause irreparable damage. But the risk in destroying those records is that your child will never have much-needed and desired information, information about their genetic identity that could help answer crucial questions they will have.

And truly, in this age of DNA testing, none of this will be possible.

Keeping secrets is isolating and lonely. It alienates loved ones and disrupts intimacy. If you think you must keep donor conception a secret, do what you believe is right for your family. However, do consider the other people in your child's life to whom you will also be lying and what you will all lose in the process. Secrets *never* stay secrets forever.

Maintaining Control over the Information

Most parents want to feel they have some control over the private information about how they had their children. For this reason, it is best that you be the one to talk to your children about the ways in which you all are connected to one another. Historically, in adoption and sperm donation, children were not informed of their genetic origins. Subsequently, in worst-case scenarios, when donor offspring or adoptees accidentally learned about their donor-conceived or adopted status, it left a lasting negative impact on families.

The term "unintended disclosure" refers to your child learning about egg donation from someone other than you at a time and in a manner you did not intend. Unintended disclosure is impossible when a child has always heard the language of family-building. Even if the child does not understand reproduction, the term "egg donor" or language about "another woman helping us" will be familiar.

No family secret is kept forever. Eventually, the truth will be known. It is not an "if" but a "when." Whether it occurs following death or divorce, in a fit of anger, or simply because it is finally the right time, secrets get discovered. In addition, most people who initially decide not to share the truth with their children change their minds at some point in the future. Feelings change over time. An early start is always easier than a later start.

We live in a time in which we can have no real expectation of privacy. There are DNA kits in every corner pharmacy and now available on many online companies. A simple cheek swab or spit in a vial can determine information about where we originated and to whom we are related. High school students routinely do DNA tests on themselves and their families. Home DNA tests have caused cataclysmic changes in donor-conceived families, whether accidentally or intentionally during a search for genetic relatives.

Conversations about one's genetic origins are very challenging to have for the first time with adolescents and young adults. It is much easier and less painful to have this conversation when children are toddlers, which allows them to grow up with the information.

The Foundations for a Trusting Relationship

Although it is true that one way or another, family secrets always come out, there are many other very important reasons it is recommended that parents be honest with their children about egg donation.

The relationship you have with your child will undoubtedly be one of the most important relationships you will have in your lifetime. And most certainly, the relationship your child has with you will be the most important relationship your child has in his or her lifetime. It is unwise to start out this relationship with a lie.

We would never consider growing a relationship with a partner while pretending to be someone we are not. We know that if we hide things such as a seedy past, an arrest record, a prior marriage, or any piece of our history we would prefer to deny, these facts will always come out. And when they do, our partners are always deeply hurt that we did not trust them enough to talk to them about those parts of ourselves about which we may be embarrassed. Pretending and denying can have dire consequences. People stop trusting us; it takes years to build trust but only a moment to shatter it. When adults discover they have been lied to, they have the defenses, intellect, coping skills, and language to help them get through feelings of betrayal. But imagine what it feels like to be a child who has none of these strategies and now must deal with trying to understand why they were not told the truth at the same time they are trying to piece together the puzzle of their genetic identity.

So although fear of unintended disclosure of egg donation may be one motivation for telling the truth, perhaps the most important reason is that it is best to start out your life in this most precious relationship with a foundation of trust.

Scripts for How to Talk with Kids about Donor Conception

Mistakes are the portals of discovery.

—James Joyce

In this section, you'll find some time- and age-appropriate scripts you can use as the basis for ongoing conversations with your children about how they came into the world. For consistency, the scripts are written with a mother and father, but they can easily be adapted for parents who used a gestational carrier or who are single or in a same-sex relationship.

Pregnancy

The simplest way to begin conversations with your children is to begin when you are pregnant. In this way, you can practice your family-building story. This is a story about how you created your family, not just an egg donation story about your child. In the beginning, the story is very simple:

> *It takes a part from a man and a part from a woman to make the beginnings of a baby. Mama didn't have the part she needed, so another woman gave her the part that she needed. We are so happy you are our precious Sally.*

Starting to practice this early helps you to become comfortable with the story you are developing. You can figure out how you want to refer to the woman whose eggs were given to you or what you want to call the couple who gave you embryos; you will not need to censor your feelings when you talk about this. Expectant parents talk and sing to their growing babies. Including a baby's conception story is no different, other than that uncomfortable feelings may come up. That may not be true for you, but sometimes women have feelings of resentment. Although she was very resolved and ready, Carole remembers saying to herself while practicing the story, "I don't want to have to be talking about *her*; I just want to be a 'regular' pregnant person!"

The most important thing to remember is that whatever feelings you have when you start to practice your story, they are normal. Just feel them, thank yourself for acknowledging those feelings, and move on. That's the point of starting early. You can't hurt anybody, and you won't have to worry that you are harming your child if you have a feeling that makes you uncomfortable.

Once your baby is born, continue the story while you are rocking, feeding, loving, nurturing, and holding your baby. Now the story is about *this* baby, with this particular name, and a particular person helped this child be yours. Express your gratitude. Tell your baby how grateful you are that Nicole gave you what you needed or that the angel brought you that part you were missing so that Johnny could be yours.

Early Childhood

As your infant becomes a preschooler, the story remains pretty much the same as the story for your infant because preschoolers are very concrete. You can share that there was a part that you were missing in order for Johnny to be yours. Regardless of the makeup of your family, whether you are a single dad, a two-mom family, or a family with a mom and a dad, the story is still the same: for a baby to become a baby, it takes an egg, or an ovum or a cell or a piece from a woman; a sperm, or a seed or a cell from a man; and a uterus for the baby to grow in. Some or all of those parts may have been given by someone else so that you could become a parent.

By the time children are five years old, they typically have come to understand that babies come out of women's bodies; until this point, they actually believe that they have always existed. Maybe they believe you went to the deli to get them or to the hospital, where babies are waiting. That's where the story of the stork and the cabbage patch came from—children believe that they have always been here, just in some other form. This can be a time when you point out pregnant women, usually the moms at preschool who are having their second, third, or fourth children. You can talk to your youngster about when you or your surrogate was pregnant with Johnny and what an exciting time that was.

Look around your community and find families that were obviously formed in different ways. Undoubtedly, at the grocery store or at your child's school, you will see children being raised in two-dad families or single-mom families. You may see two Caucasian parents with an Asian daughter and surmise that family was formed by adoption. There may be children being raised by a grandparent or families where everyone looks alike or families where no one looks alike. You can turn these observations into conversation starters by talking about families coming together in a lot of different ways—as yours did, with the help of someone who gave you a very important piece so that Sally could be yours.

The more you find ways to weave the family-building story into the fabric of your everyday life, the easier you will find the conversations that ensue. You may find your child asking questions about the parts of her she is curious about. Your child may want to know if "that lady's favorite color" is purple or if she also really likes soccer. Some of these questions, you may be able to answer, and in some cases, you may have to simply ask your child what she thinks. Engaging your child in his own questions is the best way to find out what he is thinking.

Keep every shred of information you have ever been given about the donor. Make a copy for safekeeping, and keep a copy readily available so that when your child asks a question about the donor, you can say, "You know, I really don't remember her favorite color, but I do have some information about her, and whenever you are ready, we can look at it together." Sometimes children don't really need an answer to a question; they just need to know you are willing to engage in the discussion with them.

All the while as you are having these conversations with your very young children, you can read to them the many wonderful children's books about families conceived through donor conception. (A bibliography can be found at the back of this book.) Children's books can function as templates. A pre-reading or preverbal child can look at the pictures while you fill in the blanks to match his or her particular story. In this way, you don't have to always figure out how to find opportunities to talk about family-building because the books can do it for you. Most children will not be interested in these books or the stories for a very long time, but that is not a reason not to start early. Children want to know about all kinds of things before they understand them, like where the sun goes when it's nighttime or how Grandma's voice got into the telephone.

Laying the foundation or the building blocks for understanding about how babies are created, grown, and born is a process that takes time. Learning and understanding is a gradual process that occurs in developmental stages. We can't learn to multiply until we can add and thus understand that multiplication is sequential addition. Without the foundational understanding, we would simply be memorizing times tables by rote without any understanding of what they mean. Preschoolers learn about their neighborhood. Kindergartners learn about the post office and the fire department. First and second graders venture out to learn more about their city. In the fourth grade, students learn about their state. Not until high school do students learn world geography. People can't comprehend the greater world until they can grasp the smaller community surrounding them. So it is with understanding means of conception. Obviously, children don't understand the meaning of genetics, but they can initially understand "this part plus that part equals *you*."

As noted previously, the story is the same for toddlers and preschoolers as it is for infants:

> *It takes a part from a man and a part from a woman to make the beginnings of a baby, and all babies grow inside women's bodies. Mommy needed a part from another woman so that I could be your mommy. We are so happy that [donor/helper/her name/the angel] gave Mommy what she needed so you could be my baby!*

Childhood and Early Adolescence

If you have not already begun conversations with your child, now is a fine time. You now have a verbal, inquisitive elementary schooler, someone with whom you can chat about families and personalities and likes and dislikes. You can talk about families around you and how they may have come together in different ways. By this age, your child certainly understands what it is to need and ask for help.

At this age, you can start to integrate your story as a bedtime story or work it into the family tree project assigned to every child in elementary school. You might say something like the following—again, adapting the story to match your particular family constellation.

> *Mommy and Daddy want to tell you the story of how we created our family. We very much wanted to be a family that included a child. We tried and tried to make a baby, but we weren't able to. We went to a doctor to get help. The doctor told us it takes three parts to make a baby. It takes something called a sperm, and sperm come from men. It takes something called an egg, and eggs come from women. This egg is not the kind of egg we eat in the morning; it is a teeny tiny cell that is inside a woman's body. And finally, making a baby takes something called a uterus for a baby to grow in, and this special growing place is in women. The doctor told us we were missing the eggs that it took to make a baby.*
>
> *Daddy had the sperm, and Mommy had the uterus where a baby could grow, but Mommy didn't have any eggs. The doctor told us that many women are missing the eggs they need to make a baby, and there are other men and women who do have sperm and eggs and want to help. Men can give some of their sperm to other men who want to be daddies, and women can give some of their eggs to other women who want to be mommies. A woman gave Mommy*

and Daddy some of her eggs, and we are so grateful because that is how we got to be your mommy and daddy. A baby started to grow inside Mommy [or another woman called a surrogate], and that baby was you. We are so happy that we have you and that we are a family.

There are many books available for children who are conceived with the help of donor eggs, sperm, or embryos and/or who are born through surrogacy. We have compiled some of these publications in this book's bibliography. These books are extremely helpful in opening the door to conversations with your kids and helping to promote the discussions. We recommend buying many of the books for the under-five crowd and elementary school children because they will get bored with seeing the same ones or having the same books read to them repeatedly. Also, you may not like some aspects of some books; they may use different language than you would use, and some have better illustrations than others. If you have several on the bookshelves, you can alternate, and your child can grab a different book at different times and see the story represented in different ways.

Adolescence

Adolescence is a time of extreme developmental changes. At no time other than the period from birth to age five do humans grow as much as they do in adolescence. The task during this time is to individuate, a term that means "to become an individual, to become a distinct entity." This is the time when we separate from our parents and form our own thoughts, feelings, and values, which may be very different from those of our family. The brain starts the process, which can sometimes take a decade, of thinking more like an adult. We develop abstract reasoning. In essence, we start trying to figure out who we are.

Given these huge developmental tasks, this is not the best time to tell a teen that they are not genetically who they thought they were. At the same time, if you have not yet shared this family-building story and you are now ready to do so, by all means, begin. This section is about what you might expect as you move forward.

You can expect your adolescent to have a lot of questions! These questions will not flow all at once. Initially, he may have no questions at all. Given that he is a teenager, he may just grunt. She may say, "Whatever." It may look like she is apathetic or didn't hear you at all.

But gradually, if not immediately, the meaning of the story will begin to take shape. Your teen will start to think, *If I was born from a donated embryo, then I am not related to my parents.* They may use the term "related to" even though we may use words like "genetically related to." They will begin to ask the questions that all lead to "If not you, then who?" *If I am not a combination of my parents, then who am I?*

This questioning will happen whether the child was conceived through egg, sperm, or embryo donation. Depending on how old they are, what kind of nature they have, and what is going on in their lives right then, this may a huge deal or not a big deal at all to your teen. It is best to follow your child's lead. Don't expect to tell the whole story at once with every detail. Don't focus on the assisted technology that made it happen in a lab. It is a good idea to ask your child if you can answer any questions for them, but don't expect them to ask right away.

No matter how old your child is at the time you begin discussions, these are conversations that will continue for a lifetime, if you allow them to. Processing the information takes time—sometimes a lot of time. Thoughts or questions may occur to a teenager at random times, in the same way they might for a kindergartener.

Encourage your child to come to you at any time with questions he or she might have. Here are just a few questions your teen may ask over the course of weeks, months, or even years:

"Did you meet that woman who gave you the eggs?"

"Do I have any brothers or sisters?"

"Can I meet her—not now, but maybe someday?"

"Does she know about me?"

"Where does she live?"

"Why did she donate her eggs?"

"So what am I then?" (a question about ethnicity)

As we have previously said, the key here is not the answers you give or whether or not you actually have the answers, but *how* you answer. If you are welcoming and inviting of your child's curiosity, he will feel safe including you in his thought process. She will share with you her concerns. She also may feel secure enough to let you know if she is angry that you did not tell her earlier. Remember, trust is one of the most important foundations between parents and children, so let them know that you understand this may be confusing and that you are available to help them with however they may feel about it.

Adolescence spans a seven- to eight-year period of time. A ten- or eleven-year-old will not process egg donation information in the same way as an eighteen-year-old, any more than a five-year-old will understand it the way their twelve-year-old self eventually will. Also, it is important to remember that children are as different as adults are. Some are dark and brooding and tend to see the world through a cloudy lens, whereas others have a sunnier disposition and let things roll off their backs. Of course, our children will respond to this information with their own spin on life. Some may be very curious, some may be angry or troubled, and others may think it is absolutely no big deal.

Our job as parents is not to protect our children from ever feeling pain, but to be there to help them through whatever life brings. We want to teach them coping strategies for dealing with life's disappointments and how to feel gratitude and appreciation of life's bounty. If your child is distressed by the story of how you created your family, have patience. Stand by. Be there for whatever is to come. Get help for yourself if the going gets rough. Seek a therapist who knows about various means of family formation. Clean up your own residual infertility issues so that you can really be there for your child and not feel knocked over by his process. Infertility is a chronic disease that goes into remission for long periods of time and then rears its head at various times in the life cycle. It's perfectly normal for you to feel like you might need to revisit the circumstances under which you chose egg or embryo donation. It is perfectly healthy to occasionally tap back into any grief you might have felt. You will feel better and more in control and more available to your family and yourself.

Real People Tell Their Real Stories

> *There is no greater agony than bearing an untold story inside you.*
>
> —Maya Angelou

Here is how some moms and dads told us they started conversations with their kids about how they built their families.

Joan

> *My sons turned three in January, and I have been trying to talk to them about donor egg conception since they were about two years, nine months old. They don't seem very interested—they won't read the books we have that cover the topic (*Mommy, Was Your Tummy Big?*, The Pea That Was Me, *and* One More Giraffe*), and they seem much more interested in talking about the fact that they were "little tiny babies in [my] tummy" and seeing photos of my pregnant belly than in hearing about donor conception.*

This does not surprise us at all. Of course, children are not interested in some piece of the story that is so abstract. What they love are stories about the excitement and enthusiasm surrounding their birth and the lead-up to it. They want to picture themselves, concretely, somewhere, whether in Mom's body or in the "tummy" or uterus of a gestational carrier. But that doesn't mean we should stop reading the books or talking about the helper who helped make the family complete. Eventually, over the years, the ideas will take shape, through the development of the child and the family.

Alexa*

> *I started the donor conversation with my son shortly before he turned two. That was when I pulled out our copy of* Mommy, Was Your Tummy Big? *and started reading it to him. He loves that book. When we get to the part where the doctor puts the donor's egg together with the daddy's cells into Mommy's body and a baby start[s] to grow, I say, "Just like you." He's now two years and nine months old, and he still doesn't really understand conception or what this means for him, but he does know that babies grow in a mommy's tummy. A couple of weeks ago, I decided to initiate the conversation with him without the book and said, "You know, Mommy and Daddy wanted a baby and tried for a really long time to have one. A doctor helped us find a lady called a donor, and she helped us have you." I was really doing this just as a dry run, to try and feel comfortable with it, but even so I was very nervous! As soon as I finished telling him this, he ran off to his room and brought back the* Mommy, Was Your Tummy Big? *book. He knew exactly what I was talking about, even though I still don't think he understands exactly what this means for him. I was happy and relieved to know that this story is already something that is ingrained within him. By the time he can really grasp what an egg donor is, this story will already have been a part of who he is since before he can even remember.*

Exactly, Alexa. He will never remember the moment he was told.

Frances has two boys: a nine-year-old, who is genetically related to both his mom and his dad, and a two-year-old who was created with the help of another woman's eggs. She tells us her story:

Frances

> *I've been reading* Mommy, Was Your Tummy Big? *to my son, but at twenty-three months he's actually not interested in that book. And we rarely make it through* any *whole book before he wants a new book, so it's been challenging. Maybe I'll try the* One More Giraffe *or [a] shorter book!*
>
> *I did tell our nine-year-old just a couple of months ago. My husband was dead set on waiting until he "loved" his brother. I disagreed, but it wasn't worth the battle! So I told the nine-year-old when he was asking if George had a curl in his hair because of Grammy (my mom). I said, "Actually, that's not possible because of the way we conceived George. You know we had a doctor's help, right?" He said yes, he knew that. "Well," I continued, "we also needed to have a lady's help. My girl parts that contribute to a new baby were broken, so we found a nice lady that would give me her girl parts and then mixed [them] with Daddy's boy parts and then placed [them] in my belly." He was a little sad that his brother couldn't be "just like him," but those few tears were soon dried. He was also concerned that George would "feel different" from us (very insightful for nine years old!), and I said, "We'll just have to love him so much that he never feels different." He agreed. I asked him about it a couple weeks later to see if he wanted to ask any questions, and he said, "No, I'm fine with it."*

Frances was wise to start the conversation with her elder son before he got too much older. At nine years old, he did not yet feel betrayed or lied to because he had assumed something that was not true.

Generally, we don't recommend using the word "broken" to describe the part of the mom or dad's body that needed substitution. Children can become very frightened by the idea that something is broken in their parent. We prefer to refer to eggs, uterus, and sperm as missing or to say the part just didn't work the way it was supposed to work. Or we can simply say we needed a part from another man or woman to have the child that is now ours.

Frances's son was indeed very insightful to be concerned about his brother's feelings, in particular to worry that his brother would feel different. We recommend a different way of responding to this idea of difference in families. It's really okay to be different. When we experience infertility, we must ultimately embrace the fact that we are going to have a "different" child than the one we originally thought we would have. No matter how much the donor we chose looks like us or has personality or family traits like us, she is not going to help us have a child that is like the genetic one we tried to have with our partner (if we have a partner). Genes all mixed together yield crazy and interesting results. The loss of control over when and how and with whom we will reproduce forces us to give up the illusion of control we had about the child we originally tried to create.

Healthy families embrace difference. Healthy families do not need everyone to look alike or think alike or have similar interests. When issues of difference arise in family conversations, a parent might simply say, "It's really fine for Johnny to be or feel different in our family. Being different is not at all a bad thing. You are not the same as I am, and I am not the same as Daddy. We are all different, and Johnny will be too."

Eugene recounts chats with his son that went like this:

Eugene

> *The first real conversation that I had with Logan was when he was two or three years old. We might have touched on it a few times before then as well. He was maybe two-and-a-half or so. He and I were coming back from the zoo, and while we were driving back, I told him that we [had]*

needed help to have him and that we used another lady's egg. Honestly, I don't remember the details. He was very tired after a whole day of running around the zoo, and I'm not sure how much sunk in. I told him that if he had any questions, he could ask me or Mommy. He said something like "Okay ... I'll ask Mommy" and then promptly fell asleep and never mentioned it again. I don't think that it registered much with him, but it was a good dry run for me. He's a very bright kid, and I expect that we'll revisit the subject with him soon. I think that the reason that we're not talking to him about it more is that we're still trying for a sibling and don't want him to become emotionally invested in a frustrating process (that, at this point, is unlikely to end with any further success). We'd rather he continue to enjoy the trips to San Diego (which he talks about each and every day).

Bringing up the subject in unlikely places and at unlikely times is just fine. Eventually, that is exactly what your child will do. They will ask you a question about the donor or family-building in a carpool with five other kids in the car or at Thanksgiving dinner, or just about any time a comment or question pops into their minds. There is no right way or perfect time to begin. And Eugene is so right—Logan is much more likely to remember his trip to the zoo than some random comment from Dad about his parents' needing help to have him. Still, it is fine to just start, to just bring it up, especially at that age when Mom and Dad can still practice and feel awkward and figure out how they want to refine the story.

Sandy* relayed the following about her attempts to talk with her son, now two years and eight months old:

Sandy

We haven't really had a conversation. He has a couple of books on his shelf that mention DE (An Itty Bitty Gift of

Life is one), so he occasionally picks [one] off the shelf to be read. I don't think he understands any of it yet though.

Our intention is just to include this information as we talk to him. We have often discussed the analogy of an instruction book—half comes from the man, [and] half from the woman, but Mommy's half had some pages missing, so we had to borrow her half from another woman. That kind of thing.

There are so many ways to talk about this notion of part replacement. As Carole mentioned earlier, Daniel's dad told their Daniel that the situation was like a car that needed all its parts to run. There was a part missing, so they had to go to the shop to get the part they needed so the car would run. For a five-year-old boy, this made perfect sense!

Here Chrissy describes how she has started chatting with her nineteenth-month-old twins:

Chrissy

Due to their age/level of understanding, we will sometimes talk about going to Prague, Czech Republic, where we had the donor IVF procedure. They see pictures on my laptop, and we tell them about the magical cities and castles and how we were looking for them and found them.

So in this case, Chrissy and her partner are beginning with a story about where the children were conceived and how they traveled very far to try to become parents. This is a fine beginning and a bit different, but the story will surely evolve over time. This is giving the parents the opportunity to feel comfortable with the story and to fill in blanks each time those magic castles are viewed.

Bella

> *We haven't really had conversations, but I have been practicing telling her about the nice lady who gave Mommy an egg, because Mommy had broken eggs.*
>
> *We will probably wait until she is three years old to really start talking about it, when she can better grasp some aspects of how children are made. I do worry that she will blurt out her story to family members who don't know, but that's a bridge I will cross when I get to it. There is so much more to worry about. One day at a time.*

Again, we don't really recommend the term "broken eggs," but if you have already said it, don't worry! You will have many opportunities to talk about family-building in different ways. Language will change hundreds of times over the years in which you will be talking about this.

Many parents worry about their child talking about egg donation outside the home, thereby informing friends, family members, or strangers about how the family was created. For parents who have been very private with this information, this prospect can be intimidating and frightening. The truth is that once you start to have conversations with a child over the age of four or five, there is always the possibility that the child will blurt out the information at unexpected times. Some children are like that, and others are not.

> 🗨 *Carole's son Daniel told kindergarten playmates, "My mommy used another lady's eggs to have me!" Of course, those children had no idea what he was talking about, but it led to an interesting recess of talk about sperm and penises and eggs.*

You can try to talk to your child about "family talk" or private matters. Marna and her husband used the term "four-walls talk" to help Nick understand that some things were to be discussed only among their family of three at home. The risk, of course, is that it is hard for children to understand the difference between privacy and secrecy, and they may perceive the caution about family talk to mean it is a secret, and secrets are generally bad and scary.

For many donor-created families, this is a real sticking point. So often we hear, "We want to tell our child the truth, but we don't want everyone to know." It is a quandary. This is one of the many reasons we recommend parents be as resolved as possible before choosing egg donation. The more comfortable we are with our family-building choice, the more comfortable we will be if people know about it.

It's important to remember that although this is definitely our infertility or family-building story, it is also our children's story about how they got here and, to a large degree, who they are. Eventually, they may want to share the story with a trusted friend or even a relative with whom you did not previously share the information.

Sometimes it's challenging to differentiate our needs from those of our children. We need to figure out who we are really protecting or whose feelings we are really concerned about. Children pick up on our cues; they sense our discomfort sometimes even before we are aware of it.

Josephine* has been chatting with her five-year-old about egg donation.

Josephine

> I started out with the books, and now I tell the story verbally. My second child was a miracle of nature, so I want to make sure they both feel special with their own creation stories. I tell the stories together and am very dramatic and silly. They get so excited and repeat the story often.

Every child's birth story is special, and all children, no matter how they join a family, love stories about themselves. They love to hear about the moment Mom knew it was time to go to the hospital to deliver them or the day Mom and Dad got the call that they were born and hopped on a plane to bring them home. Children are completely egocentric and think the world revolves around them; Josephine is so wise to make both of her children's stories unique and special.

Rachel C. has two children through egg donation, ages eight and five. She's been talking to them about it for quite a while.

Rachel C.

> I began telling each child when they were toddlers, using the principle of telling early and often. We have several picture books about DE, and the kids have asked to read them repeatedly at various ages. We have gone back to the topic as they bring it up or [when] I have reason to mention it. I am comfortable talking with them at the level of understanding they have right now.

Diana told us about her conversations with her two-and-a-half-year-old daughter:

Diana

> We talk about it quite openly, whenever the subject matter naturally comes up. We read all the DE books for children and draw the parallels to our own life. I think the more of a non-event you treat it as, the more of a non-event it is. It's just her origin story.

Daisy

> My twins are five years old … When they were four, I started reading a few books to them. We read One More Giraffe, Mommy, Was Your Tummy Big?, and The Pea That Was Me. They honestly were not very interested when I shared that their story was like the one in the book. They only cared that they came out of my tummy. I didn't talk about it a lot. At that time my husband and I also began talking to our [own egg] daughter about it. She just listened

and asked a few questions. I was most afraid of telling her and fear[ed] she would tell her friends (she was six or so at the time), but that hasn't happened.

Recently, one of the boys has been asking, "But where did we come from?" He would always ask at very inopportune times, but a few weeks ago he was very insistent. I literally pulled into our driveway, turned around, and told them the whole story. Again, they were most interested in how they grew in my tummy and how they came out, how they were when in my belly, etc. They were fascinated that they were once just tiny little seeds. They didn't ask a thing about the woman who shared her eggs, but as they get older, I'm certain they will.

Here are Anke's thoughts on her plans for talking with her twenty-month-old daughter:

Anke

I bought a storybook to read to her, but she isn't into stories yet, so I will read the book to her later and make the connection. I am planning on making it not a big deal and mak[ing] it a natural fact about her/her life … Hmm, that's my plan. Hopefully, it will work.

Jean and Scott shared how they started talking to their first child when she was only twenty months old (they have since had a second child):

Jean

We talk openly about the topic to each other and others in front of Karalee. She is a smart girl. How much of it she hears or gets is beyond me, but it's just another subject where we include her. She's really too young to really get it with any words, but we just treat it like we would any topic.

She knows who 'Aunt Kadie" is … they adore each other … and we talk about how she helped to make her by giving us an egg. Karalee loves eggs, so we relate it to that.

This is a great example of a way discussion about how the family was created and who helped in the process is just integrated into conversation the way other subjects are—randomly, easily, and as often as the matter is relevant or comes up.

Amy and Jack have an interesting family constellation. Jack has two adult children, ages thirty and twenty-seven, each of whom also has children, so Amy and Jack have two granddaughters and are also the parents of a nine-year-old son through egg donation.

Amy

I found PVED when my son was an infant, and it helped me immensely. I would tell my son his birth story and his conception story when we nursed or snuggled [when he was] a baby. The advice was, and continues to be, tell early/ tell often. I wanted it to be normal for him to never have known any differently. We had a few books, but the one that has lasted for us is the Mommy, Was Your Tummy Big? *book. I still catch him reading it from time to time, and he has always loved it. I like the book because it is a vehicle for conversation that is very comforting, and [it] reinforces how much we love our son. He understands that we used a helper called a donor who gave me a cell that I didn't have in my own body to help me have him and that that is a different process from most people who have babies. He understands the "birds and the bees" … we have had that talk … And right now he is still in the "girls are gross and kind of annoyingly bossy" phase … still covers his head and groans with movie scene kissing … He also understands that once that cell was gifted and he was growing in my belly, the rest of it was the same as for other people, so we don't gloss over the DE thing, but don't focus on it to death either, and move along to the birth story, the baby story, the growing-up story, etc. He also clearly states that he grew in my belly, and I birthed him, and I am Mom.*

An interesting thing happened recently when he was asking me about my eye color (hazel) and his dad's eye color (hazel) and his own eye color (extremely dark brown—can barely see pupils), and I explained on a very rudimentary level about genetics and did the typical talk about Mom's genes and Dad's genes and the possible expressions of that, very watered-down for a nine-year-old, and explained to him that because I used a donor, that was different for him, because we had to consider her genes … He asked how I knew our donor's eye color (brown), and I told him I had a huge packet of information about her from the clinic that included childhood but not adult photos. He asked if he could see it. Wow, I thought. We are here, the moment I have been waiting for.

Lindsey has a four-year-old daughter.

Lindsey

I have told her story to her since she was a baby. I read somewhere to start telling it when she was an infant, so that I could stutter over it, stop, and start, until I got it right and [felt] comfortable.

Now we talk a lot about it. I tell her how we wanted her so much and that my eggs were just no good. We found a woman willing to help us out and give us some of her eggs. I told her that we put them back in my uterus and waited and finally found out that we were pregnant. It was the happiest day of our lives. Our dream had come true, and we got this awesome kid.

I think it is age-appropriate for now, and as she grows up, I will add more details.

Here is a very cute anecdote—we were talking about siblings, and I reminded her that I don't have good eggs and she would likely not have any siblings. She told me just to go back to the store and get more eggs from the lady so she could have a brother or sister!

Final Thoughts

You gain strength, courage, and confidence by every experience in which you really stop to look fear in the face. You must do the thing which you think you cannot do.

—Eleanor Roosevelt

Those of us who have had the privilege of engaging in poignant, hilarious, and informative conversations with our children about the different ways to build a family know this: There is no greater gift we can give ourselves and our family than honesty and openness. What child doesn't want to hear a story about how much they were wanted by their parents? The details may change, and family constellations may all be different, but ultimately, the love story of people who so very much wanted to be parents that they found a unique and resourceful way to have a child is a really cool story that children love to hear. Eventually, as kids grow, they will begin to understand the meaning of donor conception, and you will have set the stage for them to come to you with thoughts, questions, and feelings about all the different experiences they will have in life. We hope you have fun exploring the language and style of your very own storytelling!

Chapter 10

THE KIDS ARE ALRIGHT

You have to write the book that wants to be written. And if the book will be too difficult for grown-ups, then you write it for children.

—Madeleine L'Engle

Susan Golombok is a professor and prolific researcher at the University of Cambridge. She, more than anyone, has researched "nontraditional families"—those with one parent by choice or those conceived through sperm, egg, or embryo donation, as well as families created through surrogacy. In her book *Modern Families: Parents and Children in New Family Forms*, she writes,

> The research reviewed in this book has shown that children born through reproduction donation (the donation of eggs, sperm or embryos, or surrogacy) and thus who lack a genetic and/or gestational link to their parents, show positive psychological adjustment and do not differ from children who are biologically related to both their mother and their father. It seems, therefore, that a biological link to parents is not necessary for children's psychological well-being.[7]

We could have told people that! Although we can point to various research that tells us in different ways that our kids are doing just fine, we prefer to highlight, as we have throughout the book, real people living in real families that were created with the help of egg or embryo donation. To that end, here are the stories, in their own words, of just a few individuals who were conceived through egg donation.

§

Dan, Chelsea, Sasha, and Nick are not your average donor offspring. All but Chelsea grew up with mothers who are reproductive professionals—both Dan (Carole's son) and Sasha have mothers who are psychotherapists, and Nick is Marna's son. From their earliest memories, they heard the language of family-building, egg donation, egg donor, and donor offspring in their homes. They heard their mothers speaking to individuals and couples who very much, often desperately, wanted to become mothers and fathers and needed the help of a woman who would contribute her genetic material to make it happen. Chelsea's parents are two of the first men in the world to have become parents through the help of egg donation and surrogacy, with both women who helped being members of their family. For Chelsea, having two dads and no mom was normal, just as Dan, Sasha, and Nick have always thought that not being genetically related to one's mom is no big deal.

Karlie's story is quite different. Hers represents the experience of many people whose parents never told them the truth as they were growing up. In her own words, she describes the pain she now feels, having discovered the truth the way she did, and describes the multiple layers of complexity the information adds to her life.

Chelsea

I never missed having a mother. My dad has a very strong feminine side and met all the needs a mother might fulfill. To me, my family is completely normal.

Chelsea is a twenty-three-year-old recent graduate of a small East Coast college with a degree in theater arts. She's come home to Southern California to pursue her acting career and is currently living with her boyfriend about twenty miles from her dads. Chelsea is used to answering questions about her family. Dad is Kevin Montgomery (who recently published a book about their family, *The Family Next Door*), and Daddy is Kevin's husband, Dennis.

Chelsea and her fathers relate that when she was about three years old, she asked where she came from. They had been advised to keep it simple and to just answer the question that was asked.

"Sandy's tummy," they replied.

Not long after that, they were vacationing in Hawaii. Lounging on the beach, the dads kept an eye on Chelsea as she played with a little girl about her own age, whom they had just met. Suddenly, Chelsea came running up to her dads, crying. When they asked her what was wrong, she said, "That girl said you were gay!"

"Well, I *am* gay," Kevin replied.

"Oh, okay," Chelsea said, and she went running off to her new friend. She told us she then apologized to the girl like this: "I'm sorry. You were right. He is gay." And off they went to play some more. Having two dads and no mom was just normal to her, but she really didn't know what "gay" meant until later. She knew her parents were in love and a couple, but she didn't realize that was anything that would be interesting to other people until she got older. By middle and high school, she would realize how unique her family was, and she would become proficient at answering questions.

In the meantime, when she was around age seven, Kevin and Dennis had "the sex talk" with her, and nothing clicked in relation to the fact that she must have come to her dads in a way other than *that*.

At ten, she finally asked her dad, Kevin, how *he* had had her. In other words, she asked, "Did you have sex with Sandy?" Once she understood that this was not how it had happened either and that Sandy was not genetically related to her, she wanted to know who had given the female part if it wasn't Sandy. That was when she was finally told that Aunt Helene had been the egg donor. Chelsea could not have been more excited and thrilled. She had always had a very special connection to her aunt, and now that connection had an even deeper meaning to her. It just made sense. She also wanted to know if she had been adopted "from" Sandy. No, they explained, the law had allowed both her dads to be the legal parents.

Auntie Helene has never been a mom to her, and Chelsea says she has never missed having a mother. In her own words, Dad Kevin has a lot of "female energy" and truly met all of the needs a "traditional" mother figure might have filled. He was the volunteer in the classroom, he took her to ballet, and he was PTA president at one point. And her fathers always made sure there were plenty of wonderful close female relationships in their lives in case Chelsea wanted to talk to a woman. But, Chelsea said, she never hesitated to talk to her dads about anything, including menstruation and puberty and what kind of pads to use. For her, their family was complete, and there were no pieces missing.

Auntie Helene has a seventeen-year-old son and a nine-year-old daughter. The subject of Helene donating the egg arises so infrequently that Helene's daughter has only just learned of it. Helene's son, being a seventeen-year-old male, is completely uninterested, and Chelsea has never really discussed it with him. She has never thought of them as half siblings or genetic half siblings or donor siblings, or anything at all other than her cousins.

Karlie*

In her own words, Karlie tells us her story:

> *My mother chose not to tell me I was egg donor–conceived. I was conceived in the '90s, a time where home-ordered DNA tests were unheard of. Perhaps my mom and dad planned to tell me that my mother was not my biological mother, but my mother admits it was too difficult after losing my father, the biological parent.*

I took an AncestryDNA test for fun last year and unveiled more than I had bargained for. My results [came] back completely different than I [had] imagined. While I thought it was strange, I still trusted the test, as I had actually matched with some of my late father's known relatives. But I also matched with someone I didn't know at a first-cousin level. I thought it was strange but just thought there was a link missing in my family tree, so I encouraged my mother to take a DNA test. When she refused, I knew something was up.

My mother sat me down and told me the truth. I was donor egg–conceived. I knew my parents had struggled with fertility. They were in their forties [when I was born] and had admittedly tried many failed IVF cycles. I [had] never had any reason to doubt that my mother was biologically related to me. All of the times that she could have told me had passed her by. I had even had my own child the year before. I couldn't fathom how she would have let pregnancy pass me by without warning me that I had a partially unknown medical history.

I felt stupid. Looking back, I had a few red flags. I was diagnosed with a mild medical disorder in my teens, one that was genetically inherited. My mother had brushed it off as being recessive or skipping a generation. I started to question everything in my life. I couldn't look in the mirror when I didn't know who I was looking at. Whose eyes were staring back at me? How could I have not realized how different I was from my mother?

Realizing my mother was not who I [had] thought she was caused me to grieve my still living parent. I had lost my father many years before, and I felt like in a way I had lost my mother too. I had built my life, my identity, around her only to feel like I lost her. I could not believe my mother could lie to me via omission for that long. I grieved for losing her and for her losing me. She had pushed the ordeal out of her brain for twenty-three years. She had never had the chance to grieve losing her chance of having biological children. I now grieved for her. I wished I was hers, for her physical traits and descendants to carry her on in one hundred years, long after she was gone. [For her] having me [had] always felt like she had a piece of my dad after he died, but what would I have of her?

I felt locked inside with my secret. I couldn't tell very many people close to me [because] they were close to my mother too. She still did not want to discuss her secret. She even resented me for causing her to tell me, thus bursting our bubble. I felt ashamed of my circumstances. In my mind, how could she not be ashamed of my not being hers if she did not want anyone to know the truth?

I know now that I should not need to protect her, and [I] wish I could be more open about my biology—but yet still I feel shame and fear that my family and friends will not feel the same about me after I tell them the truth. I wish more than anything that my mother was who I thought she was, and I love her even more for the sacrifices she made in order to have me. I know I was wanted, so very badly. I also know that if I had been told the secret as a child and [were] allowed to share my story, I would not feel like I had my identity ripped away from me.

Nicholas

Tell them as soon as possible because they are going to find out sooner or later, and they will become very mad at you if you lie to them.

At the time we interviewed Nick for this book, he was a typical fifteen-year-old student in a high school in the Pacific Northwest. He is a gifted piano player with broad genre interests. He loves classical, jazz, and rock. He has also composed a few original pieces.

Having grown up with the knowledge that he was conceived with someone else's egg, he has grown quite weary and bored with the conversation. But it wasn't always that way.

As he grew up, Nick had a lot of questions about the donor. His parents had received a typical anonymous donation, matched through the in-house donor pool at their physician's office. They knew a little about her. They knew her age, height, and weight. They had been told that she had curly hair and resembled Marna. But as Nick grew older and understood that he was genetically related to the donor, but not his mom, he had questions his parents could not answer.

Who do you think I look like?

Is she nice?

I want to know about the other invisible part of myself that you can't tell me about.

What do you think her name is, Mom?

I want to know if she's a good person.

Someday, if it's possible, I would like to meet her.

I want to know her real name. I'm tired of calling her "Nel" [Nice Egg Lady].

Does she have a husband?

Does she have kids?

If she has kids, are those kids my brothers or sisters?

Does she have a mom and a dad?

Are those people my grandparents? They don't have to be, do they?

Nick wanted to know the basic stuff that the clinic wouldn't tell his family because the cycle had begun anonymously. He knew the donor liked chocolate and coffee, for instance, but he wondered if she liked sushi the way he did. He wanted to know if she was bright, like he was, and loved books, like he did.

Given the freedom to fantasize and to ask questions, many donor offspring wonder many of these same things. As they start to put together their own identity, they wonder about ways in which they are like or unlike the donor.

With the help of the mental health professional employed at the clinic, and because the donor had indicated a willingness to be contacted in the future, the clinic finally agreed to allow the psychologist to contact her. She was asked if she would be willing to have contact with one of the families to whom she had donated. She immediately said yes.

Initially, Marna, Nick's mom, met with Jennifer for coffee. Like any courtship or new relationship, they took it slowly at first. And like any good parents, Marna and her husband wanted to make sure that before they introduced Jennifer to their son, she was stable and, in their words, "not crazy."

That was five years ago. Jennifer has since become an integral part of their family. She attends Nick's recitals and shares in celebrations, and occasionally everyone casually meets for a meal. She has met the entire extended family, and in Nick's words, she has become like an older sibling.

At ten and a half, Marna asked Nick to give a statement about his views on egg donation. This was in response to many of the members of Parents via Egg Donation who were confused about how to share information with their children. Marna's family had not yet made contact with the donor, Jennifer.

Even though the egg donor plays a big part in all these kids'
lives, it doesn't mean that they should worry that they don't
have a connection to their mom because they don't share
their mother's genes. Kids don't think about their egg donor
while they are doing homework, like "I wonder what my
egg donor is doing right now? I wonder if she likes pizza."

All I know is, even though egg donors are special, remember
that your mom is your mom, and if it wasn't for her, you
wouldn't be here.

A few years later, just shy of his thirteenth birthday, Marna again
asked Nick to address the concerns of other moms. He had known
Jennifer only about two years at this point. Her interview with him went
something like this:

**Q: Do you remember when your mom or dad first
talked to you about your origins or how you were
conceived?**

*Nick: I was too young to remember. It is something I have
always known.*

**Q: How often did your parents talk to you about egg
donation and your origins?**

*Nick: Every time I brought it up, my parents would talk to
me about it. They never shoved it in my face.*

**Q: Would you say your parents were open about
how you were conceived and about the topic of egg
donation?**

Nick: Yes. They were open about any questions I asked.

Q: How do you feel now, at the age of twelve, about your conception and that you came from a donated egg?

Nick: (shrugs shoulders) I don't really care, it's just a different set of ones and zeros—a different piece of code that does the same thing in a slightly different way.

Q: Tell me how you feel about your mom. For instance, when you think about your mom and egg donation, do you think of your egg donor as your parent, or do you think of your mom as your parent?

Nick: I don't think about egg donation at all. The woman who birthed and raised me is my mother and parent.

Q: Who is the egg donor to you? What role does she play in your life?

Nick: We have a different situation than some. We found our egg donor and got to know her. Sometimes we go out to dinner or do different things with her. My egg donor is more like my sibling. She is not a parental figure at all.

Q: For parents who have not shared with their children their origins or how they were conceived, what advice would you have for them?

Nick: Tell them as soon as possible because they are going to find out sooner or later, and they will become very mad at you if you lie to them.

Q: Tell me about the day you met your egg donor—were you nervous, scared, or excited?

Nick: I was nervous when I first met her, but by the end of the night, I felt like I knew her. She was very nice. I liked her right away. I thought she was nervous. I think everyone was nervous. We met for sushi. I found it interesting how much we looked alike. We both hate Costco. We are both introverts. We are both really smart. We both love chocolate and coffee. We both like weird things that no one else likes. We both love to read and play the piano.

Q: Do you know if your egg donor has donated to other families? And if so, what do you think about the possibility of having siblings out in the world?

Nick: I know she has donated four other times—I know I have at least four half-siblings, and I don't really have any interest in meeting them. I wouldn't be opposed to meeting them, but I really don't care.

Q: Tell me about the reaction from other family members about your conception.

Nick: Well, a lot of them didn't understand. Mom tells me there were a lot of blank stares, and our family had to do a lot of educating. They called my donor "the donor mother" and thought egg donation was where you bought eggs to make children out of. I found that quite ridiculous. Needless to say, I have no problem correcting them, and they don't feel that way anymore.

Q: Granted, you are only twelve years old, but looking forward in your life, how do you think you're going to tell a future partner that you were born via

egg donation, and do you think it's important to tell them?

Nick: I'll tell them as soon as humanly possible because there's always the risk of dating a half-sibling out there, and I don't want to have to deal with that. I'll bring it up during the first date and ask if they're from egg donation as well, and if they know who their egg donor is.

Sasha

I don't remember any one moment when my parents sat me down to talk about egg donation. They were just always very open, very normal. I don't recall any moment when I was emotionally distressed by my situation.

When we asked Sasha for her story, she was a twenty-three-year-old graduate student at the University of Oxford. She grew up in Northern California but caught the travel bug at a young age. At fourteen, she went on an exchange program in Spain, and by the time she graduated with her bachelor's degree from a four-year university in New York, she had serious wanderlust again. She fluently speaks three languages and is currently completing an internship in Turkey.

Sasha's family was created with the help of a woman who gave her eggs to Sasha's then-forty-five-year-old mom. Sasha's parents met the donor, Lara, through mutual friends at a party, where Lara offered to help them become parents. Here is Sasha's story in her own words:

While at times (in my adolescent days) I was uncertain as to whether or not I was grateful for having such a complicated family tree, now I understand that having an egg donor has really changed my perspective on everything—on what is "normal" (widening my perspective on familial diversity and diversity in general), on the importance of family.

My relationship with "my egg donor" began in early childhood. I can't tell you exactly when that was—I just always knew she was there. Because my mother is and was a therapist specializing in infertility, I was surrounded by literature about alternatively built families. Egg donation was normalized early on. I remember feeling surprised that my friends didn't all have egg donors. I was very open about it and did not feel at all ashamed. I felt completely confident about my family situation.

I don't remember any one moment when my parents sat me down to talk about egg donation. They were just always very open, very normal. I don't recall any moment when I was emotionally distressed by my situation.

I would spend time with Lara, but I didn't know I wanted to spend time with her. Of course, I did not always understand exactly what the relationship to her meant to me. I would go to her house for dinner with my parents. I knew it would be fun because she would give me gifts, and she had cats, and I loved the attention paid me. It was nice to be surrounded by people who wanted to spend time with me in this special way, and I knew she cared about me.

Going into adolescence, I realized I wanted to spend time with her because we shared many things in common. We both loved shoes and makeup; she had the same sense of humor as I did. When you're thirteen, you don't necessarily talk about the boy you have a crush on with your parents; it was nice to have an older person, not a parent, who did not have the authority to punish you the way your parents could, but [who] could give insight. I had sleepovers at her house, and we would go to the movies and shopping. It was really fun. It was like having an older sister—with a driver's license.

This contact all made me appreciate the ability to know her. I have a lot of friends now who were conceived via egg donation or sperm donation who do not want to know or don't know their donors, all completely legitimate ways to feel; but I can't imagine not knowing her. She had a lot of influence over who I became as a person and how I connect with my family.

My parents were wise enough to always keep that dialogue open, and once it was open, it stayed open for other topics of importance during my youth—sex, relationships, race, and gender issues.

Having that open connection to her made me very confident and helped me avoid the identity crisis so common in high school. Lara decided to start her own family, although she is and was unmarried. She went the route of sperm donation with a friend of hers as the donor, and she had a daughter when I was sixteen. I was there throughout the process as she was going through IVF.

To be honest, I was a bit jealous; I knew she wanted a daughter, yet she and I had this special bond. Even though I was my mother's daughter, and I always felt like my mother's daughter, there was a jealousy from being special to Lara in this one specific way, and yet she found that she wanted more. I understood why but was a bit bitter. It was a bit uncomfortable, alongside having great dialog with her. That dialog was difficult because I was only sixteen, and although my egg donor was a close friend, I could not conceptualize and grasp her need to have a child.

After she gave birth to her daughter, there was a cool baby I could play with. Now, at six years old, she sees me as her older sister, which is great in many ways because I am an only child. At the same time, I still see myself as an only child, and at times it can be a bit confusing to connect with someone seventeen years younger than yourself. It might be challenging to explain the complete family tree of sperm donation and egg donation. At the same time, I am grateful to have this channel to talk with her.

My life has been much richer for the opportunity to have this open discourse with my parents and with the donor and now with the donor's daughter. It has been challenging at times, but going forward, it will be a lot easier to figure out because my generation is the first generation to become adult offspring from [egg-]donor conception. I'm very grateful to my parents for the opportunity to grow up with Lara and to have known her because my life would have been very different otherwise.

Daniel

I'm much more concerned about passing algebra than I am that I was created through egg donation.

Daniel is currently a thirty-one-year-old who freely shares that he is "one of the first eleven people in the world to be born from donor eggs." At age twenty-five he decided he wanted an adventure, so he threw on a backpack and trekked around Europe, as so many of us have done in our youth. There he met a young woman from Germany and decided he wanted to extend his adventure to actually live in another country, soaking up the culture, the language, and the food. He found a job as a computer game developer, remained in Germany for four years and just recently returned back to the U.S. He has a fabulous job, beginning his new life back home with his now fiancée.

Dan is an accomplished pianist and can readily recite the name and composer of any classical piece, which orchestras have the best rendition, and which conductors have mastered it. He has an affable and engaging personality that readily draws people to him.

From before he could speak, Dan heard the language of family-building and egg donation. At age four, he proclaimed, "Oh, I get it, Mommy. First I grew inside the other lady. Then when I was ready to come out of her, they took me out of her and put me inside of you!" And at five years old, Daniel went to kindergarten and announced, "My mommy used another lady's egg to have me."

When Dan was twelve years old, he offered to answer questions from prospective parents on an early internet email list called Mothers via Egg Donation, or MVED. Parents and those trying to be parents were discussing the issue of whether to tell their children the truth of their donor origins. Twenty years ago there was less consensus on this topic than currently exists.

"How do you feel about being donor-conceived?" one person asked.

"I don't really feel anything about it. If anything, I feel kind of special," Daniel replied.

"Do you know if you have any brothers and sisters?"

"Yes," he replied. "I have a brother, Alex. My mom has told me the donor has a son, but he's not my brother. I don't think he's anything to me."

"Have you met the donor?"

"No, I don't really have any interest in meeting her, but I know if I want to, my mom will put me in the car and take me there."

Then he added, "To all of you out there who are afraid to tell your kid the truth, don't be. It's really no big deal. To me, it's just normal because I've always known and no one ever made it weird. I am not confused about who my parents are. My mom is my mom and always will be. I know there's another person out there I share DNA with, but it's not really that important to me. I'm much more concerned about passing algebra than I am that I was created through egg donation."

In interview after interview throughout his adolescence and adulthood, Daniel has emphasized that he believes it would have been "seriously traumatic" to have learned at fourteen or fifteen years old that he is not genetically related to his mom. "It wouldn't ever have been how

I got here that would have disturbed me," he recently said in a video. "I would have felt hurt that I wasn't told sooner.'"

"I never felt like I was missing a piece of myself," he said, "because my family felt complete."

Daniel recently told us he still is not interested in meeting the donor. "Life is busy and complicated," he said, "and there's a lot going on that I struggle to keep up with. It hasn't been something that means that much to me."

As an adult, Daniel confidently shares with partners, new friends, and neighbors what he considers to be a unique and interesting piece of his history. Twenty-five years after he first started telling people about the "lady who helped" his mom, egg donation is more widely heard of and understood. Now he is able to talk about it from the perspective of an adult who clearly understands the contribution to who he is, although he says he personally never thinks about the genetic connection. Although he readily shares the information, it is more the fact of it than the genetic link that he thinks is cool.

"I'm a pretty typical guy, so if it's any evidence for the process and whether to be open and honest with your kids, use me as a benchmark of sorts for how to just not make such a big deal out of it. You know, you can write a million books about it, and [that] will definitely be helpful. And obviously, I don't come at this from the perspective of a parent, which I'm sure is much more stressful and involved; but from the receiving end, if you are open and honest, and you were truthful with your kids and don't lie, and you share your feelings, I think you'll all be fine.

"I'm really glad my mom had me, no matter how I got here."

Acknowledgments

Marna Gatlin

There are so many individuals who deserve heartfelt thanks, wine, cookies, my love, and acknowledgment in regard to *Let's Talk about Egg Donation* that I'm not sure where to begin, so I will jump in the deep end and hope I don't forget anyone.

To begin with, I'd like to thank my mentor, writing partner, and coauthor, Carole LieberWilkins. Without her, this book wouldn't be what it is today—truly a labor of love accompanied by blood, sweat, and a few tears. Throughout this journey, Carole has been there every step of the way with me until, together, we crossed the finish line.

My family has been the glue that's kept me together. They have been my cheerleaders the whole way. They have endured the writing, the rewrites, and the edits—and also made endless cups of tea that magically appeared at my desk while I wrote this book. I can't thank them enough for believing in me and being my number one fans.

I am grateful to Dr. John Hesla, MD, my physician and dear friend. Dr. Hesla took a chance on me, partnering with me when other physicians wouldn't, and worked very hard with me, as well as my husband, to bring our son into the world. I will forever be in his debt.

"I love my son so much, sometimes I forget to breathe." I remember the first time I uttered those words to another mother via egg donation who was struggling through this incredibly overwhelming process. It was during that conversation that I realized there is always strength in numbers; and it was also during that conversation that I realized there

were many, many other intended parents who would draw strength from others' stories if only we could write them all down. Because of this mom and hundreds of other intended parents within our PVED community, we have been given the opportunity to share parents' joy, sorrow, courage, and vulnerability through their stories as told to us. We give these parents our deepest thanks because we know their stories and experiences will inspire those after them.

We are grateful to all those whom we have had the pleasure of working with during the writing of *Let's Talk about Egg Donation*. We would especially like to acknowledge Said T. Daneshmand, MD, FACOG, for his knowledge, expertise, and generosity in contributing to the "Pregnancy after Forty: A Note from a Reproductive Endocrinologist" section in chapter 3.

Without our egg donors, our children wouldn't be here on planet Earth for us to love unconditionally and thank the universe for every day. I'm not sure if our donors even realize just how significant their part in all of this is and how thankful we as parents are for their gift of life.

Stacey, Chris, Dana, Abby, Amy, Sue, and Sharon, thank you for so much—love, gratitude, and respect come to mind when I think of you seven. From PVED's very humble beginnings so many years ago to the present day, you've all been such pillars of strength for me. I am so proud to know each of you. You all have my heart.

And I thank Lauren, our editor. Truly, without her we'd have just a bunch of words on a page. She managed to take two completely different writing styles, wave her magic wand, breathe life into them, and make them delightful. In fact, the words "thank you" just aren't adequate. She talked us off the ledge, has been an amazing sounding board, told us what we've needed to hear, and has been the voice of reason, all while helping us complete something rather extraordinary. My gratitude to her is endless.

Last but not least, I'd like to acknowledge and thank all of the children conceived through egg or embryo donation. You all are the fruits of our labor. You are the first thing we think about in the morning and the last thing we think about before we go to sleep. We love you to the moon and back and everywhere in between. You were planned for, worked hard for, and so very much wanted. You are all part of a pretty special club, and we love you so very much.

§

Carole LieberWilkins

I stand on the shoulders of those who forged a path before me, and I am indebted to those who have walked the path beside me. Though I may occasionally delude myself that I have been an original thinker in these matters, history proves otherwise.

At a meeting of the American Society of Reproductive Medicine (ASRM) in 1993, I was one of only a few mental health professionals who believed strongly that we, as therapists, should not stay neutral about parents telling the truth to donor-conceived offspring. It was then that I met Dr. Patricia Mahlstedt, coauthor with Dorothy Greenfeld of the groundbreaking article "Assisted Reproductive Technology with Donor Gametes: The Need for Patient Preparation" (*Fertility and Sterility* 53 [1989]: 33–39). In 1989, these authors put forth the notion that people who were going to parent children conceived with donor gametes needed to be emotionally and psychologically prepared to do so in order to create healthy and happy families. While this seems so obvious today, at the time it was a brilliant and earth-shattering proclamation. Patty and I became instant and lifelong friends, like-minded about the need for truth telling and about the importance for all of us of facing our challenges in order to overcome them. I am grateful to Patty for encouraging me to think outside the box and to turn convention upside down.

I am grateful for the camaraderie and support of Dr. Elaine Gordon, my local comrade, colleague, and friend, and to Dr. Madeline Feingold and Jean Benward, LCSW, whose support and friendship helped support and fuel the hope and belief that the need to treat donor offspring with the same integrity long afforded those who were adopted would eventually be recognized as the standard for creating healthy families.

I am always honored to be in the company of such brilliant minds and am humbled by being included into their circle.

I'd also like to acknowledge the body of work of Ken Daniels, LCSW, author of *Building a Family with the Assistance of Donor Insemination* (Dunmore Press, 2004). Ken is, along with Dr. Mahlstedt, one of the true trailblazers in the area of sperm donation. In addition, in 1989, social workers Annette Baran and Reuben Pannor wrote the then heretical *Lethal Secrets*. Annette and Reuben had been pivotal forces in the open adoption movement and were the first to apply the notion of the toxicity of secrecy to families formed through donor conception.

In 2008, I had the incredibly good fortune to become a mentor to Dr. Carrie Eichberg, who was new to ASRM but not new to being a psychologist, already having practiced for fifteen years. Over the years, while I mentored her in the area of reproductive medicine and family-building, she mentored me, already a seasoned therapist, in psychological assessments and principles of ethical psychological practice. She has become a loyal and dear friend, as well as a fierce supporter of the work we do and our fight to maintain the highest ethical principles in our work with families. I'm honored to be able to watch her children grow and to be a part of her family. I am extremely grateful to her for allowing me to keep her on speed dial so that she can talk me down off the rafters when this work sometimes takes its toll.

For over three decades, men and women have shared their stories with me. They've brought to my office their pain and confusion, their shock and trauma at needing to make decisions about becoming parents in ways they previously never even knew existed. They have trusted me to guide them through a sometimes dark path to the other side, where they have become joyous parents of the children of their dreams, ready and prepared to be the fierce supporters for the families they created. To each and every one, I am forever moved and grateful to have shared your journey.

This book never would have come to fruition without the courage of the men and women of Parents via Egg Donation. In 2011, we started out with a questionnaire to the membership, asking them to tell us their stories about becoming parents through egg donation. Their inspirational quotes and heartwarming and sometimes heart-wrenching narratives are the foundation of *Let's Talk about Egg Donation*. The book is for all families formed through donor conception, but it is truly written through the real stories of each and every PVED member who contributed. I am grateful and honored that they trusted us to do justice to their stories.

And finally …

In 1984, my sister, Mimi, was twenty-eight years old, single with no children. Despite her youth and not having any personal experience with what had happened to me, she was the first—and at the time, only—person to instantly and unequivocally understand the devastating magnitude of my diagnosis of early menopause at the age of thirty. She was then, and remained through the years, one of the greatest champions of the family I was to build, however I was to get there. While others threw me platitudes about adoption or encouraged me to just have a wonderful life without children, my sister literally and figuratively joined me in the pain and traveled the bumpy road that ultimately led to parenthood. She was my children's first "second mother" and a much more fun one than I ever could be.

Acknowledgement and gratitude go to Paula, the most supportive, steady, and unwavering friend a woman could ever hope to have in life. Paula and I met almost thirty years ago, when our kids were in preschool. Although my path to parenthood was over by then, the parenting part was just getting started. Paula and I have ridden the often tumultuous road of life into our sixth decade. We have held each other tightly through parenting terrors, divorce, death, health scares, and the experiences that come with aging parents, as well as the extraordinary joys that growing old together can bring. Any sanity I still claim is owed to her.

Resources

Following is a list of organizations and books that you may find helpful on your egg or embryo donation journey.

Organizations

Donor Conception

> Donor Conception Network
> dcnetwork.org
>
> Donor Sibling Registry
> donorsiblingregistry.com
>
> Parents via Egg Donation (PVED)
> PVED.org
>
> Path2Parenthood
> path2parenthood.org
>
> Men Having Babies
> menhavingbabies.org

Genetics

> 23 and Me
> 23andme.com

Ancestry
ancestry.com

Infertility

American Society for Reproductive Medicine
asrm.org

INCIID
inciid.org

Resolve
resolve.org

Pregnancy/Postpartum/Parenting

American Pregnancy Association
americanpregnancy.org

Baby Center
babycenter.com

The Bradley Method of Childbirth
bradleybirth.com

The Bump
thebump.com

The Car Seat Lady
thecarseatlady.com

Childbirth Connection
childbirthconnection.org

Choice Moms
choicemoms.org

DONA International (Find a Doula)
dona.org/what-is-a-doula/find-a-doula

Dr. Sears
askdrsears.com

Fit Pregnancy
fitpregnancy.com

KellyMom—Breastfeeding and Parenting
kellymom.com

La Leche League International
llli.org

Lamaze for Parents
lamaze.org

March of Dimes — Pregnancy
marchofdimes.org/pregnancy/pregnancy.aspx

National Perinatal
nationalperinatal.org

The New Mama Project
newmamaproject.com/resources

Parenting
parenting.com

Postpartum Alliance
postpartumhealthalliance.org

Postpartum International
postpartum.net/resources

Pregnancy.Com
pregnancy.com

PVED Members-Only Forum
forums.pved.org

Single Mothers by Choice (SMC)
singlemothersbychoice.org

Twin Stuff
twinstuff.com

Twiniversity
twiniversity.com

WebMD Health and Pregnancy Health Center
webmd.com/baby/default.htm

What Is Postpartum Depression & Anxiety?
apa.org/pi/women/resources/reports/postpartum-depression.aspx

What to Expect
whattoexpect.com

RECOMMENDED CHILDREN'S BOOKS

These are just a few of the many books now available for families created by egg, sperm, and embryo donation.

The Baby Kangaroo Treasure Hunt: A Gay Parenting Story
by Carmen Martinez Jover and Rosemary Martinez

Birds of a Different Feather
by Kelly Wendel

Building My Family: A Story of Egg Donation and Surrogacy
by Carrie Eichberg, PsyD

Cookies and Cake and the Families We Make
by Jennifer Egan and Robin Gulak

Daddy and Pop (book and CD)
by Tina Rella and Monica Meza, produced by Molly Summer

Hope and Will Have a Baby: The Gift of Egg Donation
Hope and Will Have a Baby: The Gift of Embryo Donation
Hope and Will Have a Baby: The Gift of Sperm Donation
Hope and Will Have a Baby: The Gift of Surrogacy
by Irene Celcer

I Am Loved Right Where I Am
by Jason Galvez

Mom and Dad and the Journey They Had
by Molly Summer, Monica Meza, and Tina Rella

Mommy, Did I Grow in Your Tummy? Where Some Babies Come From
by Elaine Gordon

Mommy, Was Your Tummy Big?
by Carolina Nadel

One More Giraffe
by Kim Noble

Our Story: Double Donation for Lesbian Couples (singleton)
Our Story: Double Donation for Lesbian Couples (twins)
Our Story: Double Donation for Solo Mum Families (singleton)
Our Story: Double Donation for Solo Mum Families (twins)
Our Story: Embryo Donation for Solo Mum Families (singleton)
Our Story: Embryo Donation for Solo Mum Families (twins)
Our Story: Embryo Donation for Solo Mum Families (singleton)
Our Story: Embryo Donation Solo Mum Families (twins)
Our Story: Sperm Donation for Lesbian Couples (singleton)
Our Story: Sperm Donation for Lesbian Couples (twins)
Our Story: Sperm Donation for Solo Mum Families (singleton)
Our Story: Sperm Donation for Solo Mum Families (twins)
All published by the Donor Conception Network (www.dcnetwork.org)

A Part Was Given and an Angel Was Born
by Rozanne Nathalie

The Pea That Was Me: An Egg Donation Story
The Pea That Was Me: An Embryo Donation Story
The Pea That Was Me: A Single Mom's Sperm and Egg Donation Story
The Pea That Was Me: A Two Moms' Sperm Donation Story

The Pea That Was Me: A Two Dads' Egg Donation and Surrogacy Story
by Kimberly Kluger-Bell

Phoebe's Family: A Story about Egg Donation
by Linda Stamm and Joan Clipp

Sometimes It Takes Three to Make a Baby
by Kate Bourne

A Tiny Itsy-Bitsy Gift of Life: An Egg Donor Story
by Carmen Martinez Jover

What Makes a Baby?
by Cory Silverberg

What Matters Most: A Children's Book about Families
by Kristin Carter

You Were Meant to Be!
by Sherry Keen & Rosemarie Gillen

ENDNOTES

1   Ehrensaft, Diane, *Mommies, Daddies, Donors, Surrogates*: *Answering the Tough Questions and Building Strong Families,* Guilford Press, London, 2005

2   Source: https://www.sart.org; Go to the **Find a Clinic** section of the website

3   Source: http://www.cityofhope.org/blog/myth-of-closure-stephen-j-forman.

4   Source: http://www.menhavingbabies.org/advocacy/ethical-surrogacy/.

5   We have deliberately used "they," "them," and "their" as neutral, singular pronouns to refer to Erin.

6   Quoted with permission. http://www.madelinefeingoldphd.com

7   Golombok, Susan, *Modern Families: Parents and Children in New Family Forms,* Cambridge University Press, UK, 2015